Praise for *The Invisible Obvious*

'When Tim gave me an early draft [of *The Invisible Obvious*] I read it in two days. I couldn't put it down. Because it resonated with me. And I know it's going to resonate with police officers and all emergency services workers. It's written from the heart. And his theories around how we move on the continuum from one [quadrant] to the other, and how we should check in with ourselves each morning to see how we're feeling and thinking: it just makes sense. I don't think there's a police officer or emergency worker out there who's not going to get something from this book.'

—Ron Iddles OAM, former Victoria Police Homicide Detective; former Secretary of The Police Association Victoria

'Tim has such a unique perspective. His message is so strong around not only your mental health being impacted by what happens around you but also the individual role we all have to play in taking responsibility for our health. I think there's something really powerful in that. Tim's impact has been significant and continues to be. He's an extraordinary human being.'

—Patrice O'Brien, former Chief Community Officer, Beyond Blue

'*The Invisible Obvious* is a watershed, not just for the police and emergency services but for how we all look at managing our mental health.'

—Alex Zannoni, retired psychotherapist, trauma and grief specialist

THE INVISIBLE OBVIOUS

A homicide detective's story of mental health crisis and recovery

Tim Peck

CARLOW BOOKS

Published by Carlow Books,
an imprint of Schwartz Books Pty Ltd
Wurundjeri Country
22–24 Northumberland Street
Collingwood VIC 3066, Australia
enquiries@blackincbooks.com
www.blackincbooks.com

9781760645250 (paperback)
9781743823651 (ebook)

A catalogue record for this
book is available from the
National Library of Australia

Book design and typesetting by Tristan Main
Additional typesetting by Beau Lowenstern
Cover image by Baona / iStock

The power to choose to make meaningful change resides within each of us.

Author's Note

This work was never intended to be an unfiltered account of my experiences in policing and the subsequent impacts on my mental health. I have elected to disclose aspects of my story that assisted me in making sense of my experience. I appreciate that some of the content may be challenging, but to shy away from the reality of life, to remain invisible, would have been at odds with the message that I am attempting to convey.

As we all experience our internal world differently, please go gently as you read. It is important that you are aware of the resources available to you, to access support in the event that you are challenged by the content. The model described in the book is based on my experience, a model that suits my particular needs; it is not intended as medical advice.

There are many resources available. The following are simply suggestions that may assist in developing your toolkit of resources:

Lifeline	lifelinedirect.org.au	13 11 14
Beyond Blue	beyondblue.org.au	1300 22 4636
Phoenix Australia	phoenixaustralia.org	03 9035 5599

Contents

Foreword

GEORGIE HARMAN

I picked up Tim's book in the days after the April 2024 Bondi Junction attack, so my head was filled with images and thoughts of how our first responders rush towards danger to keep others safe. I was reminded of just how heroic, but also how dangerous and damaging, that profession can be.

The Invisible Obvious is a must-read for anyone interested in mental health, mental illness and the messiness of life. It is an uninhibited story of crisis and struggle, but also of hope, resilience and recovery – one that doesn't mince words and fearlessly peels back the scab on the stigma that feeds discrimination.

Although 43 per cent of us will experience some form of mental illness in our lifetimes, many people still feel deep shame about it. This still prevents people talking openly and seeking support early for depression and anxiety. This is often felt deeply for people in roles of power and influence, who we expect to be faultless.

But depression and anxiety do not discriminate by rank or role. They change our daily functioning, our thoughts, feelings and behaviours.

However, Tim's story shows us how important it is not to view people as a diagnosis or cluster of diagnoses.

If Beyond Blue had taken a closed-minded view to Tim's job application, we would have missed out working with a wise, smart, compassionate and driven person who brought deep professional and lived expertise to our work influencing and supporting change in police and emergency services agencies. With Tim's leadership and credibility, we quickly made inroads into that sector. His work benefited countless first responders and their families and friends.

And we would have missed out on something else as well: the opportunity to have someone like Tim in our team, contributing to our culture, bringing different perspectives, mentoring others. We got to watch him smile more as he navigated and relaxed into a very different, but equally results-driven, workplace and industry.

On his last day at Beyond Blue, when the whole team was invited to farewell him, there were the obligatory speeches and snacks. Tim told us that he wanted to gift something back to us: his story. Just as candidly as he does here in *The Invisible Obvious*, Tim shared how his police career had come to an end. For many team members it was the first they knew of what he had gone through. Hearing him tell it in person was incredibly powerful.

It reminded us all that hope and recovery are possible, with the right supports, people and networks around you.

People who live with and work with mental health challenges are not flawed or flaky, or a liability to be mitigated.

They often just need a second chance, sometimes a bit of extra flexibility and support, but always a respectful and inclusive culture, job clarity, and open dialogue.

Enjoy Tim's story and insights, and let them challenge and change you.

Georgie Harman
CEO, Beyond Blue

Foreword

DAVID FORBES

Tim Peck's *The Invisible Obvious* is a breath of fresh air. Tim, in this honest, insightful and nuanced memoir takes us on a rich journey, traversing his career life cycle and his wrestle and reconciliation with his experience of mental ill-health. This journey commences before joining the force, then as a recruit when he didn't even know how to identify anxiety, and takes us through his fascinating career as a detective and his shattering mental health crisis. The memoir then moves on to detail his open-hearted engagement with and reflections on his experience of mental ill-health and the transformation through the next phase of his life and work, innovating, developing and implementing mental health interventions for emergency service workers.

Tim writes thoughtfully, intelligently and with exceptional emotional openness about his experiences, including the challenges they posed to his identity, and shows the reader first-hand how he managed to integrate a new perspective on what he was experiencing.

Tim has unusually perceptive insight into the nature of his difficulties – how and why he struggled to recognise his mental health issues, what it took to engage properly with care and treatment, and how new ideas from his therapist challenged his worldview. He then shows us how he managed to integrate these, giving the reader a rare insight into how someone experiencing extreme psychological distress can incorporate this experience and alongside its pain, expand their life-view and lead a healthier life. *The Invisible Obvious* shows us how a person's mind and personal qualities are dynamic, changing and evolving over time, offering hope to readers who might currently feel 'stuck'. On the flipside he doesn't sugar-coat the challenges, instead clearly laying out how long it took him to develop a set of mental health tools, and that it may not be a battle that is ever 'over'.

Tim tackles the subject of suicide and suicidal ideation with refreshing – and necessary – candour. We need to be able to talk openly about this subject as so many people experience feelings and thoughts like Tim describes. They can often feel intensely isolated and frightened by this. Having someone like Tim share their experience so openly and break down how he gradually loosened the grip this thinking had on him with the help of loved ones, friends and intervention and treatment is incredibly powerful. While it can make for confronting reading, this kind of candour is exactly what is needed to break down the taboo and help others open up and reach out for help. As Tim explains so well, becoming visible to yourself is the first step.

Tim's achievements in being able to use his experiences to develop and improve the systems of support for police and emergency workers have been modestly understated in this book. He has brought his open and compassionate heart, his painful personal experience, his sharp detective mind and his inspiring energy to be a core and critical force for innovation and systemic improvement in addressing needs for police, emergency workers and their families and communities. It is a privilege to have worked with Tim across many of his post-police career roles and finally within Phoenix Australia – Centre for Posttraumatic Mental Health.

Sometimes we read a memoir that opens our heart, challenges our mind and inspires us to make things better in this fraught, painful and complicated world we live in. *The Invisible Obvious* does all this and I am grateful for it having been written.

Professor David Forbes
Director, Phoenix Australia – Centre for Posttraumatic Mental Health,
Department of Psychiatry, University of Melbourne 2012–2024

Introduction

Mental health. These two words were of little to no importance to me when I joined Victoria Police in 1994. Like many other recruits, I anticipated a rewarding and exciting lifelong career in policing. I never imagined it would end with me succumbing to a mental health condition. Back then, there was not so much awareness of mental health in policing, but this does not fully excuse my ignorance of the risk I faced. During my twenty-one years as a police officer, crime investigation fascinated me – obsessed me, perhaps. I was driven to solve the unsolvable, to use my knowledge and skills to reach the only acceptable outcome: a conviction in court. My dedication, expertise and experience resulted in a series of positive outcomes in protracted and complex investigations. But my career with Victoria Police ended because of my inability to identify, manage and understand the impact that poor mental health can have on us.

On 2 October 2014, I reached the lowest point I could imagine – contemplating suicide and driving my car off the road while drunk. After that crisis, which led to my departure from Victoria Police, mental health became my new fascination. Although not straight away. It took time for me to adjust to the reality that my mental health had deteriorated to a point where I could never return to the job I had loved so much. Since then, roles with Beyond Blue, The Police Association Victoria and now Phoenix Australia have allowed me to combine my two passions: policing and mental health.

One of the first things my clinician recommended I do after the crisis in 2014 was to write a journal. Over fifteen months I wrote thousands of words, and this helped me understand and express my personal experience of mental health. He also encouraged me to study, and in 2019 I completed a Master of Counselling and Psychotherapy. During this time, I also worked as a volunteer speaker with Beyond Blue. I have delivered well over 100 presentations to workplaces within Victoria Police and in the broader community. And I've spent countless hours attempting to articulate my experiences in a way that others can understand. I found that my story resonated with many – and that it opened a doorway for others to reflect on their own experiences.

There is an abundance of resources available publicly and through workplaces to better understand and manage the effects of a mental health condition. But despite the best intentions of employers, the rate of mental health injuries is continuing to rise. I believe employees and employers have a shared responsibility to proactively address mental health risks in the workplace. This is crucial to any successful model of care. Everyone has their own unique experience of mental health. Experts agree there is no one 'silver bullet' that will protect you from mental health injury. We each need to accept responsibility for developing a plan that works for us, and workplaces should support us to do so – especially if our work involves challenging interactions or exposure to traumatic events.

I am not an expert in mental health, but through combining my personal experience with my observations of the many emergency services workers I have interacted with, particularly police, I have developed a clear understanding of the frustrations experienced in these industries by people attempting to manage their mental health.

Our current model relies on the person impacted by a mental health condition to 'put their hand up' and seek treatment. Sadly, that often means the individual reaches a crisis point before taking action. It is very difficult to make sound decisions in a crisis. Both individuals and workplaces lack forward planning to identify appropriate or suitable treatment pathways before a crisis occurs. While many workplaces offer some kind of early intervention training, this sort of one-off package, usually undertaken early in one's career, is supposed to sustain them through the complex and confronting aspects of life as an emergency services worker. I believe this is unrealistic.

Mental health is often considered invisible, in contrast to our more visible physical wellbeing. But when our mental health deteriorates to the point of crisis, the impacts are suddenly very visible. I hit rock bottom before I could see what had been glaringly obvious the whole time: that I was unwell and needed support with my mental health. It was as if a switch had been flicked from 'well' to 'unwell'. I – like many others – thought I was functioning 'normally' until the point where I could no longer tolerate the symptoms. Then suddenly I had a 'mental health condition'.

This is a common theme among the hundreds of police members I have assisted through periods of crisis. We go to extraordinary lengths to maintain a cloak of invisibility around our mental health, not realising that the longer we avoid and ignore our symptoms, the greater the impact will be. This is what I call the 'Invisible Obvious' – because the symptoms of a mental health condition *are* obvious, both internally and externally. Poor sleep, lack of exercise, intrusive thoughts, nightmares, flashbacks, anger, isolation, addiction, reduced work performance, impacts on interpersonal relationships – these symptoms don't just materialise suddenly one day: they develop over time.

By understanding and developing a plan for our mental health we can be aware of the fluctuations in our functioning and identify small changes in our responses before they become major problems.

Tackling the 'invisible obvious' involves taking responsibility for how we engage with and manage our mental health. There are many resources, supports and skilled clinicians willing to assist, but it is up to each of us to develop a model that suits our individual needs. When I started to recover, I naturally wondered what would have helped me avoid this situation. What could I have done differently? How could my workplace have better supported me earlier? And I quickly realised that there were many other people out there – not only in policing but in other fields as well – who could benefit from a model of mental health that they can use to monitor their own health proactively. In Part V, 'Discovering the Invisible Obvious', I share the model that works for me – in the hope that it will prove a useful starting point for others to develop their own plans.

The simplest of solutions had been in front of me the entire time. Throughout my working life, I had come up against seemingly insurmountable situations preventing me from achieving my goals: a crime investigation that did not seem solvable, entrenched systemic cultural issues within a specific workplace, or the challenge of creating an inclusive, diverse and engaging work environment as a manager. In each of these cases, without exception, I took the time to reflect and review, to break the larger problem down into manageable components and to consider the worldview of the parties involved. I developed skills and gathered knowledge that allowed me to adopt a flexible mindset when resolving these situations. No matter how complex the task, I identified risks, employed risk mitigation strategies and achieved the best results I could in the circumstances. I understood the process I needed to follow to achieve a desired outcome. I could see what I wanted to achieve. In a work setting, this was an effective and valuable skill. Why, then, did I find it so hard to look clearly at my own situation and manage it the same way? Why do we find it so difficult to moderate our emotions, our reactions, our personal relationships, our responses to trauma? Why do we act in ways that conflict with our values? Are our mental health struggles really invisible, or do we *choose* not to see them?

On entering a career in law enforcement, I had no idea that this work would affect my emotional and mental wellbeing. Whether this was naivety or neglect is a moot point. On any assessment, I was entering an industry that would increase the risk of a mental health injury. Exposure to traumatic events, critical incidents, stressful working conditions, confronting interactions with the community, and challenges to my personal values are all identifiable risks that I either didn't consider fully or chose to ignore. I had no measures in place to mitigate the increased risk, no plan to deal with unforeseen contingencies, no thought of what the long-term impact of continued exposure might be. In a professional operational setting I would never contemplate entering into something with such brazen disregard for the risks!

I also never considered the impact my work might have on my family and loved ones. I presumed they would be proud of my achievements and that they would agree that any sacrifices were for the 'greater good' of helping others. We did not discuss this: I simply assumed it is how they would view it. This was a convenient mindset, providing the perfect guilt-free excuse to continue my pursuit of excellence in policing.

I ignored the fact that my 'normal' was different to that of most others. Exposure to trauma was a given. I was involved in complex ethical decision-making processes that would have a profound influence on the lives of others, and accepting responsibility for the safety of colleagues and the public was part of my everyday work life. I had little comprehension of the impact the cumulative exposure to traumatic events would have on me and I ignored the cluster of devastating symptoms that impacted my functioning more and more. My life was far from 'normal'.

Whenever there was a choice between helping others or taking care of myself, I would sacrifice my wellbeing and justify doing so with the notion that I was assisting others. This 'noble' stance came with a cost. By continually prioritising the needs of others over ourselves, we inevitably create circumstances where we are in conflict with the values we hold most dear. Managing our physical health, mental health, interpersonal relationships and personal interests soon become distant seconds. We can't truly help – as a member of the 'helping professions' – if we are unwilling or incapable of functioning at a level that allows us to be productive and effective. Balancing the needs of others with our own needs is an important skill that is often undervalued.

This is the simplest explanation I can provide for my personal disintegration. In response to my inner personal conflict, I retreated into a world of alcoholism, fantasy and dysfunction. I deliberately ignored the negative impacts my deteriorating mental health condition was having on my ability to be the person I wanted to be. I morphed into a functioning alcoholic, struggling to accept or understand the impacts of a mental health condition which included an unhealthy fixation on death. Isolated, anxious, overwhelmed physically and mentally unwell – this was far from who I had envisioned I would be at the height of my career.

My lack of awareness and my arrogance and immaturity nearly cost me everything, including my life.

Looking at oneself in the mirror is a great metaphor for how we assess our level of functioning. No matter what others are doing or what level of training is supplied (or not) by your employer, ultimately you need to look in the mirror each day and establish a plan that will work for you. That plan is as individual as the person looking back from the mirror.

To really look at yourself in the mirror takes courage and bravery. Not the type of courage and bravery we normally associate with high-risk occupations, but the courage to ask: are you really being true to the person in the mirror?

For a long time, when I looked in the mirror I only saw what I wanted to see: the myth, the fabricated ideal of who I thought I needed to be to be successful. This kind of reflection is deceptive, cunning and shallow, an existence where it is easier to escape through avoidance and alcohol than to have the courage to commit to your values and really consider deeply how you might achieve a life well lived.

Searching for the truth is the aim of any crime investigation. Why was I so fearful to look at the truth in my personal life? If I had applied a risk mitigation lens to my own situation, I would have made better decisions to manage my health and to care for those I loved.

It did not need to be this way. Had I applied the same level of rigour to assessing my own needs as I did to assessing those of the workplace and the community, the outcome would have been vastly different. If I had developed a plan for managing my mental health instead of simply ignoring it, I would have had greater access to the specialist supports available. I may not have avoided a mental health injury entirely, given the industry I chose to be part of, but I am certain I would have reduced the impact and severity of that injury. Reflection and review have long been a mainstay of best practice when conducting operational assessments in the workplace; sadly, for me, from a personal perspective this aspect was non-existent. I've found this to be a common worldview in high-risk industries: the notion that operational or commercial outcomes are our first priority, and our personal health and relationships second. These kinds of cultures reward dedication, determination and a singular focus on achieving successful outcomes. I know: I was a key contributor to such a culture and I lived, breathed and believed in it.

This type of thinking has a fatal flaw: if we aren't healthy, both mentally and physically, we can't be our best at home or at work.

This shift in thinking took a long time and my understanding of mental health continues to evolve. Since reaching a crisis point in 2014, I have employed many theories and strategies to better understand my experience. Of greatest importance has been the ability to become curious about how I manage my reactions and responses to different situations, and identify which strategies are effective for me.

For many years I went to extraordinary lengths to keep my secret safe – to ensure that any mental health issues remained invisible. I used the catch-all excuse that I was 'helping others' to justify my ignorance and arrogance towards my mental health. The extent to which I engineered my circumstances to maintain my invisibility was astounding – and dangerous, culminating in the ultimate act of concealment, suicide. If I was no longer here, no one would ever know of the struggle I had endured.

Having the courage to be vulnerable – to allow others to see and share my condition, to make the invisible visible – has been the greatest catalyst for change. When I am open, honest and an active participant in the process of managing my mental health, I am far more productive and live a life much more closely aligned to my values. And visibility is contagious: I now know many others who share their experiences of mental health issues, creating a network where the discussion of this previously taboo topic has become part of the everyday. In hindsight, the path to a better life was right in front of me the whole time. Many of those whom I loved and who cared for me were attempting to illuminate the flaws in my thinking, to provide safety and comfort in an environment where I could thrive. I was blind to the obvious.

Most books written by former homicide detectives detail the unique culture of policing and unpick how the most difficult crimes are solved, taking the public into the gruesome world of murder and how one brilliant piece of detective work unpicked the puzzle. As humans, we long to understand why people do the horrible things they do. We want to see inside the mind of the master criminal and find out how they came unstuck. This book is a little different. *The Invisible Obvious* is not a crime that will be solved by an outstanding piece of detective work; there will be no DNA work, no confession achieved through a brilliant interview, no arrest achieved after a complex and innovative covert investigation technique. Instead, I provide a real-life account of the toll that policing can take on those who choose to embed themselves in this world. I have deliberately avoided naming any individual in this book: no criminals, no police members, not even family members and friends. The intent is to shine a light on what can occur when we ignore our mental health in a high-stress, high-trauma environment. It is one person's experience of the impact of this trauma on himself, his wife and children, the organisation he dedicated himself to and the broader family and community he was a part of.

The process of writing has taught me that my internal world is complex, but not unusual. Writing has provided me with the opportunity to connect more intimately with my thoughts and emotions and share them with a broader audience. The story that follows attempts to capture my experience through the ongoing evolution of my thinking. To make the invisible visible.

In Part II, 'The Detective at Work', I describe how my mindset of ignoring the obvious developed: the strategies I used to conceal, even from myself, the fact that I had a significant mental health condition. This is my personal account of how my condition manifested and the extraordinary steps I undertook to hide my symptoms, but I am not the only person who has kept something so obvious invisible. While the context for me was policing, many of the themes and experiences are equally applicable across a range of workplaces and settings.

While I discuss the way the culture within policing at the time contributed to this mindset, my intention is not to denigrate my former employer, Victoria Police. I made the decisions I made, and I take responsibility for them. In fact, within my team I created a culture that was diametrically opposed to the organisational values. One of my greatest learnings has been to move away from blaming any organisation or system for my experience. A great mentor and friend of mine has a favourite saying: 'life is about choices'. I made my own choices. Nobody but me made the choice to ignore the obvious.

In Part III, 'The Aftermath', I describe the immediate fallout of my crisis – including excerpts from journal entries I wrote at the time. I hope that through these readers will gain insight into how I started unpicking my mindset and finding a different way forward. These entries may be especially interesting to those currently undergoing a crisis themselves.

Part IV, 'The Road Back', describes how I evolved and developed new strategies to manage my condition as I returned to the workforce, adapting my approach to remain visible – internally and externally – in new working environments.

In the fifth and final section, 'Discovering the Invisible Obvious', I present the tools and strategies I use to manage my mental health today.

But first let's turn the clock back to October 2014 …

PART I

THE CRISIS

1.

The Death Hours

The early hours of the morning have held a certain fascination for me for as long as I can remember: from my early days in policing and the novelty of night shift as a uniform member anticipating a major incident to pre-dawn search warrants, where every sense was alive to the reaction as you crashed through a door, the ultimate invasion of privacy. Driving home after finishing a shift, as the city slowly woke and came to life, it felt like we'd acted as protectors, keeping the community safe for another night. It was also my favourite time to exercise: swimming in a heated outdoor pool on a cold winter's morning comforted me. As did waking in the sanctuary of my family sleeping safely, anticipating the start of a new day.

But there was another side to the early hours of the morning. As my mental health deteriorated over several years in high-paced detective work, I came to think of them as the 'death hours'. The time when I would lie awake in bed, caught up in thoughts related to death in some way. Or haunted by dreams about mortality. Sometimes – but not always – I had graphic flashbacks to scenes I had visited, and death had become something of an obsession. My mind would wander from topic to topic: Is there an afterlife? Do we experience death or are we unaware of it? What does it feel like in those last moments? If the physical act of dying is all there is, what does it matter anyway?

The early hours also brought great sadness. I was by now a functioning alcoholic, and my sleep was often disturbed by my body craving alcohol: as if I had not wiped myself out enough prior to collapsing into a dream-filled coma. I would wake in those early hours with an overwhelming feeling of guilt and hopelessness – that another day had passed in which I could not manage my alcoholism.

The easiest way to avoid the death hours was to get moving. I would often exercise at 4 am in the gym at the local police station, go for a run or take an early morning swim. Hungover and ill-prepared for exercise, the physical pain at least distracted me from the mental torment I was experiencing.

The other option was to work. In policing, demand always exceeds supply. I was involved in many lengthy and complex crime investigations and there was never a shortage of targets or operations that needed attention. When you add in the unrealistic expectations and standards I held myself to, I could always lose myself in my work.

By October 2014 this functioning alcoholic had a dangerous attraction to suicide. Thoughts of suicide had been with me from my teenage years, but they were just thoughts: nothing I would act on. I would sit with them for a moment before dismissing them as something that everyone thinks about occasionally. But by early 2014, these thoughts had become more prominent, and as the rest of my life collapsed, thinking about suicide became a strange kind of sanctuary: somewhere I could find some space from the relentless feelings of fear and hopelessness that overwhelmed me. They helped me create time that was free from the crashing waves of anxiety that were like a king tide during this period. Ironically, this only created less time for the important facets of my life that were the only real pathway for me to address the mire I was in. The lure of an immediate solution was intense. Subconsciously, I knew the alternative pathway – addressing my condition – would be embarrassing and confrontational and would require courage, an attribute I was not blessed with. It was far easier to keep my condition invisible, a personal pain only I could resolve: by annihilation.

In many ways, 1 October 2014 was just another day. I was involved in the execution phase of a high-risk operation. It had not been a particularly lengthy operation but the decision to engage was critical. If the operation was unsuccessful it could lead to the disclosure of some of the covert techniques we used to gather intelligence, but a successful outcome might change the course of the investigation – and boost my ego and reputation. I was central to the decision to lead the operation, and it was me who was front and centre during the execution phase. It was not a physically threatening operation, but the ramifications for me personally of not achieving a successful outcome were massive. Given the state of my mental health, it was little wonder the operation was unsuccessful: it would have been a high-risk strategy even if I was functioning to the best of my capabilities. And I definitely wasn't.

I returned to the workplace and could feel myself spiralling into an anxious and depressed mood. The mask was on; I said all the right things, justified the risk and downplayed the potential negative outcomes. I did what I always did in such a mood: survived the remainder of the shift, found some mates, had a beer. They left, and I was alone: me, my thoughts and alcohol. Was this the chance I needed?

3 am, Thursday 2 October 2014

The next thing I recall, I was upside down, inverted, my head against the side pillar of a vehicle. Disorientated, I could not work out which way was up. If this was death, it felt much the same as life.

In those first few moments of consciousness, I tried to process thoughts I couldn't arrange in any logical sequence. Had I failed? Did I just try to kill myself? My next thought was that I had to run. Flight mode flooded through my body: it was overwhelming, but trapped in the vehicle I was unable to orientate myself and find a way out. If I had been able to extricate myself from the car, I would certainly have fled before anyone else arrived. Another act of cowardice to complement a history of decisions where the easy fix was my preferred choice.

Guilt overwhelmed me as I realised I had rolled my car and I was trapped, with the car on its side, my head against the road. Had I hit another car? Had I injured – or worse – killed someone? The fear only intensified my panic. As I came to understand my situation, I wondered if I had deliberately driven my car into another object. This had crossed my mind as a suicide plan at times, but I was far too affected by alcohol right now to be sure what had led me here.

The effects of alcohol seemed to leave me, though, as I realised this was the point of no return. It was immaterial whether the car accident had been a suicide attempt or not; I knew what I had to do next with crystalline clarity.

I could hear voices in the chilly morning air. Local residents, woken by the noise of the collision, assisted me out of the car through the passenger side window and told me the police were on the way. I looked back at the crumpled mess that was the vehicle I had been driving, prone on its side adjacent to a parked car I had collided with. I was in a quiet suburban street in inner Melbourne. There was no particular significance to the location, but it would now be forever etched in my memory.

The people who had come to assist me had no conception of the death hours or of my intentions. They were members of the public who did not know that someone whose job it was to protect them – who they invested their taxes in – was a drunk driver putting the community at risk. It didn't matter how many investigations I had solved, how many offenders I had charged or what I had achieved in life so far. The positive impact I'd made for victims, witnesses, work colleagues … it all meant nothing now I had betrayed that trust in such a catastrophic way. There are some things you just cannot come back from.

Every part of me wanted to run. Other than some minor cuts, I felt no pain. Thoughts of killing myself were prominent as I rambled aloud about wanting to leave the scene. The locals tried to convince this bloodied, raving man to wait for the police to arrive. I had to keep my head – to escape from here and gain a chance to complete my plan. I recall being on my haunches in a nearby block of flats, with people standing guard to ensure I did not leave.

The police arrived, and when I consider all my regrets my treatment of the officers present that night would be close to the top of the list.

They quickly established that I was an off-duty member. My operational policing training kicked in: I knew there was no arrest power if I refused a breath test. This would allow me to leave the scene. The consequences would be dire, but I wouldn't be needing a driver's licence if my plan succeeded. My mind was both clear and confused at the same time. In my mind, I was planning an escape while externally I was mumbling over and again about killing myself. My recollection is that my threats were audible, but this may not have been the case.

The attending police officers naturally made a formal demand for a breath test, which I refused, fully understanding the repercussions of my decision. I then walked off with a parting shot about killing myself.

I have not had the courage to read the brief of evidence that was prepared in relation to the accident. I am unsure what the witnesses or police included in their statements. Embarrassment, regret and shame are the strongest emotions whenever I relive that moment. My memory is that I told the attending officers they would never see me again, or words to that effect. I placed them in the horrible position of having to decide whether to arrest me under the *Mental Health Act* or just watch me walk off, knowing they had no other arrest power. There is a strong culture of brotherhood in policing: they would have acted appropriately and ethically, but I am certain they would have also felt a sense of sorrow and helplessness as I walked away from the scene.

In policing, there is no worse job than having to deal with one of your own in such circumstances. I gave them nothing, refusing to engage with them and shunning their offer of a lift home. They suggested they call someone to pick me up and asked me to wait so they could make other arrangements. I was belligerent and arrogantly walked away, maintaining an air of superiority where there was none. The fact I put my colleagues in that position still leaves me with intense feelings of failure and sorrow. If this was the person I had become, I was certain I wanted no part of it.

I walked off into the darkness, comforted by my plans to take my own life. It was clear: my career was over. I had no future employment prospects. My driver's licence would be gone for a minimum of two years. My relationship with my wife and children was now shattered. Too many lies, too much deceit, a failure in every sense. I had tested myself in a career sense and came up horribly short.

When I had achieved my last promotion, many wise and respected members of the police force had warned me of the need to take care of myself. As usual, I knew best and ignored them. What would they know? I had been promoted through the ranks in this state before and survived. Why would this be different?

Now the death hour was here. I felt calm: despite the alcohol surging through my system, there was a sense of peace. Fumbling with my phone,

I fired off a series of text messages to my wife, my managers and a couple of close friends, thanking them for their support and love and explaining that life had become too hard. Then I switched my phone off and continued to walk. My last operation had begun. I knew a full-scale search would be underway to locate me now I had notified my managers. I had spent the better part of fifteen years using mobile phones to trace people who did not want to be found. Without a signal, there was no way of tracking me.

A taxi into the city was my escape. I directed the driver to Melbourne's Southern Cross railway station, where trains for regional towns left. I had grown up in the country and had always intended to return to my roots. The city had never quite seemed like home. Now it occurred to me that perhaps I had never belonged anywhere. My plan was to be carried out in an isolated location, far from anyone I knew; the thought of being found by anyone I loved made me feel ill. I had gone over the reasons for suicide for so long that the decision-making aspect was not an issue. I had spent many excruciating death hours thinking about my circumstances from every conceivable angle. If you had been in that taxi with me, I could have forcefully argued my position and would not have been persuaded out of it. My family would be better off, my finances would be secure, I would not cause any further embarrassment to my beloved workplace. The sense of frustration and failure at not being able to manage an alcohol condition would be over. The memories, dreams, thoughts and images that seemed to live with me as differing shades of grey would finally be black. I could give up on ever experiencing the joy that colour brings. I could stop the fight. I would no longer have to put on a mask every day to convince others I was okay. The fire in my brain could subside.

How does an articulate, intelligent, high-functioning soul end up in a place like this?

The sense of clarity and purpose I had that night has stayed with me. It is a difficult sensation to describe. I will come to the hindsight view later, but in that moment I had never been more certain of anything. My analytical, investigative brain had removed any emotion from the decision-making process. To me, this was just another operation to complete. The preparation phase was over; it was time to move into execution mode.

I boarded a train for Warrnambool: there was a seat available and it was far from anyone I knew. It would be a three-and-a-half-hour trip from Melbourne. I paid cash for the ticket so my movements couldn't be traced through a credit card. Operational security was second nature, a product of far too many hours spent pretending to be someone else. My shirt was covered in blood as I limped to my seat. I didn't stop to consider what others on the train may have thought of me.

As the lights of the suburbs flickered past the windows of the speeding train, my mind replaced them with the images that had become my constant companion. Every light was another face, a grieving family member, a disfigured body – memories of the senseless violence that filled my gut like a mass of black worms in an intertwined moving knot of pain.

I felt a sense of safety by running, but this time was different. There was a serenity that came with knowing that my pain, frustration and suffering would soon be over.

An hour into the journey, the train stopped briefly in the regional city of Geelong and I walked the platform there, rehearsing my plan. My confidence grew as I went over the details to ensure that my last operation would be a success. a dark silhouette had formed inside me; the mass of black worms had extended and multiplied. This sensation was always with me. I had not been able to name it: it was just an internal cognitive dissonance I had learnt to live with. This morning the silhouette was a deep black colour, the worms like tentacles reaching out to encompass the extremities of my being. It felt like if you peeled my skin back you would find the real me: this black silhouette growing in strength and size from the inside out.

This felt like any other police operation, except this time there would be no debrief. I had a detached, cold, calculated persona: the same persona I had relied on so many times when I was stepping into the fear of the unknown. I did not want to think of those closest to me, to consider their future, for fear of changing my mind. By remaining in 'police' mode, I could dismiss thoughts of loved ones. It felt as if there was another me who had so much clarity and purpose it was just a routine way of thinking. Years of practice in shunning emotion and placing confronting thoughts in a place where I could deal with them later were holding me in good stead. In the months leading up to this day, I had psychologically prepared for these exact feelings. I had expected I would feel guilt and doubt, so had prepared to shut those emotions out as soon as they arrived.

I could also rely on the same thinking patterns that allowed me to continue as an alcoholic. The addiction made no sense either, yet I went to great lengths to ensure it continued. The rational, reasoned part of my being had been taken over by an expert in 'flight' tactics – hiding, escaping, distraction and numbing. When my mind turned to thinking about the consequences of my actions on others, I escaped to a distant place to plan my funeral and the contents of my suicide note. This strategy allowed me to return to the blame game of attributing the cause of my dysfunction to other factors: the workplace, the unjust court system, my genetic make-up. Safe in the knowledge that no one else could understand my experience because I was so unique. If anyone was entitled to complete suicide, it was me. That was the thinking.

The escape to Warrnambool was consistent with my regular behaviour. Freeze, fight, flight. Running was my speciality, accompanied by emotional numbing. When I was anxious or in fear, I would resort to alcohol or find a reason to stay at work. There was a comfort in the safety of the policing family and all it offered: a place where I could hide my symptoms and condition. It was easier than facing the reality of my predicament.

What was occurring? Why was I so desperately unhappy? How had I got to this point where I was so fearful of committing to living in line with my values, to easing the weight of expectation and reaching out to those around me who could provide the comfort, love and support I so badly needed? The self-imposed weight of expectation and reputation was smothering me. Life without my police family was inconceivable. I loved what I did and was good at it. Who would pay me to do anything else? Where else would I have that security? How else could I help others and serve the community in such an effective and profound way? What could be more important than providing comfort to those families who had lost loved ones at the hand of another?

Even in my darkest times, I refused to accept that my mental health condition may have been the cause of my problems. Policing was so important to me: an escape from the pain, fear and torment I experienced in reliving the video in my mind. And alcohol could push the video to the background: a symphony of broken faces, bodies, families and violence that never seemed to leave me. Sleep only compounded the intensity of the sensations. Policing and alcohol were my only escapes from the pain and confusion I was experiencing, and ironically my addiction to both only fed the mass of black worms in my gut.

To avoid confronting my deteriorating mental health, I had reached the conclusion that I could not survive without my precious policing reputation. I could not succumb to the humiliation of admitting that I could no longer cope. To do so, I would have had to accept that I was not special and that there were many competent investigators who could achieve similar results without the lies and deceit that defined me. But now my reputation was shattered, word would be out and people would be looking for me. It was as if I had conceded that of the two competing parts of my mind, the growing, writhing black silhouette had won out and I would not have to answer to anyone. Fixated as I was by the idea of death, it was both confronting and exciting.

I reached Warrnambool and reality hit. This was it. Did I have the courage to explore the final part of the journey? All the planning had been done; now I needed to record a suicide note. I had been over it in my head a million times: no funeral, no mention of my policing career, no connection between my career and my family. Time would heal, life for others would continue, but at last my struggle would be over. No longer would I spend endless hours trapped in my own mind, in a nonsensical dance that could never resolve. Surely it would be less painful for everyone; they would no longer have to watch as I slowly self-destructed.

I remember feeling really tired. The weight I was carrying was overwhelming me, my body was aching and my mind was exhausted. My internal battle had taken all my energy, my sense of self, my independence and my will. Ironically, it was one of the coping strategies I had used for so long that undermined my goal of completing suicide. As I was in such a state of hopelessness and helplessness, I reverted to the one thing I knew could relieve my pain. I went to a local hotel. I was the first customer, it was mid-morning, I have no idea of the name of the hotel and cannot remember the person I spoke with. I was in such a haze. But I do remember thinking to myself that this person may have the privilege (or misfortune) of having the last conversation with this disturbed and weakened mind.

I ordered a beer and asked the bartender to put my phone on the charger. I had intended to leave my suicide note as a recording on my phone, a surprise for investigators when it came to the coronial investigation. The recording would be a parting shot at all those who I blamed for my own inadequacies. *They would finally understand … this would teach them … imagine how guilty they would all feel …* Except I would not be there to enjoy my final glory – another glaring error in my flawed thinking.

I would like to think the phone was still turned off when the bartender plugged it in, but it may not have been: either way, I knew subconsciously that as soon as that phone had power it could be traced. The gun detective who was considered an expert in tracking mobile phones, who had solved major investigations by developing outstanding knowledge of surveillance processes, had fallen for his own trap. Offenders get lazy, they make mistakes; you just need to be there to capitalise.

To this day I don't know if it was a deliberate or unconscious action, but, sure enough, it soon ended my plan.

Not long after the bartender plugged the phone in, a couple of plain clothes police officers walked in. I knew one of them, but the conversation was disjointed. Initially I thought it was just a coincidence that they were there. I made some small talk and put the mask on straight away. I was back into my police mode: outgoing exterior, deflecting from what was going on in my mind. If I could just get rid of them, I could complete my plan.

Of course that was never going to happen, and it slowly dawned on me that I had been caught out. The game was up – they knew about the car and my messages to managers and loved ones. I was furious. My mind was on fire. How could I keep up this front with what was going on in my head? *Stay calm. Play the game. Your opportunity will come.* I was not going to give up on the plan that easily.

I needed to be smart, play along until I could create another opportunity. I was so close to the end of my final operation. I had been pretending to others for years; I could manage another few hours. *Just don't make me speak with anyone I love. That's not part of the plan.* The pain involved in speaking with loved ones had to be avoided at all costs.

I will not embarrass the people who helped me that day by naming them in this book, but they will forever know how important their love and support was to me. They took me in, kept me safe, and spoke to work and my family on my behalf. A local officer who had been my boss many years earlier drove me to Portland for a psych assessment. The threat was that if I did not do this I would be hospitalised, and I wasn't going to let that happen. I knew what to say. I was never going to disclose my true feelings or thoughts; the clinician would not have hesitated to hospitalise me had she known of the existence of the silhouette and the extent of my planning. I said all the right things, assuring her I would be safe. I even made an appointment with my own clinician back in Melbourne to ensure I had support when I returned.

A great friend and mentor travelled from Melbourne to be with me and take me back the next day. The local officer let me stay at his home that night: a generous gesture, but also I am pretty sure they did not want me alone in a motel. He washed my clothes while I was sleeping and somehow ruined my shirt trying to bleach the blood out of it. So he literally gave me a shirt off his back: an apt metaphor in the circumstances. He and his wife must have had a restless night wondering if I would still be there in the morning.

I rose early in the death hours. My mind was in full flight. I could not face the embarrassment and shame of returning to Melbourne. My mentor was coming to pick me up, having stayed the night at a nearby motel. We had had a counter meal and one final beer together (I'm not even sure

I drank it). There were a lot of tears, some laughter, but also a stark real-isation that I would never work as a police officer again.

I spent the death hours with my mind racing, planning and schem-ing. That was easier than facing the reality of what the day would bring if I returned to Melbourne. Even in my dangerous state of mind, I took solace in the fact that I had trained my brain to push away the uncontrol-lable and confronting thoughts, emotions and feelings and focus on the task at hand. Anything to avoid the anxiety, guilt and shame that was waiting for me. There were so many conversations I did not want to have; I had made my intentions clear in the text messages I sent and now the world knew all about my inadequacies. Continuing the fight with the thoughts of violence that never abated, the unwanted graphic reality of my sober waking hours, was not an option. I fired off a text message to my clinician, cancelling the appointment for 3 pm that afternoon. I would not need it.

Then I took off for a walk, determined not to come back. I would not make the same mistake as the previous day when I turned my phone on. There had been many discussions about me returning home and I was resisting. It was not as if my thoughts had changed because people knew of my intentions now: I just needed to be better at hiding them. But the death hours had started me thinking: does suicide have the same effect once people know? How could I make people feel as bad as they should for what they had done to me? This anger was misplaced: the reality was I had reached this point primarily by my own design. Many contributing factors had led me here, but ultimately this was my issue.

I fluctuated from hopelessness to thinking of a new life for myself. There had been a shift – not a seismic transition, but a small shift. Was suicide really the answer? My mind swung like a pendulum, from suicide to a new beginning and back through everything in between.

I walked to the destination I had picked for my final act – then walked away again, several times. I was manic, speaking out loud to myself. It seemed like there were a hundred voices in my head, like when you're in a busy pub and the noise is everywhere but you can't make out individual voices. I paced up and down: at times aimlessly, at times with purpose. The black silhouette of worms inside me was pulsing in time with my heartbeat, eager to engulf me and assume control. My brain felt like it was burning. a sensation of heat spread from the front of my forehead across the top of my head and into my spine. Confusion and uncertainty reigned: what to do? Was this a courage thing or something deeper?

I had spent many hours with my clinician in the years leading up to this point. But I had never been honest or open with him, and treated much of our time together like a practice for the conversations I regularly had with police informers. I would look for triggers or changes in language, concentrating on body language, sentence structure, deception detection and developing the conversation so I could protect myself from being exposed. At that time, I thought much of what I had achieved with him had been nonsense. But now, in my darkest period, with confusion rife, when logic had abandoned me, the conversations we had had were somewhere inside the firestorm in my brain. 'Sit with it. Connect with your environment. Breathe. You choose what thoughts you act on.' These catch phrases ran through my mind and created some space and distance. If I concentrated, I could subdue the sensation of the silhouette for small periods of time. I took time to feel the breeze on my face, to feel my feet on the ground. I concentrated on the feeling of my breath on my top lip as I inhaled through my nose. I have always had a strong awareness of my movement and posture. I discovered I was now hunched over, my ribs collapsed, my spine rolled forward with my head bowed. My breathing was stuck, just like my mind. Everything hurt: my brain, my heart, my body.

I made a conscious decision to stand tall. To try to imagine the shape of my spine, the feeling of it upright over my pelvis, supporting my head. This seemed to stretch or extend the silhouette and reduce the intensity of the sensation. I tried again to feel the shape of my spine within me, my ribs expanding, my head lifting, my breathing easing. It wasn't a magic cure, but it did *something*. I walked back to where I had stayed the night before, trying to maintain my posture. If I focused on that, I could make it through another minute, another ten minutes, another half hour ... Depleted, not defeated.

I didn't make a conscious decision not to complete suicide. It was more like riding waves on a surf beach. I navigated one wave, but others would inevitably follow.

* * *

Lack of choice is compulsiveness. We are not looking for freedom of choice, but the ability to choose.

—Moshé Feldenkrais

The trip back to Melbourne with my mentor was long and quiet. I am pretty sure I was silent for most of the trip, but my mind was racing. My plans fluctuated from taking off again as soon as I arrived home to facing my challenges and accepting my failures. My thoughts were hectic and jumbled and I could not concentrate on any one idea for longer than a minute. I did find some relief in connecting to my body, but this was hard to sustain. To concentrate on your breath and employ some of the techniques I had been taught felt impossible. It was a long, slow, torturous journey.

My favourite artist is Paul Kelly and all I could think of as we were driving home was his song 'To Her Door'. It might seem corny, but that's what was racing through my mind. The lyrics did not fit exactly, but the image of a beaten and broken soul returning home and wondering what the reception would be resonated with me. Returning to face the music: how could this possibly end well? The part of me that longed to be loved and valued, to feel safe and with some peace in my sense of self was battling with an intrusive, deceptive and manipulative force that raged inside me.

On the way home I contacted my clinician and rebooked the appointment for 3 pm. He is so patient and understanding. I often reflect on our time together and wonder what he wrote in his notes. 'Egotistical, self-indulgent wanker' should have made it in somewhere.

When I arrived home, the house was empty. The kids were at school and my wife was at work.

Before hearing about my car accident, my mentor had no awareness of the extent of my deteriorating mental health condition. I know that this was a really difficult period for him, and I am forever grateful for the support he provided. I am also guilty and remorseful for putting him in that position, to have him feel the responsibility for the decisions that I made, or more accurately the decisions that I allow my warped brain to make.

My clinician worked in a suburb about seven kilometres from where I lived. Since I did not dare drive to the appointment, I decided to walk. This was both a good and a bad thing. I was unfit, fat, and uninspired about exercise. Over the years I had always tried to keep fit, but recently, as my alcoholism escalated, my mental health deteriorated and thoughts of suicide increased, it had become a task without a purpose. Who would care if I died fat or skinny? This was yet another example of the illogical narratives that dominated my thinking.

Walking hurt: I was still sore from the accident. And I identified many opportunities along the way to complete my plan. My mind was back in racing mode: the flickering images of all I had seen and been involved in from a work perspective were replaying in my mind. I must have got some strange looks from the passing traffic, as I engaged in a full-on and often volatile conversation with myself as I walked.

But I got there: I met with my clinician and many tears flowed. For the first time, I opened up, honestly and transparently, about my thoughts of suicide. I had mentioned it before, but I had always been careful not to say too much, as I thought if he knew about my plan I would most certainly be hospitalised.

I wish I had had this conversation much earlier, as after months of thinking, applying logic to the decision-making process, convincing myself that it was the best way out for everyone, he brought me undone with one single sentence. After I had explained at length how my wife, children, extended family, friends and work colleagues would be better off without me, he simply replied: 'That is a very compelling argument. I just want to point out one flaw – you don't get to choose how other people feel.'

What do you mean? my brain screamed. What was all this about looking at decisions from another person's context? That was not how I operated. Decisions were about me, about what was important to me. I knew what others should feel. But his words somehow silenced my hyperactive mind. *How about I ask my wife and children about living without a husband and father before I make such a decision?* This may seem melodramatic, but it was this conversation that started me rethinking my decision and how I reached it. One thing about investigators is that we need to have a clear understanding before acting, and now my analytical brain had been challenged.

Of course, this conversation did not stop the pendulum swinging. I still oscillated from one moment to the next, between strong suicidal ideation at one end of the spectrum to starting again and finding a way through at the other. I walked home in a state of confusion.

* * *

The love, support and empathy I received from my wife and children upon my return and throughout the time that followed will never leave me. They gave me the courage and strength to search for meaning when any hope of a future had left me.

Returning home after the Warrnambool incident was a turning point. I was forced to accept that my actions had led to circumstances where I believed I was of no value. I had given up. I thought the situation I had created was too difficult to navigate and I was left with no choice but to take my life. And I had convinced myself this would be the best outcome for all involved.

The decisions I made during that period were compulsive. Is there any act more compulsive than suicide? Reaching a crisis point, whether deliberately or not, had allowed me to experience the absolute hopelessness of being left with no choice. But despite the intensity of the despair I was experiencing, there was still a choice to be made. I could connect with my body, create some time and space, even if it was only for a minute. It was not full freedom of choice – my actions over many years had funnelled my decision making into a trap that seemed inescapable – but there was still an opportunity to make a choice to live.

What that life would look like was entirely unknown as yet, but I could choose to live nonetheless.

THE DETECTIVE AT WORK

2.

Chasing the Yellow Freddie

How did I end up upside down, drunk and disoriented in my car on 1 October 2014? It's a fate I could never have anticipated when I started out as a young police officer.

I didn't consider a career in policing when I was young. I was a simple country lad who enjoyed sport, friends and family. Growing up in a small country town, part of a large family with strong ties to the local community and sporting clubs, alcohol was a constant. It never seemed like a problem: it was just part of who we were.

My wife and I grew up in the same town and met while we were teenagers. I attended the local primary and high school before spending two years at boarding school. I think the aim of this was to squeeze the maximum out of my academic ability, but sadly it failed spectacularly. Socialising was far more appealing than studying and I subsequently failed my Higher School Certificate and ended up repeating the year at home under the watchful eye of my parents, in 1986. Two remarkable things occurred that year: first, I managed to pass my Higher School Certificate and, second and more importantly, I met my future wife.

After high school, I started a primary teaching degree but I was still more interested in having a good time than anything else. We married in

1993 and maintained strong ties to family and friends in our hometown. I worked with a local building company who remain family friends to this day, before moving to Melbourne with my wife, who was pursuing a career in nursing. I settled into a job working with a steel merchant, owned by a great family who helped me immensely. It was only when one of my work colleagues mentioned he was joining the police force that the idea of policing entered my mind.

It seemed like a good idea. While I enjoyed my work, I did not see it as a long-term career, and my wife and I were looking to buy a house and starting to think about having kids. No one else in my family had been involved in policing, so it came as somewhat of a shock when I announced that I had been accepted into the police academy. I had never discussed this as a potential career with my family, and it was vastly different from the work I had been undertaking. At that stage, my only interaction with policing had been as a guest at the Collingwood Police Station cells for four hours after becoming a little tired and emotional on the drink.

To enter the police force, I needed to pass qualifying exams, reach the required physical standards and complete a psychological assessment. The focus on physical health was demanding and I trained for twelve months to ensure I was as physically fit as I could be prior to entering the academy. I never considered my mental health. Why would I? The job was about excitement, adventure and locking up crooks. They would teach us all we needed to know, and I would have a gun and a baton to keep me safe.

This was the level of naivety I had as I entered the police academy at Glen Waverley in 1994. I met my fellow new recruits in the foyer of 'C' block, in our best 'neat casual' dress. There were a couple of absolute cracking suits that stood out – one shimmering grey number left a particularly lasting impression.

I soon learnt that squad mates become like teammates on a footy team – there's an immediate sense of loyalty. We would need to depend on each other in order to graduate. This was vividly illustrated at the first Friday physical training session, at the academy swimming pool. We had been physically smashed all week and there was much ridicule if you could not meet the required standards. Push-ups have never been my strength, and the instructors took great delight in pointing out your deficiencies and questioning your fortitude based on the number of push-ups you could complete. The Friday session involved a series of exercises, followed by a pool session. We all lined up on one side of the pool. You had to swim across, climb out, do ten push-ups and then return. Then it was nine push-ups, back in the pool; then eight; and so on. If one member did not complete the sets with the correct form and to the required standard, we would all be required to start again. The cycle repeated over and over, instructors screaming at those who could not complete the sets: they pointed the individual out, asking if we wanted to work with someone like that.

This was our induction to the attitude towards mental health in the force at the time: *harden up, keep going, I don't care how much it hurts, you better make sure you keep going.* The only reason I made it through that session was because I was a competent swimmer, so crossing the pool provided a bit of a rest period. For those who struggled in the water, the exercise was torturous. Even so, when I drove home for the first weekend (during the week we lived at the academy), I thought I might not go back.

The Friday session had the desired effect: two squad members did not front on the following Monday. And an indelible message had been conveyed – *harden up or piss off.*

We had to learn so many new skills – drill, defensive tactics, firearms, operational tactics. And we studied law, communications, and policies and procedures. Mental health and emotional wellbeing were absent from the curriculum. There was an atmosphere of fear, a sense of 'do what you need to do to succeed – or leave'. Anxiety was not something I understood at the time, but if feeling like you want to vomit, sweating, having a knot in your stomach, your throat closing over so you can't breathe is anxiety, then I was definitely anxious for most of the first few weeks.

Graduating from the academy was one of my greatest achievements. Pride, relief and satisfaction were the overwhelming emotions. It was the first time I had really set myself a challenging goal and achieved it. I had experienced all those physical and emotional reactions, sucked them up and found my way through. No one had noticed: my secret was safe. Those around me were unaware that I detested firearms training, that physical confrontations scared the shit out of me and that I spent most of my time worrying whether others noticed how uncomfortable I was.

Our first deployment was to the booze buses (ironic, in retrospect). Then to the Melbourne Custody Centre and my first training station, Russell Street Police Station. The standard induction was: 'You a newbie? Forget everything they taught you out at Disneyland. This is real policing. Keep quiet, keep your head down, do as you're told, and try to learn as much as you can.'

They were heady times: the famous Russell Street complex was closing and we were about to move to the new Victoria Police Centre in Spencer Street. The culture was not dissimilar to a footy club; folklore was reinforced through the telling of war stories, and reputations meant everything. You needed to be a worker with a bit of flair, with a certain level of scepticism about command and the bosses. Most of all, you did not want to be known as a 'squeezer' – someone who followed the policies and procedures and aspired to promotion.

It was here that I learnt the great unwritten rules of policing. They didn't teach these at the academy, but these rules governed the culture. *Never pull a 'sickie' on night shift. Never lose a fight. Never lose a court case. Always back up your mates. Never 'lag' on anyone. Buy into the 'work hard, play hard' culture.* You won't find these rules anywhere in the policies and procedures, but this informal list continues to grow as you spend more time on the job. *Pay your super: you need to reach 8.4 (the maximum multiple for superannuation in the defined benefits scheme), serve forty years and leave happy and healthy.* Within the overall culture, each workplace had its own subculture. And I would eventually enter another unique culture, that of the detectives.

Carlton was my first permanent uniform station. As a young, impressionable constable with a reputation for liking a beer and being a 'worker', I was the perfect cultural fit. Working to become a detective involved ensuring you had good 'stats' and that you showed interest in crime investigation. I became well known at the local Crime Investigation Branch (CIB) and would take on as much work as I could to impress them. Through hard work, I was able to achieve good results, grow my experience and become more efficient. I was fortunate to have some great mentors who provided guidance and support throughout this period. I gravitated to those supervisors who had been detectives and worked in the 'squads'; from the earliest days, my goal was to reach the Homicide Squad.

I could not have been happier. I loved working on the divisional vans and catching crooks. We had a great team and a very supportive culture. Sure, we experienced terrible things, but we'd have a beer, reflect and move on. But the issue was I never stopped at just one beer. Alcohol became a way of managing the anxiety I felt most days.

The demands of shift work made it increasingly difficult to spend time with family and friends. If a work matter troubled me, I had senior members who could guide me through it. If I had trouble coping after a hard shift or traumatic event, there were plenty of colleagues I could have a beer with. Later I would come to call this phenomenon 'the Blue Blanket'.

We celebrated our wins and commiserated when we lost. As I took on more senior roles, I took great pride in teaching others the 'right' way – *keep your stats up, work hard, come in early, don't leave until you've finished your paperwork.* It became the norm for me to spend days off catching up on correspondence. There were not many of my waking hours that did not revolve around policing. My reputation as an efficient and effective 'worker' was growing and to say I was ahead of myself was an understatement. Looking back now, I am certain I used this persona to hide my insecurities and fear. I drew strength from those around me and committed to being the best I could be within the limitations of the pervading culture.

By the late 1990s, although the culture of drink driving had shifted, for many it was still very prevalent. One night, after a send-off for some members who were leaving the station at a Carlton hotel, I drove a mate home and stacked my private car into a parked truck. I panicked and left the scene and was later found guilty in court for this offence.

There is so much to be ashamed of in this incident – I abandoned my injured mate, left my vehicle at the scene and avoided speaking to the owner of the vehicle I damaged. I had no concept of the enormous impact this would have on my family and my relationships.

This incident only reinforced my dependence on the Blue Blanket for comfort, support and surety: well-intentioned colleagues supported and cared for me as I went through the discipline process and a court appearance. The process took a long time and meanwhile I remained at work and continued to build an impressive reputation for crime investigation.

Over time the narrative shifted from me having done the wrong thing to a sense of *how can they treat me this way?* My outstanding referee reports and my previous work ethic convinced the discipline hearing officer to give me the benefit of the doubt and let me continue with my career. From this experience I learnt that if you buckled down and worked hard, any flaws you might have could be masked. Because of the level of support available from my mates, I sought them out rather than my family. I told myself I did not want to burden my wife and family with the machinations of the discipline process. How could they understand? They didn't know policing. Plenty of people had been through discipline processes and stayed in the job.

It was easy to make excuses, to hide my fears, anxieties and emotions from those close to me, as I did not want to expose them to the horrific circumstances I had lived through as part of my work. It was much easier to pull on the Blue Blanket: in the workplace, I would never be challenged, as mental health was not a topic for discussion. It was easier to blame our bosses or the difficult working conditions for my behaviour than to accept that maybe I wasn't understanding my response to the traumatic events I had attended.

I continued on the long, arduous path to becoming a detective, working at Carlton Crime Investigation Unit and the Regional Response Unit on secondments while I built a portfolio of examples to allow me to land a coveted 'Yellow Freddie', the yellow police identification badge that distinguishes detectives from general duties members. Performing temporary duties with a crime investigation unit is like an apprenticeship – until you have the 'Yellow Freddie', you are not considered an equal.

In early 2002, I was selected for my first position at a crime investigation unit in the northern suburbs. The effort to reach my goal had been all-consuming. Earlier I had been selected for a position at the

Drug Squad, but I lost that position on appeal because of my indiscretion in Carlton a few years earlier. I moved into more complex and longer-term investigations and maintained my high work ethic. Although I had two young children by this stage, my dedication did not waver; long hours, graphic scenes and an unhealthy reliance on alcohol were my everyday life.

My first detective role was everything I had hoped for and more. I became even more engrossed in my work, and my third child arrived. My wife was managing both her own career and raising the children. While I convinced myself at the time that I was present at home, the reality was there many times when the job interfered with family life. In every decision, I made work the priority, family second. I would say the right things but do the opposite. Why did I have to take on every investigation that came my way? Why did I become obsessed with certain investigations? Were there others who could have shared the load? My personal values were telling me to be home with my family. My work values were telling me to maintain my reputation and support the community. This conflict created anxiety, and whenever I was faced with anxiety or discomfort the easiest thing to do was reach for the Blue Blanket.

A voice in my head would tell me: *of course you need to serve the community, that's what you signed up for.* We lived by the mantra of 'work hard, play hard'. We had many successes and celebrated accordingly. Alcohol had been a constant through most of my adult life, but now it was justified. We were doing amazing work, there were significant risks: didn't we deserve to be recognised and rewarded? Great friendships were built, but in hindsight I was different from the others. I lost sight of the fact that it was a job. There would always be time later to make it up to my family: I promised that things would change when I had my next days off, or on my next holiday period. I would take the foot off after the next investigation and repair the relationships I was damaging. But that time never came.

In my mind, being a divisional detective was just another stepping stone to my ultimate goal – the Homicide Squad. There was no time to relax – I had to be the best, know the most, arrest the most offenders and ensure everyone knew how good I was. I developed my skills and was adept at utilising services such as physical surveillance, telephone intercepts, listening devices and the use of undercover operatives. I am embarrassed to say that on occasion, I applied for resources just to show I could use them, not because it was the most effective way to resolve an investigation. It was a feather in my cap to say that I had telephone intercepts operating or was involved in employing covert surveillance techniques or utilising the undercover unit. Work was all I thought about, it was all-consuming. When I had doubts or felt conflicted because I had not been home and had worked another block of ridiculous hours, I justified the sacrifice because it was all part of the plan.

A cycle developed – when I was engrossed in an investigation, my sleep was non-existent, as little as three hours a night, and my alcohol intake increased. I put on weight, ate rubbish food and stopped exercising. Anxiety was a constant companion, and self-doubt and insecurity were never far from the surface. At home, I was withdrawn and disconnected: physically there, but not present. At family functions, I would put on a mask and be upbeat and engaging. I could not risk letting others see what I was becoming. By the time I finished an investigation or had some time off, I was exhausted, and it would take days before I could play any meaningful role at home. But everyone felt like this, didn't they? This was the life of a busy detective. To get results, you needed to make sacrifices, and I would make it up to everyone I had ignored later on, when I reached my next goal … Right now, I needed to be the best I could be.

There were many examples of how this nonsensical cycle affected my judgement. On one occasion I had been at the Melbourne Magistrates' Court for a bail application. Following the hearing, I left the court and walked to Parliament station to catch the train back to my office. The investigation had received some media attention, and a journalist who had been at the hearing called and asked if was still at court. I told her I was on the way back to the office. She said that was a shame as they wanted some footage of me walking down the stairs at the Magistrates' Court for the news that evening. Eager to please, I told her to wait, missed the train, walked back to court and re-enacted walking down the stairs – that was how much I wanted to be known and recognised. The word that screams in my mind as I reflect on that now is 'wanker'. It was typical of my mindset – self-promotion, ego, recognition, be the best there is.

The level of trauma was consistently high during those years; there were some very challenging and confronting investigations. Even today, I can still graphically recall images of children who had been victims of serious domestic violence.

I often wonder what I was hiding from. Was it the trauma that I experienced and my response that was causing my dysfunction, or was it my burning desire to be the best? Either way, avoiding my emotions was the priority. The irony is, those who loved me just wanted me happy and healthy: to them, my career was secondary.

In July 2004, I had my next involvement with alcohol and driving. We had started early, completed a successful raid on a house and locked up a couple of crooks. It was a good day work-wise, and we had a couple of 'knock off' drinks. Then I drove home, satisfied with my efforts and the day's results. At home, I drank a couple of beers with dinner and then went out to get dessert for the family. I encountered a booze bus less than

500 metres from home. It did not concern me. I believed I would be under the limit and I didn't declare that I was a member of the police force. I went through the testing procedure and the preliminary test showed a positive reading, so I was off to the booze bus. I completed the test and was over the legal limit – 0.068 from memory, not something I am proud of. After the test, I disclosed I was a police officer and rang my boss and advised him of what had occurred.

The reading met the criteria for a penalty notice, a loss of demerit points and a fine. Fortunately I kept my driver's licence, but I was shattered, as I knew this may well prevent me from reaching my goal of transferring to the Homicide Squad. Never mind that I had let my family down. Again. My reaction was something I had not experienced before: I became quite withdrawn, depressed. I could not let my colleagues see this, but my time at home became a battle. Sleep was never easy, but during this period it was almost non-existent. This cumulative sleep loss must have had a terrible impact on my functioning.

On reflection, perhaps the most surprising thing about this incident was how my workplace responded. The senior officer responsible for the police service area made a comment on the personnel file that I have never forgotten: 'Valued member, one of my best detectives, will learn from his mistake. Welcome back to this division anytime, any rank.' On paper, I received 'workplace counselling', but no such conversation ever took place. This response reinforced for me that if I worked hard, maintained excellent results and dedicated myself to my workplace, then there would always be support. There is a fine line between supporting your staff and tolerating poor behaviour. This was a different time with a very particular subculture, and we were a tight unit and supported each other through any challenge. This support was well intentioned, but there was never any real consideration given to the underlying cause. Was this incident an aberration or a reflection of a much larger issue?

* * *

Following this drink-driving incident, my wife encouraged me to obtain a referral to a psychologist. It's very common that those closest to you see the warning signs first. In the workplace I could hide my emotions and I laughed off the drink-driving incident as an aberration. In fact, I was struggling to understand why I made such poor decisions; this was not a one-off, but indicative of many other behaviours that had developed. When I was asked why I made such poor decisions, I would reply, 'I don't know.' That was the truth. Perfectionism and the need for recognition were at the forefront of many of the decisions I made. The conflict between my two identities – the loving father and family man and the star investigator who could achieve anything – was at the core of my discontent.

My memories of the sessions with the psychologist are vague. I contributed little, said what I thought he wanted to hear and got out of there. I lacked the intelligence, strength and courage to even try to explain what was affecting me. I told him my family life was great and I loved my work. The barriers were up, and I would not let him in. He asked a lot of questions about trauma, my childhood and what I did to cope when I felt anxious. I knew enough to answer in a way that would not lead to any further meaningful discussion – deflecting, changing the cadence of the conversation, using silence, I did all I could to ensure the conversation was disjointed and ineffective.

I didn't mention the dreams I was experiencing, the lack of sleep, or my reliance on alcohol to numb my pain. I said nothing about my fixation on death, my hypervigilance or the strategy I had developed of thinking about investigations whenever I felt anxious. To escape my thoughts, I would try to think like a particular offender I was targeting. What would they do? How did offending make them feel? Did they have regrets, or were they cold and detached? I would adopt these personas in my mind as a way of filling the space, taking away the guilt and regret I felt at being a fraud – neither a great family man nor a brilliant investigator.

I walked out of my last session with the psychologist thinking he hadn't touched me. He had no idea what made me tick or what caused my pain: to me, this was a great outcome. I had approached my first venture into the world of mental health exactly the way the culture of my workplace had taught me: *keep it in, tell no-one, don't trust anyone. If you are truthful, they will take your firearm and you will not be operational, and you can forget a career once that occurs.* I would love to see his notes from our sessions; I'm pretty sure he would have referred to me needing further treatment in the future. I deceived no one except myself.

Particularly in the early stages of my career, there was little recognition of mental health concerns in the policing context. The general consensus was: *Don't trust them – if you put your hand up, they will get rid of you.* There was no actual evidence of this, it was just folklore passed on from those who had gone before us. So instead of seeking help formally, we would cover up the behaviours of those impacted and do what we could to keep them safe. The number of people who struggle with mental health issues after a career in policing is not a surprise given this context. I can only speak from my personal experience in the particular areas I worked, but my sense was that this response was common across the workforce. *Do everything you can to remain invisible from a mental health perspective.*

I had reached a nadir – I was now aware that my mental health was an issue. Alcohol was no longer a pleasurable recreational activity but a chore, something I resented but could not live without. Something needed to change. Two words came to mind: time and space. I needed to step back, reflect on who I had become and work out what was important to me – but was I brave enough to do it? There was so much at stake. I could not keep putting my family off, making excuses that better days were ahead. I kept telling myself that if I could survive the next investigation, things would change. The cycle was entrenched and it was exhausting. I needed to take the time to learn who I was and who I wanted to be, not what others wanted me to be.

I was privileged and fortunate in so many ways – Caucasian, male, in good physical health, educated, financially secure, married with three children. I enjoyed a strong network of friends and a large, loving extended family. I had no concept of what it is like to have no family support, to be from a marginalised ethnic background, to be subjected to gender bias or have my sexuality questioned. I have no doubt that these factors would have made my situation even more complicated. One challenge of mental health is providing a resource that suits every individual, regardless of their life experience or background.

The expectation was that if I was seeing a psychologist for fifty minutes a fortnight, that would resolve the issues I was experiencing.

In January 2005, I was selected to begin temporary duties at the Missing Persons Unit at the Homicide Squad. There would be no time or space.

3.

The Big City Detective

If I was full of myself previously, this was next level. My first investigation was the highest-profile investigation at the Homicide Squad at the time, and I was the nominated informant. This increases your status and profile, as you sign the charge sheets and your name appears in the court documents. In policing, you become known for the jobs you are associated with. We were using all available resources for this case, and the media coverage was intense. It was quite a sordid investigation; it captivated the media and the public.

This was my big break – an opportunity to build my profile. I had to prove I was capable, and I threw myself into the role. I had a great team of managers and colleagues who managed the investigation. I was part of that team, but far from the leader – though to see me strut around, you would never have thought so.

My alcohol intake decreased, as there was so much to learn and focus on. The investigation fascinated me, and I was learning how to deploy resources for maximum effect and how to use the media to our advantage. It was a steep learning curve, but I thrived: this was everything I had dreamed of. All those extra hours working out in the suburbs had paid off – or had they? I was rarely home and when I was, I was preoccupied.

I didn't invest any real time or effort in my relationships. My mind was constantly racing, thinking about the next steps in the investigation. It made social functions more pleasurable, both work and family – I revelled in the notoriety, talking about the investigation at length to anyone who would listen. By immersing myself in the investigation, I could distract myself from my internal conflict.

This noble cause of investigating a significant crime provided the perfect excuse for me to move further away from my values and beliefs. How could anyone question my dedication, intelligence or output? It was a traumatic investigation that involved confronting issues and circumstances. It added another chapter to the video library of death that played in my head. As my fixation on death increased, I continued with my technique of trying to place myself in the emotional space of the offender. My head was a mix of fact and fantasy. I could distance these thoughts from my operational decision-making, but there was little room for anything else.

This was to become the pattern of my time at Homicide: frequently adding to the library of thoughts, images and fantasy. I sought recognition and positive reinforcement wherever I could get it. We investigated crimes across the state, often at short notice. Spending nights away from home became the norm. I learnt early on that to be an effective investigator you have to know more about that investigation than anyone else. Any intelligence I could absorb was an advantage, a way to impress others with my encyclopaedic knowledge of the investigation. The more I immersed myself in the investigation, the greater the chance of success.

As time passed and the investigations mounted, alcohol returned as a coping mechanism. When I started at Homicide, I was fearful of my alcoholism being exposed. The subculture at Homicide is unique: there is immense loyalty between crew members, and lifelong bonds and relationships are created through the unspoken strength and support we provided to each other to endure the unimaginable situations we faced in our investigations.

As well as having to learn to manage exposure to graphic and confronting scenes, we had to handle emotional and challenging interactions with the family members and friends of victims. The bonds we built with the victims' families and loved ones goes beyond that of a normal policing interaction. You cannot separate your emotions – turn off empathy, concern, sorrow and guilt – when you share an experience with another human in such a personal way. Maybe it was just my personality type, but this aspect of the job fascinated me. Some investigators prefer crime scenes or the court process: I was interested in the interactions I had with those impacted by an investigation. I thought deeply about how I could manage their expectations and support them in navigating the court process – through the inevitable long time frames, disappointments and potential successes. There was no specialised training for this: you had to manage the investigation regardless of your level of experience.

Interactions with family members were some of the most rewarding and testing experiences of my career. I craved the admiration and appreciation after a successful result but loathed any negative feedback. Sitting in court with witnesses and family members, I felt like I was on trial. Would the defence team discover I had made an error? I was constantly reviewing the evidence, trying to reassure myself that nothing had been missed. The investigation became a living part of me: my emotions, mood and reactions in any moment reflected how the investigation was progressing.

To be honest, I have never discussed this with any of my former colleagues. As the investigations mounted, I could feel another piece of me slipping away. The protective strategies to keep my thoughts at bay were becoming more dysfunctional. Alcohol misuse, disconnection, avoiding the library of graphic images, poor sleep and lack of physical exercise contributed to my deteriorating mental health. From an investigative perspective, I was selfish: it was all about me and how I could promote my profile. I directed my energies to protecting and growing my precious reputation.

In late 2007, I realised that what I was committing to was unachievable, so I applied for a position as an investigator in the building industry. I was searching for a way out of my predicament, a way to save face without addressing the underlying issue of mental health. It had to be a role that made more money and had better conditions: how else could I continue the charade of success? I was successful in my application, but senior managers at Victoria Police convinced me that this was not a progressive step. There was scope for development and promotion within the police force, and I had much to offer. My ego, satisfied and reassured, would never have allowed me to leave in those circumstances. It was not the done thing: folklore dictated that you stayed the course, sought promotion and reaped the rewards.

Continuing in my dysfunctional pattern, my personal importance was measured by solving difficult investigations, using specialist resources and creating opportunities through thinking a bit differently to our traditional methods. Another personal measure was the number of interstate trips I took. I can hardly believe this now, but one of my goals was to have a trip to every state in a calendar year. I am not sure why that was of value to me: I guess I believed it would show how important I was. Perhaps it was an extension of the escapism I sought through work, a way of building up this almost mythical character I had created in my mind of the detective with no limitations who would do whatever it took to solve the crime. The irony was that the better I became at my role, the greater the reward, recognition and autonomy, which only fed the beast.

But for every success, there was a downside. No matter how hard I tried, I could not remove the thoughts that I was a fraud, that I was not living by my values. I had created a persona that did not reflect who I was. Ignoring the lack of sleep and avoiding the dreams, thoughts and images that seemed to follow me everywhere. I tried many strategies to maintain some level of mental functioning – I embraced exercise, diet and sobriety with varying levels of success and failure. Despite this, the cycle continued and there was little I could do to stop the juggernaut.

By late 2008, I was just about done. I had become difficult to manage and was increasingly belligerent, condescending and disrespectful to managers. If I did not rate a particular manager or team member, I ignored and looked down on them. I thought menial tasks were beneath me and if challenged, I would make whoever directed me to do a certain task feel uncomfortable. I was behaving like someone about three ranks above my pay grade and did not tolerate being told what to do. I continued to puff the chest out, walk the Homicide strut and adopt an aura of superiority.

A new taskforce was created to address a particular organised crime threat and a member from each of the Homicide crews was required to establish the team. Our crew took turns to undertake such secondments and this time it was my turn. Looking back now, I'm sure they were glad to see the back of me. It avoided a tough conversation about my attitude and work performance. I suspect there were concerns about my mental health and behaviours and it was a convenient way to avoid that conversation. If I were them, I would have avoided the conversation as well: I was petulant, with a sharp tongue. It would not have been a pleasant conversation and given my mindset would have achieved little.

I begrudgingly moved to the new taskforce and sulked for the first couple of months. Didn't these people know who I was and what I was capable of? This work was beneath me. My mental health had taken a significant turn for the worse and for the first time the security and comfort policing provided shifted a little. In the past, results and hard work had been all that mattered – where did this accountability rubbish come from? My already significant alcohol intake increased, and I became more withdrawn at home. When I was at home, I tried to engage, but was exhausted, disconnected and attempting to slow my mind. At work, I maintained a mask, a façade – my reputation was still the most important value I held.

I got over myself, and before long I was back in the same pattern – long hours, outstanding results, increasing my reputational value and ignoring my true self. I pushed aside thoughts of my family and the conflict with my values and set about creating a new image for the legend that lived only in my head. I restored my reputation through hard work and achieving results, which in turn supported the ever-present demands of my ego.

It was during this period that I began working with a mental health clinician my GP had recommended. This was my introduction to Alex, a very approachable and comforting psychotherapist who took the time to listen, absorb and then challenge my notion of who I was. He specialised in trauma and grief but had also achieved excellent results with clients experiencing alcohol and drug addiction. Initially my reason for seeing him was to gain assistance with my alcohol dependency. In our first session I was shocked when he bluntly advised that abstinence was the only long-term solution. To say that set me back a little was an understatement, but when he followed up with the suggestion that I needed ongoing long-term treatment, my heart sank. We danced around the first few sessions like a couple of boxers, each trying to find an advantage over their opponent.

Periods of sobriety were interlaced with extended periods of alcohol dependency. I toyed with controlled drinking for a time, but as the saying goes one was too many and a hundred was not enough. So, I entered a cycle of binge drinking and abstinence, needing to go to ever greater lengths to hide my condition.

This cycle had become exhausting and repetitious and my work performance had suffered. For the first time in my career, I took a supervisor into my confidence and told him I was seeking treatment for alcohol dependency. I did so because I needed time off work to attend counselling sessions, and because when I moved into periods of sobriety there could be marked changes in my demeanour. I was relieved to find that my manager was supportive and understanding. He showed a genuine interest in me as a person, rather than the image I attempted to maintain in the workplace. Perhaps if I had been more honest with him, I would have had a different outcome. Unfortunately, at that stage, this was all the courage I could muster.

* * *

The appeal of promotion was that I thought a new start and a change of environment would help me manage what was becoming a significant mental health condition. I had previously resisted promotion, as it involved a return to uniform, something that was below my lofty self-expectation. Uniform members were 'cannon fodder' for detectives; any mistake was the fault of uniform, as detectives did not make mistakes – another unwritten rule of policing. But now, with encouragement from the management team, I sought promotion to a uniform sergeant position. This was the only pathway that would allow me to return to a detective role at a higher rank.

The stint in uniform was an opportunity to gain broader experience in management and supervision. The network in policing was alive and well. I had strong relationships with senior managers and was successful in my first application. I started uniform duties in a suburban station towards the end of 2009. In less than a week I had the message out that I had worked at Homicide, as if that was some golden ticket to superiority. I am not suggesting all the dedicated and quality members who have served at the Homicide Squad held this attitude, but this was my narrow-minded way of ensuring I maintained some reputational clout while I was transitioning.

It did not take long for me to introduce the culture I knew to my new workplace. *Work hard, play hard, dedicate yourself to the job. The rewards are there for you if you stay the course, sacrifice now will be rewarded later.* To my surprise, not everyone saw the world as I did. How could this be? How could these people survive without buying into this ethos? To manage this, I rewarded and supported those who could keep up with my work ethic, who wanted to learn and who bought into my culture. At the time I didn't do this consciously, but looking back now it's clear. I ensured that I only promoted policies that fitted with my view of what the culture should look like. Anything outside my view was met with resistance: 'what would the bosses know, they haven't been on the road for twenty years'.

As a uniform sergeant, I made no contribution to improving the culture or development of the workplace. I was very effective at getting people to like me, but being a manager is not a popularity contest. I took the time to coach, lead and develop those who I liked, but if you did not quite fit the mould, it was like you did not exist. I did not understand the impact of these behaviours on workplace culture, the divisive nature of such an approach.

My stint in uniform lasted about twelve weeks before they allocated me a position managing confidential police informers in the division. This type of work was suited to my skillset – playing a role to deceive and manipulate others to obtain important information. Building relationships was easy and this type of work allowed you to burn those relationships with no conscience; it was simply a business interaction at the end of the day, regardless of the caring, invested and empathetic persona you displayed. I jumped at the first chance to perform temporary duties outside of the uniform environment. This temporary secondment had significant autonomy, minimal supervision and you didn't need to wear a uniform. It was a position where you enlisted others from a specialist work area to assist with the role. I had completed considerable training in human source management, which included the assessment, recruitment, management and deployment of police informers. Most police informers are in some way involved in criminal activity and they have information of value. It was my role to elicit that information and share it without disclosing the source. It was a fascinating and complex field, and I was drawn to it as it allowed me to move further into what I call my fantasy world. If knowledge was power in investigations, it was even more so in the source world. It suited my analytical brain, and I could develop relationships to understand what made other people behave as they did. What was their motivation? Where was the tipping point? How could I manipulate them to achieve my own goals? I was an experienced investigator with a strong network of contacts. I could build confidence and rapport with informers with relative ease.

In hindsight this role was destined to end badly. I stopped drinking when I first took it up, but after about three months the demons had returned. With each cycle of binge drinking, the negative psychological impact increased. I would push the boundaries until I took one risk too many or did something so embarrassing, I had to pull myself up and would then return to sobriety. The cycle was so frustrating. How could an intelligent, articulate and high-achieving person not be able to control something as simple as alcohol intake? I was continuing to work with Alex, but not achieving a great deal. He challenged my thinking and I attempted to introduce parts of what we discussed into my everyday life. But the pathways in my brain were well engrained, comfortable and secure, and my motivation for change was low.

I meandered through this period; work was challenging without being difficult. I enjoyed relative freedom in a work sense, and I had a couple of active Homicide investigations with approaching court dates. In hindsight, this could have been the time and space I craved, if only I had used my time wisely. I could have reconnected at home with the extra hours I had available, but instead I developed a system of work that entirely depended on me. I introduced a model where I had to be notified about any contact or potential contact with police informers in the division. This was the perfect excuse to keep me attached to the workplace at all hours; no one but me would ever have known what my output was during this period. My goal was to live the folklore and maintain my reputation and while the strut may have subsided, the ego was still intact.

Next stop on the promotion trail was a divisional crime investigation unit close to home. The promotion, this time to the rank of Detective Sergeant, resulted from an approach from a trusted manager. I had been a uniform sergeant for about eighteen months but had only spent twelve weeks in uniform and had not managed or supervised anyone. The evidence showed that I could not even manage myself – but I was promoted anyway.

Again, I thought a change in work location would help shift things. The office was close to home. I could down tools and look forward to a relaxing period, enjoying time with my family, resolving my alcohol issues, addressing the symptoms that had not abated.

Having little sleep, intrusive thoughts, nightmares, alcohol dependency, depressed moods and panic attacks had become my norm. I thought this was the cost of being a superstar detective – a price I was willing to pay because the rewards would come. The alternative to thinking this way was beyond me, I could not see a life away from policing. There would be a time when I would be happy, worry-free and enjoying time with my family and the things most important to me. But this is a thinking trap: we never reach a position where we stop and say this is 'it'. There is always another promotion to chase, another investigation to complete, another strategy to develop. On the rare occasions I was brave enough to challenge my thinking, the risk of changing was too great. What other organisation would keep my secret and trade work performance for promotion?

The shift to a local unit worked out pretty much as planned. The big city detective arrived alcohol-free and identified some important system changes that could improve outcomes. He brought his information technology background, investigative experience, source management expertise and understanding of process and systems to make a significant impact. Easy to like, popular and trading on his hard-earned reputation. Perhaps this was the pay-off at last.

Three months in, there had been some progress. My relationship with Alex had developed, and we had started to identify and explore the thinking traps that plague me. I had developed a daily routine to improve the balance between my home life and work. My initial abstinence from alcohol had waned, but I could moderate my drinking.

I had a sense of purpose: the additional responsibilities of the supervisory role reinforced the need for change.

There were two Homicide trials I was preparing for in the background, and the lure to prove myself in a new work environment drew me back to the same maladaptive coping strategies. I gradually returned to my previous habits of dishonesty, broken promises and deception – the traits I despised were commonplace again. My home life had become difficult, as I could no longer hide my condition from my family. I spent nights awake pacing the lounge room, talking to myself, insomnia driving anger and sudden mood changes; and I had a complete lack of empathy, insight or compassion.

Alex asked me to write down the four most important things to me in my life. I identified them in the following order: my wife, my children, my family, my health (physical and mental). He then asked me how many decisions I made each day where I put those values first. This hit me right between the eyes. There was nothing I did that did not have work as my driving priority. If the phone rang when I was off duty, regardless of the circumstances I would answer and respond if required. If that meant going back to work, I would, even if I wasn't on call – this was the level of commitment required to maintain my precious reputation. There is nothing you will find in Victoria Police policy that demands such a response; it was just the policy in my head.

This never-ending conflict was the source of my pain. I wanted to be the best husband, father, brother, son and friend I could be, but I was always relegating my values to second-best in my inane pursuit of excellence. I didn't trust anyone else to make a decision, conduct an interview or take a significant statement. It had to be done by me; that was the only way I could be certain it would be right. But if we consider my mindset during that period – sleep-deprived, alcohol-dependent, anxious and insecure – was I really the best person to be doing the most arduous tasks? The unwritten rules were well engrained: *it's your job, your responsibility, do it yourself and do it right.* This was the mindset I was exposed to in my formative years of policing and, in hindsight and with regret, I continued that thinking for a whole new generation.

The big city detective was popular and able to achieve impressive results. As I slipped back into the old cycle, my contact with Alex would drop off or I would attend sessions but not contribute in any meaningful way. I easily translated the skills I had learnt as a source handler into the therapeutic setting. *Show him enough to keep him interested but hold back the important details.* The culture of not trusting clinicians was strong. My GP had given me the referral to Alex, and I paid for the sessions myself. I was clear in my instructions to Alex that my workplace could not find out I was seeking help. I would do anything to ensure they would never find out. And I would never make such a disclosure myself. It was a taboo subject, from my perspective: a mental health injury was a sign of weakness, and trauma was not a concept I understood. Given my influence over the people I managed, I am certain they would have adopted this approach too. *If you can't see it, it can't hurt you.*

Perhaps all I achieved in this workplace was to inflict my chaotic reliance on the most destructive aspects of policing culture onto a new generation. I considered myself an excellent teacher. I took time to assist others to develop their skills, but only those who bought into my rhetoric. If you were not willing to work ridiculous hours at the drop of a hat, able to work as fast as me or understand new concepts, you were left behind. I would never state that openly, but actions speak louder than words. As a manager, I meted out subtle punishments to those who were not like-minded. Additional weekend shifts, allocation of the mundane and boring investigations, exclusion from the exciting, high-profile and challenging investigations. These were the methods I employed to maintain control and reinforce the culture I was so familiar with.

Performance management conversations with my managers did not occur. I would just receive an email asking if I agreed with what was said in my professional development assessment. The feedback was always positive. Perhaps this was because there were very few performance management issues on a superficial level. I made sure that I hid my issues from any managers. I had an amazing ability to put the mask on, remain upbeat and get through difficult times. But the longer I stayed in any one workplace, the harder it was to conceal my issues. I cannot recall having a truthful performance discussion with anyone in my time in policing. Folklore dictated that we looked after each other, we said nice things even if we didn't mean it. This was the essence of police culture at the time: avoid the tough conversations to maintain our safety and security. It was also reputational; I did not want to be known as one of those managers who actually managed.

In my experience, staff development was focused on those in whom we saw potential. *Grab them early, take them under your wing and teach them well.* This tradition continued with the staff I managed. But what if what I was teaching was flawed? What if my methods were not in the best interests of these members or the organisation? I had accepted my experience without question and had never raised concerns about it. In my mind, I was complying with the organisational values and I was being rewarded with promotion. This model leaves out those who do not comply with the way of thinking I have explained. What if their family and their own health were their most important priorities and they realised that to be the best version of themselves they needed to make decisions in line with those values? We shunned and left behind those people who did not fit the 'all in' culture. Turn down one early morning search warrant and you were not a team player: *I don't want to hear your excuses, that's just the way it is.*

How could I expect to think clearly and reflect in the state I was in most of the time? It was a white-knuckle ride to make it through most days without the mask slipping. There was no time for reflection or development.

In mid-2013, I was approached to apply for a Detective Senior Sergeant position in covert intelligence. The role involved the supervision and management of high-risk human sources. My application was successful, which meant that I had progressed from being Detective Senior Constable in 2009 to a Detective Senior Sergeant in 2013. Such a rapid rise is an anomaly in policing; this progression normally takes many years and many attempts. This only confirmed my belief that the sacrifices I was making were justified, regardless of the personal cost.

Privately, I was relieved. Not only was this the position I had been craving, the cracks were showing at my workplace, and my personal life was disintegrating before my eyes. Trading on my reputation was wearing thin. My dark secret was in danger of being exposed. If the organisation knew the depths of my condition, I was pretty sure they would not consider me for any work, let alone promotion. Of course I had years of experience in hiding my various symptoms and conditions, and building relationships and confidence in those around me came naturally. But my internal world was dominated by my thoughts and images of traumatic events, and doubts were creeping in about others discovering my secret. Now I was anxious about being anxious.

I traded on my rapid promotion; the strut returned – this was my time. The role came with major responsibilities and good people had entrusted me with them. As a leader and a manager, I needed to set the standard. Perhaps this was the ticket out of my dilemma? I could stop drinking without losing face. My work with Alex was starting to make some sense: perhaps managing my mental health was a bit like managing my physical health – I needed to train regularly and with purpose if I wanted to reach my targets. If I exercised, ate well, used my sleeping medication, continued with my clinical sessions, abstained from alcohol and concentrated on my relationships with my family, I could pull this off. I could manage all the pain and inner turmoil I had suffered if I followed the plan.

There was one major flaw in my thinking. I felt this role was the trade-off for all the work I had put in; my faith and belief in the organisation had been justified. While I still fell back on this thinking and dysfunctional coping strategies, I could never be free. Policing would always return me to my old pathways; my brain was wired that way. The security of the workplace – and the Blue Blanket – was so much easier than challenging myself. The mask had served me well: look where it has carried me. No other occupation would allow me to earn the same sort of money or level of respect and recognition.

This was the essence of my battle. Taking responsibility for my own mental health required bravery and courage and would mean fundamentally changing my worldview. Sadly, these were not traits I was blessed with at that time. In an operational setting, my decision-making was concise and considered, and I gave great advice to others, but when it came to managing myself I was scared and avoidant. What would be the cost of letting go of my reputation? I did not have the courage to find out. Lying to myself and those I loved had become an artform. I could justify anything in my warped mind. When in doubt, I would return to one of my favourite sayings: 'There is nothing you can't do!'

* * *

I sincerely believed that my faith in the policing system had paid off. My hard work had been rewarded: I had achieved the rank I had always strived for. This was a role I was passionate about and that provided the opportunity to have a significant positive impact on many high-level crime investigations. My ego had been suitably stroked. I could select staff for the workgroup and had a supportive management team. The years of sacrifice and dysfunction would be worth it now that I could say I had made it.

I had a simple plan: I would stop drinking, start listening to my clinician and GP and take steps to manage my mental health. This included allowing for time with family. I would repay them for all the sacrifices they had made along the way. Repay them for having to watch me disintegrate before their eyes over recent years. All I had to do was be true to myself, set good boundaries, appreciate the small things in life and live by my values. It was a solid plan. I had been very fortunate to have this opportunity presented to me. I had kept my secret safe and still achieved my goals. Maybe I was so special I could make this work?

I underestimated the extent of my mental health condition. A voice in my head whispered, 'There is no reward, you've just done a Bradbury. All the other qualified members have been removed or sidelined and you were the last one left. This promotion is just a ruse to keep you working.' My internal voice said: 'You will never live up to the role. There's no support, it's every man for themselves, you'll never cope. Look at how the last group of people in your role were treated. If you are going to survive this, stick to what you know.'

My thinking was confused during this period. On the one hand I was grateful that they had selected me for such a sought-after position. On the other was searing self-doubt. Did I have the spirit and energy to put the mask on and go again?

The role was challenging. I approached it the way I had all the other roles in my career. After all, this method had served me well in the past; why change something that wasn't broken? My initial aim was to impress everyone with my knowledge and understanding – a 'subject matter expert' was the phrase we used – then be popular and likeable with the staff. My management style was more about pleasing people rather than challenging norms that were not healthy. I selected staff I knew and trusted. In hindsight I made safe selections: people who looked like me, thought like me and would make for a pleasant workplace.

At the same time I was now acutely aware of the difference between my policing persona and who I wanted to be. Alex continued to challenge me on my values. I could easily write them on a whiteboard but I did little or nothing to live up to those values. If work, colleagues, selfishness and ego had been my values, I would have been performing perfectly.

The conflict between who I wanted to be and the police culture that had been driving me for so long had created the perfect storm. I was able to show up each day, make sound decisions, perform at a high level, train and educate others and present as an authentic leader, But beneath the mask I used to survive each day was surging anxiety, racing thoughts, a feeling of wanting to vomit, alcoholism and the fact I was functioning on three hours' sleep a night.

Small things became massive in my mind. I felt as if I was a fraud: landing my dream role had been a fluke and now everyone would discover I was not up to it. Managers would find out my diary was not up to date, or I had outstanding property items, or a brief of evidence had not been completed. Despite this, I took on any work that came my way and then some. I created new projects and took a keen interest in the training aspect of the role and found some peace in lecturing and sharing my operational experience with others. I was making a difficult situation even worse. In the past I had pushed all my worry and anxiety aside, but now I was seriously doubting the purpose of my role and aware that I wasn't being the person I wanted to be.

As the weeks rolled on, I could feel myself being pushed further into the abyss. I was drinking heavily, sleep was almost non-existent, and my mental health continued to deteriorate. Intrusive thoughts, flashbacks and dreams became more prominent. I was paranoid that I was being watched or followed, unsure if it was crime groups or my employer who had worked out that I was a fraud. Either way I was forever vigilant about cars, people, places, phone calls, almost every aspect of my life. In my mind, others were building a dossier to use against me and my world would soon come crashing down.

Instead of two versions of me, it now seemed like there were three. There was the family man who longed to be a great husband and father, physically and mentally well and at ease with his place in the world. There was the good corporate citizen, the prototypical copper, who had an unrelenting work ethic, high standards, could solve problems and was easy to be around and collaborate with. Then there was the self-destructive, insecure, frightened and scared me, who was unable to comprehend the seriousness of my condition.

Many people in other high-risk occupations faced the same pressures I did – long hours, hard decisions, ethical challenges, managing staff. We worked alongside other emergency service personnel – ambulance workers, fire brigades, the SES – who also faced difficult and confronting circumstances. The list went on: emergency department staff, nurses, doctors, corrections officers, lawyers, barristers. Each had their own specific challenges. Each of these occupations carries inherent risk and involves serving the community and unrelenting demands on individuals' time. But I did not witness any of them breaking down with anxiety or a lack of self-confidence. Why couldn't I cope? Why did I feel like every day was a personal attack on me, that situations I confronted did not happen to others? That my experience was extraordinary, and therefore I could use extraordinary measures to cope?

As the cycle became more destructive, my thinking became more blinkered, focusing only on surviving each day and maintaining my precious reputation. It was as if I had no peripheral vision. I was deploying all my available resources to the area of crisis, much like when our body limits blood flow to non-essential areas when a traumatic event occurs. I felt as if I was physically shrinking, stooped over, with my shoulders rolling forward and chest sinking. My pelvis would tilt and collapse with my ribs. Every part of me was in pain – physically, mentally and spiritually. Limited head movement emphasised my lack of peripheral vision and recognition of an outside world. I reduced eye contact and displayed behaviours that were the exact opposite of what I had been taught about body language and engagement. Surely it would not take long for someone to notice – I needed to act first ...

4.

The Silhouette Awakens

I was exhausted. I knew I could not continue as things were. The noise in my head had reached a crescendo; there were so many competing voices. My logical, practical brain tried to analyse the challenges and keep a sense of normality in the workplace. The true me wanted to walk away and be with my family, to start living again. The confused, frustrated, angry and irritated me could not accept or understand that it had reached this point. Arguments went around in circles in my mind. It felt as if my entire head was burning. I often wondered whether others could tell. Was my face red? Could they see I was sweating? Did they wonder why I asked them to repeat their questions? Did I seem distant and disinterested?

In my head contradictory voices competed with each other:

You're intelligent, articulate, high-functioning — why can't you stop drinking?

Be a man and leave the job if that's who you want to be, live up to your values and leave the job.

You don't know how to do anything except policing — how will you pay the mortgage and keep the kids at school?

VicPol owe you. They've caused this mess. You've given so much, you deserve to be looked after, go to the media if they don't.

Your family can wait: look at what you've achieved, one day they'll be proud.
You're not an alcoholic, it's just for the next little while to get through.
Once you settle in the role you can take the foot off and repay everyone.

There was no sense to any of this thinking. There were no solutions, just more questions.

My role involved high-level access to intelligence products, and I was an expert in covert investigation techniques. This only fuelled my paranoia: I was fearful that I was being watched, listened to, monitored or followed. I knew that many crime gangs had sophisticated surveillance techniques and access to confidential information. With no evidence, I created a scenario in my mind where I needed to be hypervigilant about everything and everyone.

I could not be truthful with anyone; I could not tell my managers or colleagues I was not coping; I did not want to let my wife and children down and take time off; I could not tell Alex how I felt as I was sure he'd have me hospitalised. I did not know what the truth was anymore. Every moment was a juggle of emotions and anxiety trying to appease the different voices in my head.

By early 2014 my mental health had taken a significant turn for the worse. My mind rarely stopped and I had become what I would describe as manic. I experienced panic attacks and would pace the lounge room in the early hours of the morning trying to find some peace. I would imagine I was in an exercise yard at a jail as I stepped out the six-metre length of the room, turned and continued the monotonous motion. I felt anxious all the time; it was like I could have thrown up at any moment. I avoided contact with my extended family and friends, because outside of work I had no reserves left to keep the mask on. When I was home, I disengaged from everything. The world moved past me like I was watching a movie, with no emotion or connection to anything or anyone.

As my condition deteriorated, memories and images of incidents I had been exposed to flooded my brain. I have heard this described in many ways, but I cannot think of a more appropriate descriptive phrase than a 'tsunami' of images, conversations, words, faces, emotions and physical reactions to the experiences I had been exposed to. It was like a never-ending film of flickering images that went with me wherever I went. They consumed me. When I describe myself as being detached, this was the world I was living in. I feared sleeping, as this only enhanced the imagery. What little sleep I achieved was when I was passed out after a bender. The continued alcohol misuse only amplified my paranoia, and the cycle continued.

I could not understand what was happening. No one else I knew had described this sensation to me. I thought mental health problems were for weak pricks who could not handle the job. This could not be me. Who would believe me anyway? There was no one in the workplace I could turn to – at least in my messed-up state of paranoia and egotism. I had no capacity to be honest with anyone. I was so fearful my secret would become known and everyone would learn that I was a fraud. It was terrifying to realise that alcohol could no longer soothe my anxiety. Maintaining the invisibility of my mental health condition had become impossible.

One night during this period I woke up drenched in sweat and leaping out of bed. I would often have nightmares or relive some real or fictional scenario in my mind. I would act out, fighting people off, running, hiding, talking in my sleep. But this night was different. I had dreamed that there was a dark body inside me that was taking me over from the inside out. I went out to the lounge room, still manic and very emotional. I started walking and could feel the sensation of this dark figure inside of me reaching internally to the extremities of my skin. It started as a blob in the centre of my chest and as I became more agitated and hyper-aroused, the blob felt like it was spreading through me like ink. If you took an X-ray, it would look like a black silhouette that sat inside the outline of my body. I considered cutting myself to find out if the black substance was real. I had no fear of the pain or of how this might look to others. I convinced myself I was losing my mind.

There was no one I could talk to about my experience. Who would believe me? And if they did, what would become of me? This incident scared the shit out of me, more than any operational policing incident I had ever faced. I fell asleep on the floor, woke a couple of hours later, then drove myself to work and pretended nothing had happened.

For what seemed like weeks, I played with this black silhouette in my mind. I had no definitive conclusion about this sensation. If this force won, I could forget a life of family, love, contentment and exchange it for an alcohol-filled, ego-driven fantasy. I regularly had sensations of the black ink inside me growing and shrinking depending on my mindset, like it was in my veins and would course through my body when the symptoms intensified. This coursing sensation is how I would best describe my most manic times, panic attacks, waves of anxiety, trying to gulp them down like you gasp for air when you have been underwater for too long.

I also considered that the black silhouette was in fact an image of death and that it was a part of me that was preparing me for the end. If this is what death was like, why had I not read about it or heard it described or come across it in any of my investigations? This sensation increased my belief that I was unsafe and disconnected from reality. I knew nothing else, I had to push through, no one would believe me and there was no one I trusted enough to tell. The reality is there were plenty of avenues to gain help and support. It was the extent of my condition rather than any lack of resources that was leading to my demise.

At work I spent most of the day trying to keep the pulsating sensation at bay. Outside of work, I used alcohol as a way of coping. Inevitably, I would reach a relaxed and calm state, even if only for half an hour, and then it would take off again. The alcohol amplified the coursing sensation, but it was all worth it for the half hour of relief. This is nonsensical but was all I knew to do to survive.

At home, I was exhausted, but sleep would not come. I was detached, alone and isolated in my mind, worrying and anxious about when the next coursing wave would hit me.

* * *

By March 2014 I was having serious thoughts about suicide. Before then, when I had fleeting thoughts of suicide during different stages of my life, they had remained just thoughts. I cast them aside, believing everyone thinks like that at some stage. But it had crossed my mind that my fascination with death was unusual: I spent considerable time thinking about the concept of death, and my time at Homicide had only increased my fascination. Now I was also struggling to make sense of my dreams and thoughts about the silhouette, and I could not find any peace in the overactive thought machine that was my brain. I tried to concentrate on work by creating fictional scenarios of being the target of whatever operation I was managing at the time and try to live a day like that person. When did they wake? What did they eat? How did they see the world? What was their motivation, how did they align with their values? A recurring cycle of dysfunction.

Now, for a fleeting moment I thought about a solution. There was a glimmer of hope that I could dismiss the thoughts and stop the coursing sensation of the black ink that was attacking me in waves. Rather than trying to find a workable way to live with the silhouette I thought of an ultimate solution that would stop the cycle of dysfunction. I dismissed the thought of suicide almost instantly, but it had started a new process – a shift to thinking about a solution that would disempower all the other forces that were consuming and destroying my life.

It surprised me how quickly the suicide idea took hold. The more time I spent allowing myself to move into that space, the less manic and confused I became. I knew my work performance was deteriorating, although it may not have been evident in my output. I could sense I was struggling with tasks I had once completed with ease and my memory, decision making, and concentration were deteriorating. I had an amazing capacity to absorb operational intelligence and recall and reorder the information as required. I could develop investigation strategies and determine which resources would give us the best chance of a successful outcome. But as I became more absorbed in my chaotic internal world, my capacity for strategic and analytical thinking decreased.

Suicide gave me an end point to work towards. It had been so long since I felt like I had experienced any emotion other than anxiety, having a time frame gave me some structure and brought clarity. This is a ridiculous concept, but it provided relief. It was like my little secret, a safe place where I could contemplate an end to the misery and suffering that I was causing others while offering a dignified way out of my torturous existence. An end to the cycle of images, dreams, thoughts, paranoia, guilt, regret and shame.

In policing, suicide was seen as a weak way out – unfortunately a reflection of the broader societal view. a selfish and short-sighted solution to a problem that one did not have the courage to stick around and resolve. I had attended the aftermaths of many suicides, where loved ones had been left to pick up the pieces of a shattered life. I had been involved in an instance where I was named on a suicide note as the reason why that person took their life. At the time, I shrugged it off, thinking, 'What a weak prick, he must have been guilty as I suspected. Why else would he choose this resolution?' I had not thought at the time that my actions may have led to the death of another human, more that I was right and everyone else could suit themselves. This incident comes back to me when I least expect it: a thought I cannot remove. I have unresolved guilt, anger and embarrassment at my complete lack of empathy and regard for another human life. A bit like my alcoholism: another dirty, grubby little secret.

Now I had a new secret. I felt sure it was not the easy way out; I was looking after those who loved me by taking away the pain I caused. If others knew the torture I endured to survive each day, they would understand my thinking. The cumulative lack of sleep had compounded my mental health issues; I could no longer think clearly. But with this solution, I thought everyone could move on, time would heal the pain and in the long run everyone would be better off.

I spent hours thinking about the experience of death. How would I know when I was dead? If I was dead, how could I recall the experience? I focused on the act as I would only have one chance to experience this event. You never get to share the aftermath of death with anyone – but in my case I had the other characters in my mind to share and debate with.

I was concerned about the damage to my precious reputation if I could not continue to perform to the highest standard. In my mind I was the high-flyer, the gun detective. Others aspired to be like me. This was just another part of the fiction created in my mind, but it was a key driver in why I continued to push to remain at work and enhance the legend. Suicide offered me a way out; I knew I could make my death look like an accident. I would then receive the plaudits of being the courageous protector of the community who died in tragic circumstances. My family would be none the wiser. As tragic as it would be, it would be an acceptable narrative. The accident could be blamed on my dedication to the job, long hours spent chasing the worst of the worst. In my mind the plan was coming together.

At first I was still aiming to make it through to the next block of planned leave. I told myself I would return to sobriety and spend time with my wife and children to make up for the hurt I had caused in the previous weeks. If I could just push through to that break, I could make things right again. But in reality recreation leave was not much different to being at work. I had set myself up as being irreplaceable and constantly monitored my emails and took work-related phone calls. Court cases or other pressing engagements that could not be avoided often interrupted my leave. In truth, I could have avoided them; it was only my ego and need for control that kept me working.

As my battle intensified, the conflict in my mind took me further away from any meaningful engagement with anyone. I was living in a parallel world, physically on the same plane, but miles away mentally. Conversations would flow around me; they were just jumbled words and background noise as the fire in my head raged. I often felt like I was a third party to a conversation, even though I was an active participant in that conversation.

Then I reached a point where I was just trying to get through each day, let alone make it to the next period of leave or days off. I channelled my energy and resources into making an acceptable appearance each day at work. Days off were spent slumped in a heap, exhausted, frustrated, agitated, angry and disconnected. Not a very pleasant person to be around, I could not risk letting my colleagues see this persona. As much as I wanted to be connected and loved, I did everything I could to push people away. Somehow it was alright to be like this in the privacy of my home, but not outside it. The ones I love the most saw the absolute worst of me.

As the weeks passed, the idea of suicide moved from being a faraway fantasy to a realistic solution to a very complex problem. As I spent more time thinking about the possibilities, the pieces came together. I was building a forceful argument in my head that was bringing me some peace and a way to reduce my anxiety to a somewhat liveable level. While I was disconnecting from others, my mind had never been busier, racing through the possibilities that suicide would bring. My analytical, investigative brain was alive with strategies of how I could end the cycle of pain and dysfunction I was causing. I knew my behaviours were having a devastating effect on those who loved me. I could not change my behaviours, despite my best efforts, so there needed to be another solution.

There was a stark irony in the way my mind was functioning. I had always feared being alone. I needed to have people around me, to be busy, to be productive. Suicide is the ultimate act of being alone. Yet even as I retreated from others, I did not feel alone, as my mind was a constant chatter of nonsensical planning between the different aspects of me. Did I create the silhouette, my ego and my relentless desire for perfection and reputation as a defence against being alone?

Throughout this period, I continued to meet with Alex regularly. I didn't mention the thoughts of suicide. I was far too skilled in conversation management and deception detection to allow him to see the real me. I was such a wanker. I actually believed that shit. I listened attentively, but I was careful not to give too much of myself. I lied a lot. I educated him about the world of policing and spent hours explaining why the police force was dysfunctional and why I was the only one who could see the need for change. I recruited him like I would a human source into my world, to be a private advocate, to provide positive affirmation of all that was wrong with policing.

Alex would have a very different view of these sessions. He was more skilled than I cared to acknowledge at opening me up and testing my boundaries, at calling out my shit behaviours. When we first met, he was very clear with me that there was much work to do; he would guide me, but the work was mine to do. This was not just six sessions and then a review. To resolve my issues might take years. He asked if I was up for the challenge. And of course he told me that the drinking must stop: abstinence was the only solution.

Of course, I said yes to all of this, agreed wholeheartedly, and then did the opposite. I would often turn up to sessions unprepared, thinking I could bluff my way through. I never admitted the true extent of my drinking. My initial goal was to find a quick fix, a minor change to allow me to return guilt-free to my dysfunctional way of being. This was not the place for that type of solution. Alex challenged my values and my behaviours. It was uncomfortable, but I stayed. There was something in his calm and intelligent manner that intrigued me. But I still believed I was more intelligent and that he had no clue about the life I was leading. He had never been a copper: how could he understand?

It is clear to me now that you do not have to experience policing to be a good clinician, and that he has a bullshit detector that is second to none. There is no debate as to who the most intelligent person in the room was – and it certainly wasn't me.

* * *

The constant churning in my head had reached a crescendo. The symptoms I was experiencing had intensified, but I was too frightened to disclose this to anyone. I thought my circumstances were too absurd and too challenging for anyone else to appreciate. My 'normal' – a life surrounded by death, trauma, stress and expectation – wasn't the norm for anyone else.

I had adopted many strategies to break the cycle, to change my thinking, to rid myself of the conflicting voices in my head – nothing had worked. For the first time, I was doubting if my commitment to the cause would really be rewarded with the peace and happiness I craved. I lacked the desire, energy and resolve to commit to it again.

Something had to give. I could not continue the cycle of destruction that had become my life – binge drinking then sobriety, catching up at work then falling behind as the workload became unsustainable, personal relationships that ebbed and flowed based on the status of my mental health. I sought solace in thoughts of suicide, planning my inglorious exit as a lesson to those who I felt had treated me poorly.

As the year progressed, the second voice in my head became more prominent, taking a stronger role in developing the suicide plan and considering contingencies that may arise. There was so much going on in my brain that I could not reconcile: Why did I have certain images and thoughts that kept repeating? Why did I have physical reactions to particular locations? Why did certain aspects of work remind me of previous events? Why did I push those who loved me away? Why did I refuse to listen to the advice of those I trusted and take time away from the workplace?

The mythical, secure, safe place that was to be my reward for hard work and dedication felt further away than ever. My whole life's purpose was being challenged. There was no contract that rewarded me for going the extra mile. I had to face policing alone. In my mind the workplace was now the enemy, watching me and waiting for me to slip up so they could expose me for the fraud I was. I could not share this with my family, how could I show such weakness and vulnerability? Policing had taught me to work to my strengths; it would be catastrophic to admit to my shortcomings.

If I continued on this path, what would become of me? I would have to leave my family as I could no longer tolerate the pain and damage I was causing. What then? Without that stable foundation to keep me safe, I would spiral further into alcoholism and the dark thoughts that plagued my thinking. I imagined myself retired, in ill-health, on a pension, in a caravan on a river somewhere, drinking a box of stubbies a day, pondering how long death would take to arrive and what the experience would be like. A slow, desperate slide into destruction: this scenario was not for me.

I had lost the capacity to live in the moment; I was either engrossed in my past or thinking about the future. Guilt or anxiety? Take your pick. Neither was a great outcome. I had lost the ability to sit and just be present. With my mind in overdrive, suicide was the cleanest, most practical and achievable solution.

In August 2014, after enduring another tumultuous week at work – long hours, alcohol, stress, critical decision-making to reach the weekend – I went for a walk with my wife. She was always encouraging me to do the little things – eat well, exercise, sleep, control what you can control. She provided great advice, but I had no capacity to act on it. These conversations generally resulted in more conflict, confusion and anxiety. We were sitting on a bench looking over the Darebin Parklands in inner-suburban Melbourne and I could see out over the suburbs. Instead of connecting with my wife, I was thinking of the different places I could see from my vantage point that related to some type of trauma. Car accidents, family violence, suicides, assaults, murder scenes: these were the images that came to me in a highlight reel of graphic violence. I was distraught, emotional, guilty and trapped.

When I tuned into the discussion, she suggested I take some time off work. I had ample leave entitlements available – nine months' long service leave, weeks of recreation leave and over 300 days of sick leave. The conversation turned to creating time and space, those two words again. We had been over it hundreds of times before and I slipped straight into my defensive mode and provided all the usual excuses for why taking time off was not possible. Who would take my position? They're reliant on me – what if they fuck up what I've started? So many people depend on me, how could they cope if I wasn't there?

What I didn't mention was my greatest fear – what if they exposed my shortcomings while I was away? How could I manipulate and cover up if I was not there to protect myself? I had seen it happen to others – I needed to be there to make sure they did not cast me aside.

No other type of work would do. I could not take such a hit to my reputation; I had committed too much of myself to simply take a step back. We had discussed a role outside of policing, but what else could I do? Who would pay me as much? Who else needed someone with my very specific skill set? But in reality, my mental health condition in a high-risk environment was destroying me. What's the point of being financially secure if you have no one to share it with or you can't reap the rewards?

It was during this discussion on the park bench that I disclosed for the first time that I intended to complete suicide. Until I verbalised it, it had seemed like just another idea, another fantasy bouncing around in my head. Now it was out, there was no turning back: I had to keep my word. This was not a cheap throwaway line to keep the wolves at bay, or a manipulative strategy to buy some time and convince my wife to stay. This was me at my most vulnerable, expressing a desire to end the hurt for everyone.

The fact that I put my wife in this position is unconscionable to me. What was she meant to do with that information? Ring my boss, tell him I should not be at work? Contact my GP or clinician? Tell my parents or family, contact a colleague or friends?

I had made sure that these options were off-limits. Any disclosure would only bring the plan forward. She knew I was smart and agile enough to create circumstances to complete my plan: after all, that is what I had been trained to do. Manipulation, deception and creating fabricated circumstances were some of my best skills.

I had created a scenario where work was the enemy – the extra hours, after-hours contact, time away from home and the utter exhaustion when I returned: work was the scapegoat for all my flaws. I was smart enough to deny any suicide plans – if my GP or clinician asked, I would say it was a throwaway line, just me blowing off stream. I knew they could not hospitalise me if I was not actively suicidal. I deliberately kept my parents and siblings at arm's length. If I'd disclosed my intentions to them I would have been met with disbelief; this was not the person they knew. Unconsciously I had ceased almost all contact with my parents and siblings: in hindsight this was a protective factor. The less I thought about them, the easier it would be to complete my task. If work colleagues or friends attempted to approach me, my skills in deflecting and creating space to complete my task came to the fore. I was a practised, competent and deceptive manipulator, a master at portraying myself in whatever role the circumstance dictated. After all, this is what crime investigation and human source management is, essentially: living multiple personalities and personas simultaneously to create opportunities to achieve your aim.

The die was cast and there was no turning back. I had been waiting for the opportunity to commit to my plan, and the disclosure to my wife had steeled my focus. I started looking for opportunities to carry out my plan. This was a distraction from the other turmoil in my mind. I had stopped completing work tasks that required a response in the coming months, as I had decided I would not be around for Christmas.

Although I thought I had planned my finances, my death would have left a financial mess, even though I convinced myself that my family would be compensated after I made the ultimate sacrifice.

I speculated about who I would have my last conversation with, and how I could make my death seem like an accident rather than suicide. This may have been a subconscious protective factor, as my plan was to take an opportunity when it arrived rather than create one. I knew that any investigation into my death would need to have as natural a lead-up as possible to make it believable. Ironically the heat in my brain dissipated during this period. It was too painful to connect with the real me; there was so much pain, I would go to any length to avoid having to think about it. This included continuing to work at a manic pace and ensuring that no one detected any change. I had convinced myself that my family would be better off without me, so I had only superficial contact with them. I am not sure if I was trying to protect them or if it was simply easier to disengage.

I was waiting for the perfect opportunity. One of my concerns was that if I was too affected by alcohol, I may miss the experience of death. I had spent so much time thinking about the final act: I wanted to understand what others had been through, to find answers to the questions that had been running through my head for so many years. My planning was often interrupted by my inability to manage my drinking. Alcohol increased the risk of a spontaneous action that might end it all without the opportunity to consciously experience death.

I stumbled during the month of September; I know that this was the most terrible period for my wife. After the disclosure of my intentions, every time I didn't come home or was late, she feared the worst. Putting the person I love through such an ordeal is my greatest regret and something that can never be forgiven. Was it domestic violence or psychological torture? I did not intend it that way but that may have been the impact. I thought it was a step I had to take to cement my intentions in my mind – until I said it, I would not be able to do it. That she could tolerate this pain and continue to love and support me unconditionally speaks to her enormous humanity. Amazing.

PART III

THE AFTERMATH

5.

The Only Certainty Is Uncertainty

October 2014

My return home was torturous. By the time I had travelled from Warrnambool and walked to see Alex, I felt drained, numb, embarrassed, ashamed and withdrawn.

I didn't know how my wife had explained what had happened to the children, but I knew my managers had visited her at her workplace to try to identify places where I may have gone. This was a very terse exchange (management were the enemy from our family's perspective – I had skilfully painted my workplace as the enemy) and my wife's message to them was clear – leave him alone, he will return, he just needs some time. Despite my text message being very direct about my intentions, she always believed, no matter how dire the circumstances and despite all I had put her through, that I would find a way to survive – she had an unshakeable belief in me and our relationship.

My children knew I was in crisis – they had seen my deterioration first-hand, and they understood that this was more than me making bad choices, that my mental health condition was impacting every part of my functioning. They may not have described it in this way, but there was an awareness that the symptoms I presented with were part of a much broader condition. I had been attempting to hide my symptoms for years, in hind-sight with little success. It had been frustrating for my wife to watch me self-destruct, attempting to downplay or hide the trauma I had experienced in a hopeless attempt to maintain my façade, but it was remarkable how she managed the children. Perhaps she had been preparing for this day for some time, knowing that there would come a time when my capacity to absorb my internal world would reach breaking point. I never cease to be amazed at the level of confidence and support my wife provided, even in the darkest periods.

Alex had suggested in our meeting that I write a journal, and I vividly recall my first attempt. It was late in the evening on the night I returned from Warrnambool and my family were in bed, no doubt worried about our collective future. Sitting on a couch with only a lamp on, hoping I might drift off to sleep, I took out a notebook and tried to capture the mess that was my mind. My writing was shaky and disjointed. Trying to write caused my brain to burn. Guilt and hopelessness were the overwhelming emotions. I had lost the will to fight. I had been fighting an invisible enemy for years, throwing punches in the dark, hoping to keep the threat at bay, without really understanding what I was fighting. I had no appreciation of the magnitude of the challenge I faced to return to some semblance of healthy functioning.

This is what I wrote that night:

Guilt, shame, isolation, overwhelmed – no way forward.

    Cannot process the magnitude of what I have done.

    Have ruined my reputation and that of my family.

    Caused guilt to others who are feeling like they were somehow responsible.

    This was my doing, no one else to blame.

Needed alcohol to make the pain go away.

Absolute frustration at having tried so hard and failed.

Regret and failure to perform the job I had been given.

Weakness for not being able to manage.

Stupidity for not listening (to wife) who saw all the signs but could not make me see.

This should not be about me. My fault. I will face the consequences.

It is the things that I cannot control and the effect on those that I love I cannot cope with.

Messages of support mean nothing. Do they understand the magnitude of what I have done? There is no way back.

(3 October 2014)

This first journal entry is far more coherent than I remember my state of mind being. I described the situation I was now facing accurately. I had suddenly stripped away every resource I had used to avoid facing my internal pain – no work, no alcohol, I was no longer 'special'. The mask had been removed and there was deep pain with no immediate solution, only a realisation that my life had changed forever.

Could my flirtation with suicide be the wake-up call I needed to regain some control of my life? I woke the next morning, looked in the mirror and hoped that everything was going to change – that I would live a life in line with my values, reconnect with those I loved and beat my alcohol addiction. That the suicidal thoughts I had experienced would disappear now I had failed so miserably and that I would somehow be magically 'cured'.

This was far from the case. In fact, I had added an extra dimension to the symphony that played in my head: now I had no future, no job, no driver's licence and a family in tatters. My relationships with my wife and children seemed irreparably damaged and without my job we were facing financial insecurity too. Returning to policing was a fantasy, but not returning was a concept I could not contemplate yet. Without the escape clause of suicide, I don't think I would have remained rational during this time; there had to be a release valve. Ironically, the comfort of suicide became a protective factor, a high-risk strategy that I did not contemplate or comprehend, but one I needed to maintain some level of functioning.

> Don't want sympathy or support. It is my fault. I had been taught the skills to cope and ignored them. WHY!! That is the most frustrating part. I cannot understand or comprehend why I would make such a decision. It made no sense.
>
> Just want to be alone, wish the world would swallow up my pain and embarrassment.
>
> Wish I had died, can't even do that properly.
>
> Still an overwhelming sense of wanting to run away.
>
> Will be reminded of this every day; it will have so many impacts.
>
> I want to be punished. I accept responsibility, not looking for a cop out. I took the role, was not good enough to carry it out. Too stupid to ask for help. Too proud to acknowledge my limitations.
>
> I am a shit bloke. Lies, deception, avoidance – not characteristics that make me proud. But that is me.
>
> Can give good advice, shit at listening to it or following it.
>
> (4 October 2014)

My greatest challenge was that I had no certainty. The court and discipline processes would be lengthy, and I did not know if my marriage would survive. In my mind, I had no employment prospects and a head full of useless police intelligence and information; there was no freedom of choice, only compulsion. But although it was unpalatable, I did still have a choice – I could wallow in self-pity, or I could attempt to make some sense of my existence.

I had no 'safe' space to retreat to, too ashamed to reconcile the mess that was my personal life, too proud to have contact with my workplace, too embarrassed to speak to my broader family and network of friends. Uncertain and isolated because of my own actions, I was experiencing a mental health crisis, but this was a concept that was foreign to me. I had accepted my inner turmoil as my 'normal' and saw the symptoms I endured as the price I needed to pay to maintain my 'specialness'. Far from an obvious solution, there was only confusion.

My mind moved to the question of blame: was this my fault? I was responsible for my actions, but what caused me to become the person I was now? My thinking was so black and white. I would oscillate between blaming Victoria Police for my predicament and reducing myself to a bumbling, blithering mess for not being strong enough to find my way through. There was no middle ground; it was all or nothing: either VicPol caused my injury and every action that followed, or my ambition had exceeded my capability and I had taken one risk too many.

Writing the journal was a confronting experience. Expressing my feelings did not come naturally. As a police officer, I had learnt to write about what I had seen and done, not what I had felt. Keep it short, simple and accurate. The investigations I was involved in required statements that detailed my actions, not my feelings. When you give evidence at the Supreme Court, they are not interested in how you managed your emotions. In the thousands of words I had written during my police career, not once had I written about how I felt.

I packaged my memories of investigations into the narratives in statements, summaries of evidence, and affidavits. These were the stories of the investigations, not of my emotional experiences, combining all the facts and intelligence to build narratives that would stand up to review and examination. This was challenging when the dreams, thoughts and images of those same investigations came back to me in different contexts. The process demanded that I put aside my experience of the trauma, that I deny my genuine memories; instead, my memory became what my statement detailed, not those fragments of recreation that contained emotion.

Now the journal was giving me a place to dig a little deeper. But it was still not a 'warts and all' account of my experiences. I attempted to honestly capture my thoughts and emotions, but my state of confusion and disconnection made this almost impossible and often I could not accurately articulate the dreams, memories and flashbacks of the events that troubled me most.

The days that followed were a blur: meeting daily with Alex, ensuring I was not left alone, and formulating a plan to manage my suicide risk. I couldn't see a way forward. The problems seemed insurmountable; any hope was extinguished. I wrote in isolation, embarrassed to let even family members know my pain. Themes of heat and fire were prominent in my writing, and I was still using suicidal thoughts as safety, as a 'get-out clause'. I was paranoid about expressing my suicidality for fear of it being used against me if anyone ever found my writing; the seriousness of my mental health condition was becoming starkly clear.

I was incapable of making a plan to manage myself alone. It was only through the support of my wife and Alex that I was able to maintain some structure – diet, exercise, attempting to sleep and abstaining from alcohol.

Detox is a demeaning process, as you know your own actions have caused the physical and mental pain you are experiencing. But the thought of returning to drinking was terrifying. I made a pact with myself that I would only drink if I revisited suicide as the solution (the idea of one final bender before the last tragic act was alluring). Attempting to find ways to distract my mind was challenging with my go-to coping strategies of alcohol and work removed.

Medications were a challenge for me. I convinced myself that the medication prescribed to subdue my cravings for alcohol was ineffective: that it was a placebo and that any side effects were only in my mind. In the past I had also been prescribed medications to manage my anxiety and to assist with sleep, but I had either refused to take them or pretended to do so and thrown them out. I was convinced that they were just a new vice I would become addicted to. And I worried that the sleeping pills would intensify my dreams and intrusive memories. My GP was very supportive in allowing me to make informed choices. He explained the risks and benefits of various options clearly, but my ignorance and arrogance fed the rebellious desire to avoid assistance. Subconsciously, I think I was resisting the realisation that I required medication to manage my condition – I didn't want to accept it was that serious.

However, my inability to sleep exacerbated my symptoms and after this incident I relented somewhat. Although I was not fully compliant with the sleeping medication regime, it did provide some relief during the detox period.

Text messages and voicemails of support from colleagues flooded my phone, and family members were reaching out to offer support. Accepting help was not in my nature; I was the person who solved problems. I simply ignored the contact or deflected it. After so many years of dysfunction, it was a huge step to concede that perhaps I was the issue, not those around me or the job that I did. Trying to be normal in such an abnormal situation, I was like a raft going down the rapids, being taken wherever the water flows.

> Sent a message to my manager, my wife thought it sounded rude. All I wanted to get across is that this is my problem, and I can never accept that things will ever be the same again. This is much bigger than VicPol. This is me. Why am I like this? I can accept I am an alcoholic. I have many faults. I push too hard. I do not accept mediocrity at all. High functioning alcoholic, that should be. How did I manage all these lies and maintain my persona? Why did I do that?
>
> Why couldn't I say that I was struggling and needed a break? Could have taught at the academy. I certainly have an interesting back catalogue.
>
> (6 October 2014)

In this state, I navigated the weekend and prepared to attend a meeting at the union, The Police Association, on Tuesday 7 October, to learn my fate. There was no way I would meet with managers from Victoria Police without first consulting the union. I had been avoiding contact with my manager, sending ad hoc text messages to keep him at bay. There were so many obvious questions to ask, but I had no capacity to retain or process information.

The black knot in my stomach cramped as I walked across the park to The Police Association building. Falling back on my old instincts, I had arrived early and located a vantage point in the park across the road to observe who was entering and leaving the building. I was in work mode, checking for exits, analysing those around me and considering how

I could disappear without leaving a physical or electronic footprint. The anxiety was crippling. I wanted to vomit to rid myself of the black knot, as my mind went into overdrive. Every part of me wanted to run, to escape and finish what I started. Fortunately, I had discussed such a scenario with Alex and planned how to handle it. I exchanged text messages with my wife and somehow found the courage to attend the meeting.

Most of the discussion was a blur, but I came away with two clear pieces of information. First, I was suspended from work, not able to attend any police facilities or access IT platforms, but I would continue to be paid. Discussions about WorkCover, the discipline process, pending criminal charges, superannuation and the pension went on around me: I retained very little of them. The second takeaway was that I had worked my last day with Victoria Police. Their advice was to look after myself, avoid contact with management and string out the suspension with pay for as long as possible.

I had observed a senior officer from Victoria Police entering the building as I sat in the park and when the time came, I refused to meet with him. The suspension notice was served on a representative from The Police Association; I was too embarrassed and ashamed to meet anyone from management face to face.

During the meeting with the staff from the Association, I did everything I could to remain disconnected – no eye contact, short answers, long periods of silence. I felt like a fraud, and I felt cheated. A fraud in that I had not been able to live up to the expectations I had set myself, and cheated because I had dedicated so much time, energy and effort only to be discarded in my time of greatest need. This thinking is nonsensical, but it reflects the inner turmoil I was experiencing. I walked out of that building like a hollow shell, thinking that the black silhouette had eaten me from the inside out, leaving an exoskeleton devoid of purpose or meaning.

Life at home was challenging. There was no escape from the litany of mistakes I had made. Promising that I would change my ways carried little weight; they had heard it all before. I attempted to explain what had happened at the meeting at The Police Association, but all I could share was that I was suspended and had worked my last day with Victoria Police. My wife asked about the length of the suspension, the court date, financial help for my treatment, and I responded with a blank stare — a common response, a blank face with no explanation. I had no capacity at that time to navigate the complexity of the systems I was now entering: workers' compensation, the discipline model, Medicare, private health insurance, criminal court appearance, superannuation and ill-health retirement; it was overwhelming.

> Sleep will not come to me. When I sleep, I have bizarre dreams that I dismiss as that. Last night, it was a kid who shot two of his mates. We were in a motel room when he told me he needed to confess to me. Woke up and only my wife there. Not sure what to make of these dreams.
>
> During the night had a strong feeling of wanting to lie on the floor. Want to feel the cold of the floorboards against my skin. Think a lot about burial or cremation. Reinforce ways of making sure no Police attend my funeral or memorial service.
>
> (8 October 2014)

It felt as though I had trained myself not to sleep. Bed was at once the most secure place and the most frightening one. When I climbed into bed, I felt comfortable and secure and sleep was possible for short periods: perhaps two hours, perhaps five. But after I woke again, there was no return to sleep. My mind raced — thoughts, images and emotions flooding my brain with no pattern or logic. Lying awake, watching the backlit digital clock, it seemed as if time was standing still. I was no longer secure, but afraid of where my mind would take me next, imagining the physical sensation of being shot or attempting to create 'a day in the life' of whichever target I was working on. Attempting to make sense of the violence and fear that accompanied most dreams. Without work to occupy me, there were many sleepless hours pondering the uncontrollable.

6.

Reality Sets In

October–November 2014

A week on from the accident, I was still in great confusion. As I tried to reintegrate into my family, my mind dwelled on the futility of my circumstances. I was very self-conscious out of the house. School drop-offs or visiting the supermarket caused my hypervigilance to shift into overdrive. I was fearful I would meet someone who would recognise me or ask me how work was going. I constantly checked my mobile phone, as if I was still at work, but did not respond to anything.

> I am really uncertain at the moment. Don't know how to feel –
> still have an overwhelming sense of impending doom. It is like
> the first explosion has gone off and now I am waiting for the
> next. This time it won't be what I do that causes it, it will be the
> consequences of what I have done. So where does that leave
> me? Do you run and disappear? Check out from something you
> have no control over. Easy to say it may not be as bad as it
> seems – just as easy to say it may be considerably worse than
> you ever expected. Although it has been a week, it all becomes
> very tiring, can't sleep, sick of running scenarios through my

head, sick of continually putting off any thoughts of hope. At the moment, I think of myself as an ex-police member.

(9 October 2014)

Alex had explained that it takes the brain seven days to dry out after a bender, to regain cognitive capacity. My feet needed to find the ground before I could consider a path forward. But at times I could wrestle control of my thoughts, even if only for short periods. I was exercising daily, walking or riding for hours along the Yarra Trail, attempting to exhaust myself, hoping this might improve my sleep.

These were difficult times for everyone, and when I was alone I was vulnerable. I felt like I was in a cocoon, like a grub hiding from the world. It's strange trying to be a parent when you are the weakest link in the family unit.

Do I want to be the grub inside the cocoon forever? Trapped but safe. I can manage my own thoughts – I can love my family, we can survive. If I try to extend outside the cocoon, the risks are too great. What if I relapse? What if all the preparation counts for nothing? I have tried to be the butterfly for everyone to see and judge – and failed miserably. But if I stay in the cocoon, I hold my family back. They need to fly and soar and show the world how wonderful they are. They are not me. Think I will just make the shell thicker for a while.

(11 October 2014)

I shelved much of what the Association had asked me to do in relation to the workers' compensation claim: it was just too difficult, and I did not understand the process. Completing a claim form, engaging with my GP, participating in independent examinations, the information was inaccessible and overwhelming. My strategy was to avoid and ignore everything outside the cocoon. I wanted to return to policing and show everyone I could cope. This shit storm was a mistake; surely, I must have enough credits in the bank to turn the clock back a couple of weeks and forget it all happened? It was my actions that had caused this mess, now it was up to me to resolve it. To me, help was invisible – I could not see I needed it, nor could I see it was available.

> My conflict relates to what led me to the position I am in.
> The absolute frustration that will not abate. My mind races all day
> with scenarios and ideas about how I could improve how we deal
> with people in my position. I cannot shake my default position.
> Of this all being my fault - I must wear the consequences,
> however difficult that may be. I fear I am too materialistic - but all
> I want is the best for my family. I am frightened of retreating into
> my shell and becoming a wasteland.
>
> (14 October 2014)

I walked along the Yarra River for hour after hour, lost in my thoughts with only the voices inside my head to keep me company. Who was right and who was wrong? What was the point of all this? Troubling thoughts plagued me. The reflection in that mirror was a disfigured, ugly, black blob – without shape or meaning. Was this what I had become?

* * *

The cycle I was in had become repetitive: moving from hope and a solution to frustration and uncertainty. I focused much of the time in my internal world on theories around mental health that I would then discuss with Alex. We developed mind maps of the models I created, and I attempted to apply them to my circumstances. I wasn't sure if they would benefit me; applying logic to the dysfunction in my brain seemed incongruent. How could I ever balance the past, present and future?

My life, and my mind, appears to be split into two distinct categories:

My home life with my wife and children that can be so complete and fulfilling. I can read and think and have time to develop some concepts that come into my mind. I eat well, sleep (sometimes), exercise and I know my mood has changed significantly since I have been off work. I am no longer manic. I am present in the house, rather than being a stranger. With clarity, I can now see what effect I was having on them.

The second category is that of my working life. Why do I need to work? Because I cannot sustain this family without an income. But it was more than that. It was a way of escaping, using alcohol to hide my guilt and shame. If I could perform at work and receive the plaudits, that was all that mattered. I could function at a high level, despite my alcoholism. But what was I really running from?

(20 October 2014)

I established a daily routine. Sleep was still a precious commodity, and I spent many hours listening to passing vehicles and checking that they were not slowing down to enter my street. Nights were a mix of unwanted thoughts, images and dreams, combined with restlessness about my future. Much of the time, I felt like a stranger in my own home, despite the genuine love, care and support of my wife and children. It seemed so long since I had been part of the family without my police identity as the main character.

I had several discussions with The Police Association about a workers' compensation claim. The consistent advice was that any claim would be rejected and pursuing a claim would take a significant personal toll on me.

I had not yet been interviewed or had any contact with Victoria Police in relation to the driving matters. I was advised that it was likely to be twelve months before any internal discipline hearing and they could cease my pay at any time. While well meaning, my managers had no answers. They offered the support they could within the framework of a dysfunctional and cumbersome system. Undermining their efforts was my reluctance to engage; without any evidentiary basis, they had become the enemy.

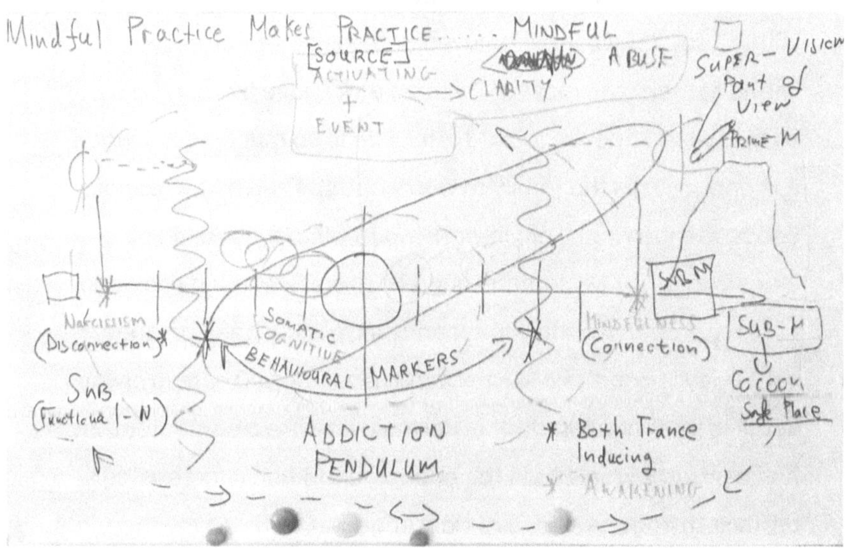

To avoid the challenging and uncomfortable thoughts about the future, I spent hours examining my internal world. This diagram sums up my mindset: striving to be relevant and trying to develop a concise model to explain my downfall. At the time I wondered who, other than Alex, would understand the model. In hindsight, this process enabled me to explore solutions that might work for me. I started thinking much less about who was at fault, exposure to trauma, and work-related stressors, and more about who I was and how I interacted with those I love and care about.

But I still needed an 'escape clause'. Suicide was the safety net that allowed me to tolerate much of the internal dissonance I experienced. It was still beyond my capacity to see a positive future. I was convinced that I was different to everyone else, that no other person had endured what I had experienced.

> I cannot resolve my feelings of guilt and shame at what has happened. It would be easy to wallow in self-pity and the reality is that I soon will be unemployed and possibly unemployable. I need to make the most of the time that I have left and be sure all the loose ends are looked after. Life is so much easier when it is only me and the family to worry about. There is no fear of consequence when I am in work mode, almost a feeling of indestructibility. My famous quote – 'There is nothing I can't do.'
>
> I have been wondering recently if my mind goes on once your body is gone. It is like my mind never slows, there is always some idea or concept that is ticking away, like a computer that has a program running in the background. I find it increasingly difficult to engage and to remain engaged, at times my thoughts totally envelope me. I am not sure whether that is stress, or whether it is because I have more time on my hands, but it becomes increasingly irritating to me and those around me.
>
> (25 October 2014)

It took three weeks to summon up the courage to meet with my parents. I knew their love was unconditional, but shame, guilt and embarrassment had seeped into every part of me. It was important to me to show them that I could find a solution to the problem I had created. I was not open about the seriousness of my condition or the effects the symptoms were having on my everyday functioning. I had no genuine answers about my future. I wanted them to know I was okay, but I couldn't be fully honest with them about my circumstances and the extent of my mental health condition.

The end of the month was challenging. Although I knew my claim might not be accepted, I still wanted to pursue the workers' compensation claim, as doing so stilled some of my internal battles. On the one hand, I wanted to take responsibility for my actions; blaming Victoria Police for my predicament made me feel like a fraud. But then I would skip to the other end of the spectrum: my role with Victoria Police had clearly had an impact on my mental health. The condition I was now suffering from was not because of crashing the vehicle and the events that followed. It was clear to me now that I'd been unwell for some time and that my work was a big factor in that.

I met with lawyers on 28 October, and on their instructions submitted the workers' compensation claim the following day. I described the injury and cause on the claim form as 'acute anxiety and depression, mood disorder resulting from exposure to traumatic events over an extended period while working with Victoria Police'. The explanation made no sense: it was so generic it could apply to any officer who ever worked with Victoria Police. Perhaps I structured it that way to suit the workers' compensation process, but it told little of my story or my experience.

I had returned to swimming – early morning in the death hours, following a black line, just me and my thoughts. Feeling the warm water contrasting with the chilly morning air on my back, I wondered what other swimmers thought about as they chased the black line. Had they contemplated suicide? Had they seen what I have seen? How would they react if they knew I was a drink driver who could have killed someone? I would experiment with how long I could hold my breath before I was forced to gulp for air. On other mornings, it was almost a spiritual experience, the quiet sounds of the splashing water and taking the time to feel my body move against it. A place to explore my random thoughts, to shift my thinking from the images of negativity, trauma and death to a future. There was much work to do.

* * *

As November began, the workers' compensation issue was at the front of my mind. We had a family holiday to Queensland booked, which provided some respite. This was the holiday I had been aiming to reach to recharge and reassess my goals: it came a month too late. Despite my intentions to make this time as 'normal' as possible for my family, there were long periods of silence and distraction, and outbursts of anger. I had no illusions: I knew a brief holiday would not resolve the issues my family was experiencing.

Alex encouraged me to read widely on the topic of mental health; any insight to make sense of the thoughts that flooded my mind would be beneficial. I had a habit of grabbing a thought and running with it until the next thought came along. This led to many hours of analysing things that had little relevance. I slowly developed a practice of concentrating on a single thought and deciding if it was worth pursuing or not. This was my form of mindfulness: taking the time to accept each thought, consider it and then decide if I needed to pursue it. This process allowed me to quieten some of the anarchy that would over-whelm me in moments of free thinking. Dreams, images and flashbacks were far more difficult to process than thoughts. Something as simple as the sound of a motorbike in the street was enough to send me into a panic attack, believing outlaw motorcycle gangs were sending a mes-sage. My thoughts of violence manifested in my dreams. It was easier to stay awake than to relive the graphic detail that was so real it felt as if I was fighting for my life.

Small changes had improved my outlook – time away from work, a consistent routine, exercise and abstinence from alcohol. I was so con-fident of returning to my previous self, I started applying for jobs. I didn't know how I would explain the circumstances I found myself in, but I threw myself into researching possible roles and imagining my life returning to normal. I ignored the fact that I was getting medical certifi-cates from my GP stating that I had no capacity for work because of my mental health condition – and I put the workers' compensation claim out of my mind. I was seeking a short-term fix to salvage my reputation and avoid the stark reality that I was being dismissed from Victoria Police. Unsurprisingly, I was not selected for an interview.

> Has been a time for reflection and realisation. Had a meeting with my manager last week and it just reminded me of the hopelessness of my position at Victoria Police. That organisation will go on, there is nothing I can do to change the perspective that they have in relation to the offence I committed. I accept and understand their need to protect the brand and no one person is bigger than the organisation.
>
> I feel free in mind and spirit this week, like I have an acceptance that I will find a way through this, just letting go of

all those negative thoughts that restrict me and, in turn,
dominate me. I have a meeting with the WorkCover psych
tomorrow that has been playing on my mind a bit. I am not sure
I will find the right words to describe my experiences.

(25 November 2014)

The consultation with the WorkCover IME (independent medical examiner) was the first tangible step in moving through the claim assessment process. An IME, in this case a psychiatrist, was sought to determine if I had a diagnosable condition and, if so, whether the workplace had caused the condition. One step at a time, I told myself: a linear upward path to a better place. If this was as bad as I was going to feel before an important event, then I could survive. But I would soon learn that recovery is anything but a steady upward gradient.

I compiled a list of the key topics to cover with the IME. I built up a picture of how the conversation would unfold and how I would explain that VicPol had caused all this. But as so often happens, what I forecast in my mind did not play out. How could I have known what to expect, what a qualified psychiatrist might ask? It is human nature to prepare for the unknown, but I was next level. I had a clear set of points I wanted to articulate, but I was reluctant to disclose many of the symptoms that had been impacting me. I didn't mention the suicidal thoughts, sleep deprivation, nightmares, flashbacks, intrusive thoughts or alcohol dependency. Perhaps I did not want to admit the full extent of my condition or accept that I was one of those who could not handle the job.

It has been a very difficult past 24 hours. I had no insight into
the internal conflict that the psych session with the WorkCover

rep would cause. I have been over it a thousand times in my head, second guessing what answers she was after, wondering why she did not ask the questions I expected. Disbelief that she could form an assessment of my current circumstances based on the questions that were asked and the responses given. I did not think it would matter to me at all, tell the truth and let them decide. The reality was very different. I have slipped back quite a way and feel very distracted, withdrawn, depressed and frustrated. Really had to force myself to exercise this morning. Wanted to curl up and hide from the world. I sense a lot of anger and frustration. Some of it is based on the realisation that I may have a mental illness. I had never really considered this before, not in those terms. I knew I was having some issues, but never considered myself to be mentally ill. If WorkCover approves my claim, does that mean I have a mental illness? If they reject it, am I okay? More doubt in my life is not what I need.

(27 November 2014)

This was my first experience of a significant negative event since the incident in October and it involved my workplace, something I had tried to isolate myself from. I had limited knowledge of the workers' compensation system, but I was willing to condemn it out of hand. Surprisingly, despite the setback, I remained sober and dismissed any suicidal thoughts, which in hindsight I see was a considerable achievement.

It amazes me how contained the entry following the aftermath of the IME seems to be. My recollection is that I was erratic, moving to thoughts of suicide and escape, without realising I had developed a method for dealing with crisis. It did not feel like it at the time, but having a simple plan to enact when I was confused and frustrated was beneficial. For the first time in a long time, I was experiencing a sense of myself, regardless of how confronting that was.

7.

Home Truths

December 2014–March 2015

I hadn't anticipated the impact of the workers' compensation process. As a middle manager in a large government organisation, you might expect that I would have had some understanding of the process. But in my world, workers' compensation was for freeloaders who wanted to take advantage of the system or for officers who were in the shit, a category I never thought I would find myself in. At the core of my discontent was that I felt like I was looking for something or someone to blame, while feeling intense guilt knowing that I could have killed or injured an innocent community member because I chose to believe I was infallible.

> The start of another week, I am feeling a range of emotions, none of which can be resolved. I guess I am trying to learn to live with uncertainty. I have no idea what the future holds, but I must continue to look after myself each day. I feel safe in the place I am in at the moment. I have so many ideas for the future, but no idea of how to make them happen or if they would even be worthwhile.
>
> (1 December 2014)

I had survived the first major challenge. If this was the worst I would feel, I could tolerate the pain and move forward. How wrong I was. To my family, I was withdrawn and quiet, trapped in my internal world where there was no capacity to be open or vulnerable about my mental health.

When we consider our own values, we generally put work at the bottom of the list after marriage, children, family, wellbeing, physical health. That does not mean that it cannot be a major factor in our minds and our thought processes. In fact, because we spend so much time at work, it dominates our thought processes almost exclusively. Yet how mindful are we of the goals we have at work? I mean the actual goals, not the corporate ones. How can I expect to make contingencies against risk when I have not even identified the conflict? The workday may start clearly but quickly descend into a smoky haze and depending on what is happening, there could be many fires burning that are dragging my attention away. What do I do when this becomes too much? How do I escape the flames? I shelved my original personal priorities, not put into the background to be considered as new thoughts come in, but actually shelved, to be unwrapped at a later time.

(2 December 2014)

On 3 December 2014, I was notified that my workers' compensation claim had been rejected. And that was exactly how I felt – rejected. The meeting with the IME ate away at me. How could that clinician have made a realistic assessment of me or my condition from the time we spent together?

The scariest part was realising there was nowhere else to go: I would have to sit with and endure the pain of failure. Guilt and embarrassment reinforced my strategy of avoiding everything and everyone. In any case, Victoria Police has a force-wide policy that suspended members cannot be contacted unless the member has an exemption. Even if I wanted to, I could not reach out to my colleagues without breaching policy.

> I have been very overwhelmed in the past week. In discussions with Alex, he suggested I consider a Bachelor of Social Work. I had a long discussion with a close friend and although I do not know if anyone would take me on, it is the type of work that was of interest. With my background, recent lived experience, exposure to counselling and interest in assisting others, it would be a perfect fit. Unfortunately, I have no say in that. I have eroded my choices with my past behaviour. There are a lot of 'what ifs', but something had to give. My choices led to that, and I need to resolve that in my mind.
>
> (14 December 2014)

This was a contemplative entry; it reflects my thinking patterns for most of this period. I was swinging between despair and hope – and making no apparent progress. Suicide was never far from my thoughts. I had broken my options down to a choice between experiencing the pain and accepting my failures or checking out and teaching 'them' a lesson. Whoever 'they' may be.

At Christmas my aim was to make it through family events without the topic of mental health, my work life or the car crash being raised. But as with many of the experiences we fear most, I was surprised at how others reacted. My immediate and extended family members were only concerned about me and offered unconditional love and support. Alex's catchphrase rang in my ears: 'You don't get to choose how other people feel.'

> I have given up counting the weeks, concentrating only on myself and my family. I made it through Christmas at home with the parents, extended family and in-laws. There were some awkward moments, some dark thoughts, but on the whole, it was a positive experience. Had it not been for my wife, I am not sure I would have made it through. She is very understanding and appears to know when I am down and encourages me through that time.
>
> At no time was my current situation raised. It was like a taboo subject and while I am thankful for that, it is an interesting insight into human nature. To me, it still seems unresolved and maybe that is the best place for it until I can find a way forward and move on. I enjoy the company of those that love me, I think I put too much pressure on myself and worry too much about what others are thinking. That is their right to think about what they want. I just need to concentrate on myself and my wellbeing.
>
> (24 December 2014)

I remained invisible during the Christmas period. If anyone had asked, I had no easy answers about the car accident, my work prospects or the discipline process. Being visible to myself was challenging, let alone sharing my experience with others. But by focusing on observing my thoughts and reactions, I could navigate this period without relapsing. The small actions I could control were my greatest asset – diet, exercise, sleep, abstinence from alcohol, maintaining my sessions with Alex. There was so much in my life that was out of my control; by concentrating on what I could control, I maintained some value and independence.

* * *

I spent the death hours of the first morning of the new year sitting alone on the back steps, contemplating what might have been. Last year I had reached my goal of becoming a Detective Senior Sergeant – and then thrown it all away. It was a bizarre way to begin a new year: awaiting the outcome of decisions others would make.

I was also concerned about how I would be remembered by the families of victims I had helped during my time with Victoria Police. The question they most often asked was, 'How does your wife cope?' I would provide some lame response about how we had a great relationship and the long hours were just part of the job. What I failed to mention was that the long hours and commitment to the cause were a way for me to avoid the internal turmoil that enveloped me most days.

> Almost three months to the day since my life changed forever. Have been alcohol free and am starting to feel alive again. It is 7.51 am and I have just done an hour on the bike. It is ironic that one of my girls asks me to check her room every night for monsters. Alcohol and I were the monster, and it has been invading our lives in some form for as long as the kids can remember. We went out for tea last night and it was so comfortable.
>
> (1 January 2015)

Pondering new horizons inevitably drew me back to my old life and I would start developing strategies for a triumphant return against all odds. How could I work for Victoria Police now that they were aware of my suicidal thoughts? To be operational I had to carry a firearm – and it was unlikely they would grant me access to a firearm any time soon, given the state of my mental health. Were there any non-operational roles I could perform? This nonsensical thinking absorbed me for hours at a time. I would often withdraw from those around me as my mind explored the various possibilities.

As I reached the three-month mark, my long-term future was front of mind. I had spread my wings a little, met with family and friends and some close confidants from my workplace. But I still didn't know how the disciplinary matters or court process were progressing.

One casualty of my previous years of recklessness was my closest childhood friend. Even though we remained in contact, I had subconsciously pushed anyone close to me away in the chaotic period leading up to the car accident. I was too embarrassed, or perhaps fearful, that he may notice my decline.

> It was great to catch up with my closest friend, he has a refreshingly independent view of what I face. Yes, I made a mistake. It will not change our relationship and there is an entire world of opportunities out there, the hard part is picking the right option. Keep as many options open as possible and listen carefully to what is being offered. In his own way, his advice was to 'sit with it' – that mantra keeps on coming back. Ultimately, do what is best for me and understand that there is a world outside VicPol if that is what I choose.
>
> (6 January 2015)

As the month progressed, I returned to the dark periods of helplessness that seemed to absorb me for days. My sleep was poor, as I ruminated on the unfairness of my position, and intrusive thoughts and memories were with me every day. I am not sure which caused me most concern – managing and understanding my mental health condition or my frustration with the workers' compensation and discipline systems.

> I have had a very disturbed period, feelings of frustration,
> lethargy, anger and a sense of helplessness. I can feel these
> moods as they wash over me. I do not seem to make progress
> in anything I do. My frustration has seen me argue with my wife
> over trivial things. I am realising how difficult it is to be
> suspended in time, with no future to plan and a lack of
> confidence to decide about my future.
>
> (9 January 2015)

Despite the fluctuations in my mood, I continued to work on strategies I had developed with Alex. In our sessions we talked a lot about staying in the moment, accepting difficult feelings and recognising that not every day will be perfect. To develop these skills requires persistence, patience and practice.

> The priorities list can be viewed as a bird's nest. The more
> time and effort you put into it the stronger the construction
> will be. It takes many individual, repeated actions to make
> a strong and sustainable structure. However, if we neglect
> the nest and don't put the time and effort in, or take
> shortcuts, or choose poor materials, then the nest will
> crumble. Like any bird's nest, a catastrophic event can lead
> to failure, but it can be rebuilt. If we have a weak structure, it
> is much more likely to break down and leave us exposed. We

> can check for weakness. We need to review how our
> structure is holding up. Is it prepared for today's activities?
>
> (12 January 2015)

This may well have been my first attempt to explain the concept of 'everyday attention' when considering our mental health – which I explore more in Chapter 16. The need to reflect, review and adjust daily, to build habits through repeated actions regardless of how challenging this may become. After much procrastination, I took the plunge and applied to the Cairnmillar Institute to undertake a Master of Counselling and Psychotherapy. I attended an interview and was accepted as a mature-aged student. I was open about my current circumstances and detailed the series of events that had led to my plight. This was the first time I was fully open about my condition with anyone aside from Alex and my wife. What had started as an attempt to ease some of the noise in my brain from the policing world had developed into an opportunity to learn and understand my world from a different perspective. My primary aim in studying was to gain a greater understanding of what went wrong and why.

With every positive, there is a negative. I took a small step forward in beginning the course at Cairnmillar, but then I was advised of the reasons why my workers' compensation claim had been rejected. I had requested a copy of the documents to assist in applying for the workers' compensation conciliation process. The workers' compensation report shattered me. It included witness statements from managers and a copy of the report from the IME. I felt betrayed. There was no consideration of what I had sacrificed. It felt like VicPol had used my high-end skills, exploited my willingness to overcommit to the cause, reaped the benefits in the results I achieved and then abandoned me when I needed them most. Never had my one-sided view been in such sharp focus. The truth was my employer never gave me permission to drink-drive, to take risks with the lives of others, or to relinquish all responsibility for my mental health. In the past, I would have held onto this perceived wrong-doing for many months and either brought it to a head somehow or sought ways to undermine the people involved. I am pleased that I did neither.

Instead, I applied to take my workers' compensation claim to formal conciliation. I did not understand the process or know what to expect. Naively, I hoped that if an independent arbitrator heard my story the claim would be accepted. If I had known the toll the process would take on me, I may well have made a different decision.

In contrast, I was excitedly nervous about my first day in the psycho-therapy course. I had little sleep the night before as I was worried about the 'ice-breaker' exercises, of all things. I had developed a cover story for my previous life, a skill I had thought I would never need exercised again. Sweats, churning stomach, tight chest – all these sensations were familiar, but for once this was a pleasant apprehension.

This is it, the first day of the course I have enrolled in. Feel somewhat apprehensive, as if this could be the start of something I love or it could be the biggest waste of time and money I have undertaken. I feel comfortable within myself. I will remain quite reserved initially, as it feels strange being back out in the public. I can meld in with everyone else. I am not that bloke on the train who lost his job because he made a shit decision.

The WorkCover mediation is sitting in the back of my mind, but I am not too concerned about it. I am more interested in starting this course and challenging my abilities and testing my

theories. I do not know where this will lead. I will never know
what I can achieve unless I put myself out there. I read recently
that you should follow your passion, do what you enjoy. To me,
helping others has always been my goal. I do not think that
VicPol offers me that scope anymore. I need to learn, develop
and become better at what I do. I am hopeful additional study
will provide me with that opportunity.

(29 January 2015)

Throughout the fluctuations and challenges I experienced, the support of my family remained a constant, and this was particularly powerful as I approached my return to study. Without saying as much, I think they were relieved that I had started something new. It may not be the solution, but it was a starting point.

* * *

My journal writing lapsed during February as I got used to life as a student. I struggled with reading and comprehending text: these simple tasks now required my full attention and concentration. It was also new for me to take public transport everywhere. I would spend most trips observing others and imagining what their lives were like, usually fabricating an ending that included some type of graphic and violent death. The newfound enthusiasm and positivity that came with moving on to a new stage in my life was short-lived. It was not long before self-doubt and negative internal chatter were once again my constant companions.

I have been thinking about my predicament and took some
action to move forward. I will never take the meaning of that

term lightly again. To be 'suspended' – in time, in thought,
in movement and in ambition – is one of the most difficult things
I have had to try to manage.

(3 March 2015)

Being 'suspended' was an apt metaphor for my experience. An object in space and time with little or no control over its destiny. Being moved with no control or direction, the best I could do was prepare for when I had greater influence over my future.

Each time I seemed to make progress, another part of the 'system' would rear its ugly head. I had engrossed myself in study and it was providing new areas for my brain to explore. Policing was no longer the centre of every thought I processed. My thinking had shifted a little: as Alex had suggested, it would take time to realign some of those neural pathways. On 6 March 2015, I travelled to The Police Association to meet with a Victoria Police representative and they served a summons on me to appear at the Melbourne Magistrate's Court on 2 June 2015 and a notice to immediately suspend my driver's licence. I had known that I would have to appear in court and that my licence would be suspended for a minimum of two years, as I had refused a breath test. But even though I had anticipated this, the interaction had a significant negative impact on me. I had expected to be interviewed about the driving offences prior to being charged, or to be interviewed for a disciplinary offence. Instead, I had no contact with any investigator until the summons was served: a brief two-minute exchange where I received the documentation and walked away. There was no discussion about the suspension, no information on my pay entitlements, and no enquiry around my mental health or whether I was receiving treatment.

We had a lecture on existentialism yesterday, and my response
to it concerned me. We spoke about death anxiety and what
impact that can have on people. I have no death anxiety, or at
least I don't think that I do. I could die any time and that is the
way life is. It does not concern me. I know my parents will die
and I will lose people close to me, but you cannot change what
is inevitable. My concern is that although I am comfortable with
death, I still think about what it would be like to die most days.
I do not have a feeling of living every minute as if it is your last.
I am just surviving and that is all. I am trying to make things
better for myself and my family, but I would not say I am on top
of things. Far from it.

(13 March 2015)

I was really concerned. I had all the support I needed. I was not working, I was having no alcohol, it was just me and my mind – and still
I thought seriously about suicide. I had justified my previous suicidal ideation as a response to my abnormal working environment and alcoholism.
These aspects had been removed, and yet I still could not find a sense of
worth. Despite the love and support, I could not comprehend why I felt
the way I did. As this sense of unravelling continued, I became more
invisible to those around me. I could now use study as an excuse to be
detached, to retreat to my world of fantasy. This became a common
response to challenging times.

There has been much frustration at home, adjusting to life
without a driver's licence and the change in roles that brings.
I am mindful of how my wife is feeling, but I react to the smallest
hint of her frustration coming to the surface. My usual ploy is to

shut down and retreat to my study. I want to give more of myself and let her know how I feel, even if I don't understand why I felt that way. I guess one advance I have made is that I can recognise my own emotions and feelings during those periods.

(17 March 2015)

This was a period of great uncertainty. It was exhausting, as I swung from hopelessness and despair to believing in a new beginning several times a day. Any reminder of policing or my past would take me straight back to the negative and pervasive thoughts. Seeing my wife smile or a positive interaction with the kids would spur me to continue – to be the best version of myself, whatever that may be. I have heard this sensation described as a 'rollercoaster', and I cannot think of a more accurate descriptor.

I find it very difficult to remain motivated, to find things to do that have meaning. It is far easier to drift away and live in my world with my thoughts and just let the days wash over me. There are only so many times you can tell yourself that everything will be okay. The reality is nothing has changed. I may be fitter and healthier, and my relationships have improved, but my circumstance has not changed. I am still in that terrible state of 'Suspension' waiting on the decisions of others. What will become of me?

I shot myself in the hand with the nail-gun on Saturday. The pain was intense. When I was in blind pain, I took the time to try to feel what it was like. I could feel my finger being pulled off the nail. I wanted the cold water to run on my hand to have the contrast between the burning pain and the soothing water. I did not mean to do it, but I am not upset that I did. I have little care for my safety or well-being. I believe that what will happen will happen. I do not want to die, but if it happens, so be it.

Just filling in the days, finding things to do, missing my previous life. Just me and my thoughts, it is a very sombre time. My thoughts are not always good company and I find myself fighting to redirect my thoughts away from places where I do not want to go, but somehow keep getting drawn there. It is like a sadistic fascination to see how far I can let my thoughts go without acting on them.

(23 March 2015)

One of my great frustrations was that there was no one I could share my concerns with who fully understood the entirety of my predicament. This is not a slight against my wife: how could I expect her to understand the intricacies of the police discipline system, workers' compensation or the court process? And Alex could never fully comprehend my personal relationships and my interactions with my broader family and colleagues. My former colleagues had no appreciation of my mental health condition and how this devastated my working and personal relationships. I was the one who would have to find the key – and there would be no single solution to such a complex problem.

8

The Six-Month Shame

April–July 2015

Returning to study had broadened my horizons. I often discussed topics raised in lectures with Alex and he always provided a new insight or perspective. Alex had been successful in moving me away from my operational policing experience: not every conversation needed to be examined for mistruths and signs of deception. The dark times of the previous months subsided but the pressure of my impending court appearance and discipline hearing lingered on.

It is six months tomorrow since my incident and subsequent fall from grace. I have remained anonymous for much of this period, cutting off friends and work colleagues, but becoming closer to family and treasured friends. What have I learnt? No two days are the same. Each day has its own challenges. Many thoughts still play on my mind, although I have a better capability to identify and manage those thoughts. I feel much fitter and healthier. My previous way of life seems so distant, but I am very guarded in that I know it would be a slippery slope if I ever went down that path again.

I have enjoyed studying again and there is much to learn in
that field. Today is a good day. I know there will be bad days
ahead and that is okay.

(1 April 2015)

False dawns were common. Whenever I thought I had made a positive step forward, something would remind me, brutally, of the fleeting nature of any perceived improvement. When I thought I had one aspect of my life under control, a crisis in another area would challenge me. Having hope is an important part in managing the worthlessness that anxiety and depression bring. The stark realisation that my choices, and my choices alone, had led to the position I was in undermined any hope I had.

My inability to drive had a major impact on our family unit. Whenever I took public transport or had to walk to the supermarket, it reminded me of my flaws. It felt as if everyone was watching me, knew my history, and this was my ultimate shame.

Instead of systems issues relating to policing affecting me, now my personal relationships had come into sharp focus. The day following my positive start to the month, my wife attempted to have me consider our position from her perspective. I reacted in the same old defensive way.

I am just trying to articulate how I feel right now. I feel as though I
want to be physically ill. My stomach is churning and already
I can feel my thoughts compounding in a negative way. I want to
run; I want to escape this pain that I have. My first reaction as
normal is to escape. I have no clue how I can come back from
this. My mind is racing, and it is like I cannot keep up with the

thoughts. Death thoughts come and go, guilt and anxiety are my primary feelings. I am embarrassed and ashamed. Worthless. How can I have hurt those I love so much? It feels like I have regressed six months. The pain I feel is unbearable. My mind is full of smoke and my head feels like it is on fire. I know that these are immediate reactions and if I can sit with it, I can manage this. It is just so uncomfortable. If I am feeling uncomfortable, how is my family feeling?

(2 April 2015)

A key component of any relationship is trust. My previous behaviours meant I was coming from a long way back – broken promises, dishonesty, deception and manipulation were my stock in trade. Although I had decided that I would change my ways, expecting those I loved to accept this on faith was naive. I had spent years breaching the trust they had afforded me. Now, because I had decided to change, I expected my wife and children to believe I would not relapse. The only way to truly win back trust is through repeated, consistent actions in line with your shared values. This would take time. I had little capacity to put myself in the shoes of my family members. They must have wondered who this strange – isolated, short-tempered, reactive, reclusive and agitated – person living in their household was.

My wife can move between stories and adapt her behaviour and narrative. I get stuck. I go to that place where conflict in my mind dominates - where the smoke and fire don't allow me to see the stories and the sub plots with such clarity. Again, my mind wanders regularly to escapism, suicide and death. I picture myself in another life as an alcoholic without responsibility, being homeless or suicidal. They are all so negative and places that are incongruent with my true story – but that is where my free thoughts take me. I spent the rest of the day in my cocoon, trying to free myself but not being able to. In some ways, I think there is a part of me that wants to feel those thoughts and emotions, that it is something I need to experience. To see what those dark places look like and feel like. The day passes as a blur. My only explanation is that I cannot control where my mind goes.

(20 April 2015)

Any conflict would cause me to retreat and isolate. It must have been like walking on eggshells. If anyone in the family expressed frustration or disappointment, I would return to my sulking and petulant ways. I had placed my family in a horrible, uncertain and scary predicament. Their only sin was providing unconditional love and support. This is how I responded after a minor disagreement:

My actions have left a permanent scar on this family and there is nothing I can do to erase it. I went to my room and hid under the doona. My mind was racing. I fantasised about having a knife and stabbing myself in the heart, bleeding to death before anyone found me. The warm blood keeping me safe until death came. But I could not continue with that thought process. It was too painful to think of how the family would cope with that scene. I would be fine, but what it would leave behind? I was exhausted. It was as if my mind wanted to keep delving into those dark places to search out solutions that I knew were not suitable.

(20 April 2015)

This was a most difficult day. I did not mean to escape to thoughts of suicide every time I was challenged, but invariably this was my response. This was the dirty secret that was the most difficult to dislodge.

* * *

Despite the depths of my depressive episodes, the level of anxiety I endured and the looming spectre of suicidal ideation, I was making progress. I had taken small, painful, slow steps and there was a sense of gradual improvement. The one thing I could definitively hang my hat on was that I had stopped drinking. I no longer needed to count the days of sobriety – it was the decisions I made each day that mattered. There was no set target date: by focusing on each day, the length of my abstinence would look after itself.

Today is a struggle. For several reasons, some I could list, others I am yet to identify. There is a very negative cloud around me, and I cannot seem to clear it. I feel like I have come so far, but I have not moved. There is no resolution to my 'problems in living' – that is the external circumstances that control my future. Conversely, I feel well, I am appreciating this time with my family and have finally found some semblance of peace and happiness.

(8 May 2015)

I have been fortunate to have an understanding of depression and the effects it can have through my dealings with Alex. It has been a complex and difficult period, with many mood swings, uncontrolled thoughts, unchecked emotion and a strong feeling of hopelessness. These thoughts have been countered by my own self-examination, living the moment, wanting to experience where these emotions come from and what they feel like.

(15 May 2015)

It was a measure of my improvement that I made the above entry in the week that I had met with the barrister who would represent me in the upcoming appearance at the Magistrate's Court for the driving matters.

My barrister was a close friend, and her empathy and non-judgemental attitude towards my predicament provided great comfort. She could have easily referred me to another legal representative, but such was her level of support and compassion she took on the case herself.

I reached out to some former managers to request statements of support for my court appearance. This type of interaction would normally have led to a cycle of self-destruction, but I had developed a greater understanding of my responses and was able to handle it.

The court date was set for 15 July 2015. It would be acutely uncomfortable, I knew, and I would need to plan well to prepare myself for the difficult period ahead.

I am slowly attempting to reintegrate into the outside world, but it is not easy or comfortable. I have met several friends, and it is interesting to watch their reactions and monitor the conversations. Unfortunately, every conversation starts from a position of me being a victim. How are you doing? How are you coping? Often, by the end of the conversation, I wonder who the victim really is. I feel privileged to have had this time to explore my inner self, to get to know my deepest thoughts and fears, to learn to overcome the anxiety, to develop a sense of resilience that did not exist before. I constantly feel conflicted. I cannot look forward to the future because I do not know what it will be. I have nothing to plan or prepare for. Yet I feel vibrant, as if these last seven months are preparing me for whatever comes. Maybe that is the philosophy behind suspension – to force the person involved to look at themselves, to find out who they are and who they want to be. For so long, I looked at this period as a punishment. Then I considered it to be a waste of time and resources. Now I look at it as an investment in my future – I will be a far better person for this experience and will make those around me better people.

(22 May 2015)

I had always been scathing of the suspension process, the 'suspension trap' as I referred to it: once it has you in its grasp, there is no escape. I developed a different view of suspension from writing about being 'suspended in time' in my journal. As time progressed, I was able to consider the suspension process a positive, an opportunity for reflection: it was bringing me closer to my family and giving me permission to step off the policing treadmill.

* * *

There was a shift in my outlook. I had explored options outside policing to make myself relevant again. This may not have been discernible to anyone but me, as I did not dare share any of this hope or enthusiasm with anyone else. I suspect that my external demeanour remained much the same; I was frozen by the fear of becoming visible.

> There have been so many emotions in the last eight months, but today I am calm and confident about my future. To others it may seem hopeless, but to the contrary, I see a new beginning with many new experiences to be lived, enjoyed, evaluated, assessed and endured. I will do this with my wife and family beside me on my own terms. I am free to determine the way forward.
>
> (2 June 2015)

I applied for an investigative role external to policing, an example of my determination to find an opportunity to save face, to teach VicPol a lesson and show them I had landed on my feet. I was still considering pursuing the workers' compensation claim through the courts. I was suspended from my current workplace, had a pending Magistrate's Court matter and was undergoing treatment for a significant mental health condition. Unsurprisingly, I was unsuccessful in my application.

> There have been a lot of thoughts around my future, how it could all change with a phone call. I may get an interview for a job that I applied for, I may have to try to stay with VicPol and endure the discipline process. The theme through all of this is uncertainty and restraint. When my mind wanders, I need to pull it back to the reality of the situation. Speculation gets me nowhere, trying to anticipate what the feelings might be like if I go a certain way is of no benefit to me, as it may never happen.
>
> (3 June 2015)

As the court date approached, I became more reflective and took some steps to be more visible about my mental health condition. First I had to work on being visible to myself. Until I could accept and understand my internal world, I did not have the language to explain it to others. There were many people who were available to support me; all I had to do was ask. But what could I say to them? That I believed a black silhouette was taking me over from the inside, that I had several voices in my head that I could not explain, that there was a magical solution that would take away all my pain regardless of the circumstances? Little wonder I remained in my internal space.

> I continue to exercise and be mindful of my moods. Depressive thoughts are never far away, but I am far better at identifying them and limiting the length of those feelings. At times, I just have to experience those feelings, knowing that they will dissipate if I do not feed them. Continue to notice the times that I feel good and what occurred to make that happen. An example is this morning when I arrived home from swimming and just sat on the couch and noticed the daylight on the deck. a small thing, but immense pleasure. Today will be what I make it. I am disappointed in my actions that led to this, but there will be no more shame. It does not have to be a secret. In some ways, the more I put it out there, the less chance that I will go back to those ways.
>
> (29 June 2015)

* * *

As the court date approached, I had a sense of calmness. My former managers had provided character evidence for me and this support had buoyed me. I had placed them in a terrible position; they had made a career of policing and had well-earned reputations for their commitment, ethical strength and sacrifice in serving the community. Asking them to support a colleague who had behaved in a manner that was contrary to every value they held was confronting. It is a mark of their compassion and integrity that each of them did so without hesitation – they did not condone my actions, but they supported me as a person, as a human who made mistakes.

My barrister was a source of great strength and comfort. She kept the details I did not need to know away from me but included me in every aspect of the plea submission.

To prepare for the uncomfortable court experience, I spent many hours with Alex discussing what my reactions might be and what strategies I could use to address my responses. *Stress, anxiety, guilt, regret and anger will all be part of the experience. I will accept them for what they are, it is my choice how I react. I can be patient and sit with the uncomfortable experiences, or I can return to my old strategies of escaping and avoidance. That is a choice only I make.*

During this phase, I was in contact with my parents, siblings, work colleagues, family friends and, of course, maintained relationships with my wife and children. It felt now like they were like satellites orbiting my world. They did not have to understand my world, but they could provide unconditional love and support. Always present at a safe distance, available to me should I choose to engage with them. I only developed the capacity to do so once I had removed myself from the stress and chaos of my previous life. They had always been there; I just could not see them when my sole motivation was to hide the condition I was experiencing. I was invisible to myself and offered no visibility to others. On gaining a deeper understanding of my internal world, these options became viable. I was like a lone star, shining in my own dys-functional way, but burning so brightly that I obscured the other stars in my orbit.

> The court date approaches, and my feelings and emotions are moving quickly. The theme of avoidance has become much stronger, whether that be going into my cocoon or wanting to physically escape, those thoughts are never far away. This experience has brought me closer to some of my siblings, my relationship with my parents is still strong, yet I still choose to keep them at arm's length and not show any real emotion. I think this is a protective measure so as not to hurt them or let them know my level of distress.
>
> (10 July 2015)

My appearance at the Melbourne Magistrate's Court on Thursday, 16 July 2015 will stay with me forever. The contrast to my previous times there was acute. I felt a wide range of reactions and was able to sit with them and experience them, almost from the lens of a third person. The shoe was on the other foot: I was the accused, the shift in the power balance palpable. In the past, I had been full of confidence, presenting evidence to support the case I had built. Now I was a shell of my former self, embarrassed to have to sit through a summary of evidence that detailed far more than a car accident; it was a dramatic deconstruction of my life.

As I sat behind my barrister, on the wrong side of the courtroom for the first time, I felt like the enemy. The police informant sat on the opposite side behind the prosecutor, in the seat I would normally fill. Court had always been a challenging experience for me, as anxiety was a constant companion. I spent many hours in the informant's seat planning how I could escape and have my fill of alcohol to find some peace. But now I found that while I was acutely anxious and stressed, I could take a step back and experience the reactions as they occurred. Alex was right: they were not pleasant and it takes practice to experience the physical and emotional reactions and resist the urge to escape. The flow of negative and pervasive thoughts was as terrible as I expected it would be. I felt like I wanted to vomit. My shoulders were raised and tense, obscuring my neck. My stomach was tight and my left leg nervously bounced in a rapid, repeated up and down motion. It was mid-July, the middle of a Melbourne winter, and I was covered in sweat.

My barrister presented my case with grace and humility. There was no stepping away from the seriousness of my offending or the need for an appropriate punishment. We agreed that my role as a police officer was an aggravating feature of the offending and that whatever sanction was imposed would need to act as a deterrent to others. This was tough going. Listening to others speak on your behalf was not something I was accustomed to. The experience made me very self-conscious; the intersection of my actions, my mental health condition and my role as a police officer increased the complexity of what should have been a straightforward court process.

I was fortunate to have outstanding character references, both personal and professional, and supporting reports from my GP, a psychologist and Alex.

After discussions with Alex and my barrister, my wife and I had decided that I would sit in the court alone. This was not because my wife did not support me. It was more about me; I wanted to shield her from my professional world, as this was not her fault. I alone needed to be judged for who I was and what I had done.

I received the mandatory loss of licence and fine, but a conviction was not recorded. The magistrate's comments were balanced and she encouraged me to continue with my studies, my sobriety and the work with my clinician. The seriousness of the offence was not downplayed, but I took some comfort from the thoughtful and positive manner in which the matter was resolved. I only have respect and admiration for the police members who handled my matter. Although I did not engage with them, I put them in a horrible position. They were professional and courteous throughout the process.

> Outside of the emotions I felt during the hearing, which ranged from shame, remorse, guilt and sometimes pride in what I had achieved prior to the incident, the most interesting emotion was how I reacted to other Police members present. I was determined to have no interaction and viewed them as the enemy. I felt a lot of anger toward the members who were present but not involved in the matter. There was a sense of abandonment at the lack of contact with command, but then again, I would have resisted anyway.
>
> The strongest emotion was that of my love and respect for my wife. The hearing really troubled her and she believed to the very end that I may go to jail. Because of my past involvement with the courts, I knew that this was not a possibility, but despite my assurances, this was still a live issue for her. She travelled in to meet me. She filled in the awkward time prior to the hearing, just having her with me was immense. I did not want to expose her to the court scenario, I guess it was my way of protecting her. I am not sure how keen she would have been to be in there at any rate. I knew she was with me spiritually and that was the most important support I could ever have.
>
> (17 July 2015)

The time I had taken to prepare for the court case meant I avoided an immediate relapse into the maladaptive coping strategies that had caused so much harm in the past. The court case was uncomfortable, but something I could endure and reflect upon, another step in my journey. My routine of diet, exercise, sleep, study and treatment with Alex continued and my values were at the forefront of the decisions I made. However, the rollercoaster did not abate.

A dark mood looms today, feeling very alone and finding it difficult to resist the lure of just shutting everyone out and retreating to my cocoon. There is much to learn and observe during a period like this, but it is a fragmented picture due to the old maladaptive thoughts that return. The court appearance was massive for me – so many emotions, but a chance to see a way forward. My expectations have changed somewhat. I realise I am a tiny part of a much bigger problem. If I can contribute, so be it. What is the worst that can happen if I share my story? At least it has given me access to people who decide about these issues.

(21 July 2015)

Every step of the process was unexpected. I thought they would progress the discipline process, interview me and set a date for a hearing. But two weeks on there had been no contact from Victoria Police or The Police Association. I wondered if they knew I had appeared at court. My frustration was building.

On the other hand, I could appreciate the unique opportunity that my circumstances had provided for me to reconnect with my children. In the past, I had seen them every day, but I was not 'there'. Now I was involved in all aspects of their lives. I never took for granted how difficult it is to regain trust. Building a catalogue of memories to enhance my relationship with them was my priority.

> I have been letting the feelings of frustration wash over me, feeling abandoned by VicPol, feeling isolated from others because of the secret I have, feeling regretful for the hurt I have caused and the damage I have done. I am putting today down to the normal human experience. We cannot feel at our best all the time. There will be times when I am more pessimistic than optimistic, when my mood darkens. The important thing is that I am aware of these feelings and am thinking about some of the reasons why they occur. A short argument with one of the kids, a disagreement with my wife, frustration at not progressing my assignment as I hoped – it is okay to have a response to those issues. They are isolated incidents, drawn together only by time. It is okay to feel anxiety; it does not have to cause fear or evoke that feeling of escapism. Today is another learning day, to notice my feelings and let them develop. Safe in the cocoon, there is no need to act.
>
> (29 July 2015)

I never appreciated the amount of work required to process these thoughts, to set new pathways for my mind to follow. I was making considerable progress, yet it still felt as if I had not changed at all. But these small, incremental steps over an extended period allowed me to gain a greater understanding of my mental health condition. Repeatable steps well practised.

9.

The Dark Anniversary

August–October 2015

The letdown after my court appearance was significant. I had invested so much time, energy and effort into preparing myself for the experience and the immediate aftermath. Alcohol was not a consideration. My suicidal ideation was at the lowest level it had been for many months. I was well physically. Taking the time to experience and reflect on my thoughts had a purpose, as there was a concrete goal I was aiming for: learning to tolerate and observe discomfort without reacting in my usual negative and avoidant manner. And it had worked: at court I had been able to experience difficult emotions and contextualise them as just that – something to be endured, but not catastrophic.

Following my plan had also allowed me to reintegrate into family life. Even though it was far from perfect, significant progress had been made in re-establishing relationships that were precious to me.

But as the weeks passed with no contact from anyone associated with work, I became more disillusioned. I had no goal now, nothing to plan for, just an extended period of uncertainty. Despite my best efforts, thoughts about my future once again dominated my consciousness. I was constantly checking my phone, waiting, hoping for some contact.

It is difficult to explain the stress that I am feeling. It stems from not having an identity and having that taken away from me – that is, my work role. The longer the process goes, the more confused I become about who I am and where I belong. I am sure others see my life as a breeze: not working, getting paid, no responsibility. I am concerned about my future and what it holds. I feel like I want to escape the world, to retreat to my private world until I can sort through this. I feel like I have tried so hard to change, but it has all been for nothing – I am still stuck in my cocoon, much the same as I was ten months ago, only this time, alcohol does not mask the pain. It is raw, and it is real. It wears you down; it reduces your want to fight. Who am I anyway?

(3 August 2015)

This is one part of my experience I found hard to articulate. I was craving my old identity while also working extremely hard to move on. Study had provided a new lens with which to observe my world. I was far more aware now that it was not only me feeling the way I did.

I continue to travel on this rollercoaster that greatly affects my moods and emotions. I often feel like I am on the edge of a cliff, waiting to fall back into the mire that was my old life. I want to stay on top of the cliff, being mindful of myself and others, knowing and believing that I can be the person I want to be. Earlier in the week I felt lost, today I feel as though I can feel the breeze on my face, but I am aware of what it is and where it will take me. I don't have to brace against it, I just need to feel it and know that it is okay. The breeze will subside, and I will still be standing.

(5 August 2015)

I was caught in a trap: if I reached out and asked for a timeline for a resolution, it would bring on my inevitable dismissal from Victoria Police. The advice I received was to keep my head down and wait for the process to take its course. The fear of being unemployed and without an income was real and I was not convinced I could return to full-time work, even if I wanted to: part-time study was hard enough. My levels of concentration were poor and often compounded by extended periods of poor sleep. I felt like a fraud, being paid to do nothing and not contributing in any meaningful way to any objective.

Assignments are due tomorrow, yet I still leave it to the last minute to complete. I have had plenty of time but have not been able to put into words what I wanted to say. There have been massive self-doubts, as if my position will somehow be wrong. What if I attempt to become a therapist and fail? Is it the expectations of others that drive me? So many have said it does not matter what I do, I will succeed. I wish I had their confidence. I feel an animosity toward VicPol for not valuing me, particularly since the court date. But what does this achieve? I feel trapped and without direction. I feel vulnerable.

(12 August 2015)

I think I underestimate the effect of all of this on the family. I am very aware of my quieter mood, my distraction and self-analysis that takes much of my time. It is okay for me; I am in the process, thinking, considering, hypothesising. I am sure my wife wonders what is going on inside my head. Easy for me to say, 'I am fine, everything is okay, I just need my time.' I am sure there are times when she thinks I am in crisis, or close to it, and becomes very concerned about her future and our future. The stress on her in recent days has been increased. I speculate it is because she has recognised the old pattern – my feeble excuse not to exercise, working to an impossible deadline, little sleep, becoming more introverted. Little wonder she has doubts and concerns. Interestingly, I respond in the same way – 'it is okay, I am fine, you are worrying about nothing'. It must be like a recurring nightmare for her. She has seen the behaviour and heard the excuses so many times before. What other logical conclusion could she possibly reach? If it is not this time, it will be next.

(14 August 2015)

I am changing, and while I feel I am making progress, I often think about how my family perceives my current condition. My internal world has shifted, I know and understand this, but how does this appear externally? I am still withdrawn, lack patience, have little sleep and my symptoms intensify when I am under pressure. How do they interpret my moods? I still find it difficult to engage when I am affected by my symptoms – a tough place to build a platform for trust.

So I return to the day-by-day existence. The ongoing battle in my mind about what the future holds. Contemplating a life that is on hold. Financial concerns about my future – can I really ask my family to sacrifice their goals and dreams so I can follow mine? If I can manage my mind through this, I am sure I can manage a job or a life that may be that of a 'sixty percenter'. Then I could be like all those others that I see as incomplete, inferior and dissatisfied. I can grab a number and join the queue.

(17 August 2014)

The old narcissistic traits that had dominated me previously were returning. A 'sixty percenter' is a reference to those who could not work as fast as me, were not as intelligent, or were not willing to sacrifice themselves for the cause. This was a phrase I coined for those I perceived as lazy and not committed; it did not occur to me that they might have had the balance in their lives that I was craving.

I had now completed a Graduate Certificate in Counselling and Psychotherapy and the court matters had been resolved, yet I was still stuck in a process I could not control. The only agency I had was over my internal world and remaining committed to my everyday plan to give me the best chance of being the best version of myself. I had to keep reminding myself that I was making progress, despite the negativity and frustration that surrounded my future.

* * *

In my head, I had imagined finding a position with VicPol or The Police Association, assisting others who had shared similar experiences. My frustration was that I could not create a meaningful story of who I was. My past persona was clear – the gun detective who would go to any lengths to achieve a positive outcome – but what did I stand for now? It is difficult to focus on a positive future when you feel as though the past is a deep, dark secret. The reality was that while the anchor of Victoria Police was sitting on my chest, I would never be free of the doubt and dysfunction that dominated my thinking.

As inevitably happens, my mood has taken a dark turn
today after being quite content for a period. There is
a lingering frustration and anger that decisions I want to

make are out of my control and so heavily influenced by the decisions of others. It has been seven weeks since my court date and I still do not know what the next step in the process is. The long wait with no control over the outcome has caused me to lose my hopes of a future trying to help those in a similar position to mine. I have a feeling that the time has passed, that what I have been through will be forgotten, a blip on the radar that while significant to me is of no importance to others. The organisation has continued on without me and it will be easier to continue with new people facing the same risks.

(4 September 2015)

At the time I felt as though my world had collapsed, but when viewed from a broader perspective, this was just another normal human experience. But it was becoming tiresome – I was difficult to live with, angry, withdrawn and isolated. I had retreated somewhat from the advances I had made at the time of the court date. I had no answer to the inevitable questions about my future and I was sick of lying about the present. The past was a dirty topic that no one dared touch.

I started to second guess my strategy – did it make any difference if I drank or not? What was the point of exercise? Were the sessions with Alex changing anything? Motivation was difficult to find; I was now dragging myself out of bed in the morning instead of looking forward to a new day. Mindfulness was a pointless exercise that led me to a place of anger and frustration, my mind continually wandering to the unfairness of the situation and the futility of attempting to change. I felt like I had been swept under the carpet as another unfortunate soldier who did not make it through.

Finding motivation is proving difficult at the moment; I feel a bit scattered and disconnected. I can lose myself in a thought or some reading, but it is invariably interrupted by the reality that I have other things I should be doing. I am reading an article, 'A crisis of identity', which is giving me another insight into my predicament and providing much scope to let my mind wander and explore the number of complex different 'selfs' that I am trying to serve. Anxiety sits in the base of my throat, just at the top of my chest, waiting to spew out - in the true sense of the word.

(11 September 2015)

The Police Association contacted me on 24 September to advise me that my pay was to be suspended. My immediate reaction was anger. This was the first contact I'd had with anyone since the court date. Had the twelve-month anniversary of the incident set off a reminder? Attempting to explain the timing of this contact to my wife and broader family was futile. From their perspective, witnessing the extended periods of uncertainty, not know-ing my future and not understanding the processes and systems at play, they could come to only one conclusion – that my employer did not care.

Following the news that I had to attend the TPA to discuss my financial position, my mind went into a full open narrative, images and stories of my life recurring at a rapid rate. My wife asked why I was so quiet, yet there was an orchestra going on in my head. Every embarrassing, demeaning act I had been involved in, my conflict with alcohol, the guilt and shame over the pain I have caused my family. Regular thoughts of escapism, a return to alcohol to make this go away, the need to remove the images from my mind.

(28 September 2015)

The weekend was brutal. The uncertainty and fear led to many arguments about our future. I could not help but sink back to that terrible feeling of guilt and shame. It was like I was standing on the precipice in Warrnambool again, determined to make everyone pay for what they had done to me. It would not have mattered what support they offered to me in that instant, there was no reconciliation with VicPol. They were the enemy; I had a chance to leave a lasting symbol of the destruction they caused. When I was in this mode, my story was always about the gun detective who had sacrificed so much being thrown to the wolves when his use-by date arrived. Going back to this story was my choice. There were healthier alternatives.

I then had the strangest recall that I have ever had, which I shared with my wife. This incident occurred during the middle of the day, not during a dream at night. I was trying to stay in the moment, trying to feel every part of me, my body, my mind, my internal organs – the physical reaction of such a state. I was cocooned in a curved body shape, ironic given that I wanted to shrivel and disappear. I felt helpless and alone. There was a feeling of a child inside of me, a younger version of me. The child was a black corpse, and it was under my skin like a smaller version of me. It is shrivelled and lifeless and just residing within my body. It has decayed and is soulless, but it just stays there, doing nothing. I realise then that I have had this image many times before, but not known what it is. It is the safe part of me that no one can hurt because it is already dead. I can drown it in alcohol, no effect. I can shame and humiliate it, no effect – it is always there, just a dead black space that can never be filled. I need to keep that shape inside of me to keep me safe when

I am challenged or confronted. This is the space I return to.
It has not been the good me and the bad me all this time.
It has been this black death that lives inside me, the useless,
shameful, guilty me that is always there to eat up the pain I feel.
Somewhere there is a hope that there will be some good to
come from all of this, but right now that is buried deep within the
black corpse inside of me. The corpse will hold my secrets. I sit
in the sun and feel the anxiety well in my abdomen. The thought
that I should have finished this twelve months ago is at the
forefront of my mind. This is exactly what I wanted to avoid,
a long-drawn-out process that leaves me bitter with everyone
and living the struggle between the corpse that wants to
become one and a soul that still wants to live.

(28 September 2015)

I had thought I had reached my lowest ebb many times in this process, but this feeling was next level. Still, there was no guarantee that this was the bottom: somehow it could always be worse. The hope that I had attempted to maintain, the new story about myself that I had tried to create, the changes I had made to become a better person all seemed to have been an exercise in futility. All that effort and I was in the very place I had wanted to avoid.

I could not appreciate it that weekend, but all that work I had undertaken – all the time with Alex, the investment in relationships and educating myself about mental health – had paid off. I may well have reached my nadir, but I was still here to write about it and experience it.

* * *

The one-year anniversary of my self-destruction passed with no real acknowledgement from anyone, except my wife, who mentioned it in an understated way. There were long periods of silence as I attempted to process the changes to my life. While it had been a terrible event and I had hurt those I loved, there had been positives in the aftermath. I had remained sober for twelve months now, no small achievement considering where I was coming from. And my physical health had improved dramatically, as had my understanding of myself and my mental health condition.

But despite all the progress, there was still a part of me that wanted to keep the extreme aspects of my mental health condition invisible.

> The anniversary caused me more anxiety. I know my mood changed significantly, often without reason. Since writing about the corpse last week, it has been a constant reminder, but the actual physical sensations have diminished somewhat. I still think of it as a place to hide my feelings, a part of me I can go to when I feel I need to shut down. I don't think it is a very healthy place. The feeling of a dead object inside me scares me somewhat. I have been reluctant to discuss this with Alex as I fear it may prevent me from returning to work and I could not tolerate another extended period of uncertainty.
>
> (5 October 2015)

The issue of my pay was still being considered after I made a submission to review the decision, and my frustration with the system was growing. During my next meeting with Alex, I opened up about the corpse and my ongoing fascination with suicidal thoughts. I am not sure what Alex made of this session, but it felt different to me. It was not as embarrassing as I had expected, and in his calm and intelligent way he reframed the idea of the corpse and proposed an alternative way of looking at the sensations I was experiencing. What did I expect? I had almost reached the point where everything I had dreaded – losing my job, having no income and being unemployed – was a stark reality. Periods of anxiety were inevitable given the circumstances, but there was progress: I was sitting in front of him, discussing my deepest emotions and sensations. This was one of the most difficult periods. On any measure, I was in an infinitely better state of mental health than before, but this did not mean that I could avoid the pain of the circumstances I was facing.

The sense of helplessness I feel is overwhelming. There appears to be no way out, I keep trying to tell myself that everything will work out – but it seems the longer this drags on, the relevance I have to anyone is diminished. I feel like I am living a lie – how long can I continue the charade that I am on long service leave or extended leave. People must realise that I don't have a licence. I miss interacting with people and trying to make a difference. Instead I am left to battle my own mind, the continual flow of thoughts that has me on a rollercoaster every day. I feel anxious most of the time. I am training most days and eating well, but I feel physically ill most of the time.

(6 October 2015)

My pay was ceased on 9 October. Initially I wanted to appeal the decision and find a loophole in the administrative process. I requested that the discipline hearing be expedited, but there was no response. The days and weeks dragged on. I knew there was a process to follow, but the uncertainty and doubt consumed me. I thought I had done the hard work and that the worst of my experience was behind me: another thinking trap, longing for an end date when it would all be over. This experience was now part of me, it would always be with me: there would be no magical point when my life would be free of anxiety, thoughts about alcohol, or memories of the traumatic events I had been involved in.

> My frustration continues to grow. The lack of control over my future, combined with the uncertainty, is a toxic mix. I find myself continually having to check my thoughts and mood to prevent a complete disconnection. That overwhelming feeling of guilt is never far away. Why should I be upset at the TPA or the organisation when this circumstance came about only because of my actions?
>
> (23 October 2015)

I could sense my anger building; my sleep had deteriorated to about two to three hours a night. The intrusive thoughts, nightmares and thoughts of violence increased, vivid reminders of what I had been exposed to in the past. Although it had been twelve months, this period reminded me that although you may improve, there will always be new challenges and periods of adversity.

10.

A New Start

November 2015–January 2016

I was in the midst of my worst-case scenario, awaiting my fate with no control over my future and still clinging desperately to the idea of remaining in policing. I was willing to accept a demotion, work in uniform and take up a position with the police welfare team. I was desperate to repay my colleagues and the organisation for the harm I had caused. Anything to show that I could still be of value. I could not conceive that I was of value outside the organisation.

The wash up is nothing has changed and no-one cares. I can make all the arguments I like in my mind, but they mean nothing. My viewpoint is worthless. I have and probably still am suffering from PTSD. I had a substance abuse problem. I am therefore worthless in the eyes of my employee and nothing that I do will ever change that view. You are nothing but a number after all, and there will be somebody to replace you. There will be others that face this very same fate, but that is the cost of doing business. Why do anything as progressive as trying to identify the reasons behind why people behave the way they do, when the system that is in place works just fine?

(5 November 2015)

As I prepared for my 'last stand', I continued to develop strategies that would allow me to present myself in the best possible light at the discipline hearing. The systems issues were frustrating, and the interminable wait seemed like it would never reach a conclusion. Thinking about a return to Victoria Police started me pondering what I could do to effect change. Had anyone considered the plight of a member with a mental health injury from their perspective? There were many aspects of a very complex model that were only ever considered from the siloed perspectives of the respective stakeholders. Was there an opportunity to bring a voice to those who were silenced by a disjointed and ineffective response?

They advised me on 20 November 2015, almost fourteen months since I ceased work, that I would need to attend a formal discipline hearing. The hearing was listed for 4 December – after all this time, I had two weeks to prepare. I had never been interviewed or formally spoken to about the incident and why it occurred. I had been expecting the hearing for months, yet when I was notified it was frightening.

After 14 months of complaining and ruminating, they finally served my discipline notice yesterday – and it makes it no easier. I can see the effect this has on my wife; the guilt and shame over the hurt I have caused is overwhelming. When I first saw the notice, I wanted to be physically ill – I think I may have had a panic attack. I was not prepared for the details of the events of that night, and I felt as if I was back in that moment. I knew that this would have a devastating effect on my wife, however her support and dedication to me has been phenomenal. My physical reaction was startling. Even as I type this the next day, I can feel the dryness in my mouth and the tendency for my heart to race. Immediately following the email, the physical sensations were enormous: shaking, racing pulse, nausea. There was the initial reaction to take off, the reaction to take the easy way out and make it all go away.

(21 November 2015)

The lead-up to the hearing passed quickly. I had exams and assignments due for my course and I needed to contact referees and get reports from my treating doctor and clinicians. Life at home was a blur: we tried to be as 'normal' as possible. At times I was quiet and disconnected. My family understood that in the circumstances, that was my way of managing. They had seen the alternative, and nobody wanted a return to those dark times. In preparing for the hearing, I was opening myself up to being questioned about my experience of a mental health condition, suicidal ideation and alcoholism. For the first time, I was willing to take the risk of being visible and vulnerable. Not because I wanted to keep my job, but because I wanted someone to hear my story. The most important part of this picture – the individual affected by a mental health condition – had no voice at all so far.

The hardest thing to let go of was a policing career. All parties had made it abundantly clear to me that the likely outcome of my actions was dismissal. But I had not accepted this fate. I wanted to have my say. I had an unwavering belief that because I had made so many sacrifices I would be exempt from the standards that applied to others. The difference now was that my reason for wanting to have a voice had shifted. No longer did I want to complain about the perceived unfairness of my situation, the lack of recognition for the sacrifices I made or the heart-lessness of the workers' compensation and discipline processes. I wanted people to hear an authentic story, so that perhaps we could learn and improve outcomes for those who make the choice to enter such a challenging work environment.

* * *

My reaction to the discipline hearing surprised me somewhat. Although I had wanted to help others by sharing my experience, and to be a better person, to forgive and move forward, I reverted to my old thinking traps when it was obvious things would not fall in my favour. I spent the weekend after the hearing in my internal world, going over every investigation that I had been involved in, creating an inventory of what they had exposed me to. I recall sitting on the deck at the back of the house, feeling helpless and overwhelmed, running the videotape of my career through my mind for the last time. Every gruesome crime scene, grieving family, physical confrontation and ethical misstep appeared in a neat chronology – I was grieving.

Although they had adjourned the final decision, dismissal would be the outcome. Dismissal. Dismissed as a person with no worth. Dismissed like an inanimate object that could be cast aside and replaced.

> Well, it is done. The build-up was so slow and drawn out. In the end it happened so quickly and unfortunately was everything that I expected. In the end, my behaviour was inexcusable, and I had to go – that type of behaviour, regardless of the circumstances, cannot be tolerated. What was so disappointing was the method in which it was done and the thinking behind it.

The only agenda at that hearing was to belittle me and ensure
that VicPol could not be seen as having any fault in the matter.
To be told that my mental health counsellor was not qualified
enough, that my GP did not support the rest of the evidence,
that I had fabricated my suicidal thoughts to simply try and get
out of a sticky situation was reinforcement of all the
stereotypes that exist in Victoria Police with regard to mental
health. To be ridiculed and to have my integrity questioned as
to the issues I was dealing with was the final humiliation.

(7 December 2015)

The final verdict was to be delivered on 14 December. Leading up to
it, I swung between expressing vitriol at Victoria Police to looking towards
a new future. Policing was still luring me back: I was desperate for that
warm, familiar embrace. But there would be no coming back. I finally
realised that my career was only a job, others would replace me, and it
was my actions and my actions alone that had caused this mess.

Knowing that I would be dismissed, I asked whether I could resign
before the hearing, but I was advised that this was not in line with policy
and I would need approval from a senior officer for the resignation to be
accepted – another frustrating systems issue.

I have just been notified that my resignation will probably not
be accepted. The challenge now is to remain aware of my
thoughts and my response. My immediate thoughts are of
frustration and anger - what else do they want from me? Why
are they continually pushing me, refusing to accept that there
is some culpability for my position on their hands. I can feel my
chest tighten and I am all of a sudden very hot, like I am

sweating. The room seems smaller, and I have a sense of being trapped. But it will pass. The coffee is making my heart race, but I only have to breathe, I have been through worse. Tomorrow will come and at some stage my time will come – patience and persistence.

Did I like who I was as a person prior to the accident? Most certainly not. Am I a happier, healthier, better person as a result? Most certainly yes. It will cause some embarrassment and discomfort to tell others about my departure from VicPol, but in a way, it is a new beginning. a chance to make a difference again, without all the baggage that I carried around previously. To be a better husband, to be a better father, to be a better son, a better brother. So today I will attempt to resign before I am dismissed on Monday – they probably won't accept it, there will be rules no doubt, but I will give it a crack.

(11 December 2015)

We reached an agreement on my departure, and I resigned on 14 December 2015. Twenty years and seven months since I entered the academy, it was all over. A star that burnt too quickly and too brightly before fading into oblivion. Maybe I was never cut out for a career in policing, maybe it was a miracle I lasted as long as I did. Hindsight is a wonderful thing. Perhaps the hearing officer made the correct decision. I had to go; there could be no dispute about the facts. My worst-case scenario had eventuated and I could sit with it, control what I could control, and look to the future. I could not have achieved this progress without the support of all those people who stuck with me through this period. All those who were simply there, not necessarily knowing the right thing to say, but being present and available.

After such a long period of waiting, it ended so quickly. It felt like I was never heard, that I never had the opportunity to explain how I ended up in the position I found myself in. I am not sure why it was such an intense feeling, but there was much sorrow and a sense of loss. It hurt. A lot.

I cannot settle on a narrative of who I am anymore. Do I need a job that will satisfy the external expectations that I can find something else after VicPol and just move on? A job that will fit into the societal expectation of who I should be – a safe environment, guaranteed income, financial security, a narrative that the kids can be comfortable with. Or do I pursue my goal of trying to make a difference to the lives of those who are struggling with the daily complications of life? If I can assist just one person in identifying a pattern that prevents them from following my path, I would be satisfied. But there is so much to do and no appetite for it. Speaking out about mental health is too hard, too confrontational, too far out of the comfort zone of those who want to live in their secure worlds, walking over others to reach the nirvana of a house, 2.5 kids and a Mazda 9. My aim is not to get bogged down with the millions of thoughts that fill my mind every day. There needs to be balance. If I keep dismissing the thoughts, they just regroup and come back in a stronger form. This, after all, is life. Which raises the question, if this is life, if this is my battle every day, if I am alone in my thoughts and opinions, is that a life at all?

(18 December 2015)

Now I had no income and no driver's licence. I was unemployed, had a court record for driving offences and significant financial pressures.

It was approaching Christmas, and I had no good news to share. But all the effort I had spent on learning about myself and my condition stopped me from relapsing. I had experienced the most difficult period of my life and I was still here. A little bruised, but still here.

Now that my worst-case scenario had eventuated and I had survived, I found to my surprise that the suicidal thoughts abated. Uncertainty was a constant, but our family life was enjoyable. I realised and appreciated that they did not mind what I did to make a living, so long as I was healthy. My family will never realise how much this phase altered my thinking about 'success'. It was not about how much I could promote myself or show I was the smartest in the room: it was about what I believed was worthwhile.

> I have seen an advertisement for Beyond Blue – a liaison
> position for first responders. I doubt I have the qualifications,
> but it would be the perfect role to allow me to continue with my
> pursuit of making things better for emergency workers.
> Interstate travel, not like my previous work trips. No requirement
> to work weekends and in line with what I am hoping to make
> a career out of. It is only a twelve-month position, so job security
> is an issue, but it may open doors at TPA or back with VicPol as
> a consultant.
>
> (29 December 2015)

* * *

Despite my predicament, there was hope and enthusiasm. I had applied for the position at Beyond Blue and was fortunate to progress to the interview stage. On 14 January, I travelled to their offices in Hawthorn for my first real interaction in a workplace since October 2014. This would not be like my previous interviews. It was not an opportunity for me to provide example after example of my successes and how important I was to an organisation. Instead, I was approaching the interview as an opportunity to share my story, to promote myself as a conduit between those who experience mental health conditions and those who design systems and programs to manage them. At the core of my intention was the need to be honest and to be visible about my journey and the ongoing management of my condition.

My first entry for 2016 – could there be light at the end of the tunnel? A scary thought, but I cannot help but have a warm contented feeling, one that I have not felt for a long time. I dare not dream or consider a future – it could all be very different – but an opportunity has arisen that excites me and provides a vehicle to achieve my goals. To share my story, to help those who find themselves in a position such as mine, to prevent others from getting there. Beyond Blue is a larger scale of the concept I was proposing. Better resourced, better educated, better expertise, but the ideas are similar. It is impossible to stop my mind racing, as much as I try – the thoughts continue to flow. I am taking my time to identify them and let them sit. I guess moving from such a long period of uncertainty to having a potential future is going to create a range of thoughts and emotions. It was interesting as I travelled to and from the interview yesterday. My thought pattern fully activated the link between a workplace and alcohol. I noticed every pub, bar and bottle shop. I thought of contingencies to meet people for a drink, the ease of the public transport access. My mind map drawing me back to my old work life, that dysfunctional thought pattern that so devastated my life. I could sit with those thoughts, like they were a pathway that had to be noticed but not acted on. For every thought of that nature, I had a counter thought – where will I put my bike, could I run to work?

The excitement of being able to tell my story and introduce the new me back into the world. Not the new me, the renovated me: the same pieces, just put back together in a more functional and effective manner. The thoughts of being known as the bloke who used to be a copper with a drinking problem who found a way through. I must check myself again. This may not happen. But it has given me hope that there are others who see the merit in what I am trying to achieve. It was nice to speak of my skills that had served me so effectively in the past, engaging in a positive way – to feel that I could be a worthwhile contributor to a team. If this opportunity does not eventuate, I feel more comfortable that others will become available. This is not just a meaningless crusade; it is not vengeance or retribution that is spurring me on. There are mistakes and regrets on both sides, more on mine than anywhere else, but the time for change is here – I just need to be part of it.

(15 January 2016)

If there was one skill I had developed, it was patience. Waiting for a call back following the interview was another step along the way.

I thought the interview went okay, but what does that count for? I knew that there were many people out there who had more experience and better skills and who were not burdened by my history. From a personal perspective, it provided me with some confidence that there was a way forward. Perhaps my plan was working. By paying attention every day to the small actions that I could control, I could make significant change. Repeated action, practice and persistence.

My core principles of exercise, diet, sleep and abstinence from alcohol have sustained me. Although sleep continues to be a problem, it would be worse without the other three. I have read so much, written a lot and pondered my various theories - but is this just a stocking filler to ease my mind and take it away from the tension and anxiety of the position I find myself in? To move on from my memories of the past? Is this all part of the ruse of maintaining balance, being able to find suitable, harmless stocking fillers to prevent the negative and pervasive thoughts?

(19 January 2016)

That I could reflect on how I managed my thoughts during this period is a further example of the progress I had made on many fronts. I am certain there is a psychological term that better describes this experience, but 'stocking fillers' made sense to me. I did not need suicide as an escape plan. It becomes pretty simple when you ask yourself what is most important – partner, children, mental health, physical health, and ensuring that whatever decisions you make have those four components at the centre of the process.

I completed the last entry in my journal on 16 February. I was sitting in a coffee shop in Hawthorn, about to begin my first day with Beyond Blue. It was such a strange sensation: nervous anticipation coupled with a quiet confidence that I had an opportunity to contribute to a cause that was important to me – improving how we understand the experience of policing from the perspective of the 'troops'. At the time I never believed this journal would see the light of day. It was just the confused and rambling musings of a mind attempting to make sense of an uncertain and confronting world. But I was pleased I was still around to write it.

Sixteen months and thirteen days since I last attended a workplace – so much has changed, so much is different. I am different. I will always have my battles, but that is normal. Accept them for what they are, experience them, learn from them, and move forward. So much fatalism. Believing that my world would collapse. That I would never have a feeling of self-worth again, that there was no way through the smouldering tyre stack that was my mind.

Don't get me wrong, I still have some of those feelings. I still think about my past, mostly looking back with regret at how I could have done so much better. Then I consider the other side – did I like the person that I had become? Was I ever going to be satisfied? What would have become of my family? How long would my body have lasted with the abuse I was putting it through? So I sit here today with a new opportunity. Feeling fit, healthy, motivated and most of all wanting to make an easier pathway for those who are having 'difficulties in living'. I have no real expectations, just a desire to be the best person I can be, to continue to develop my relationship with my wife and kids and, most importantly, to be happy.

(16 February 2016)

11.

Making Sense of the Shadows

It was many years before I could go back and read over the journal. When I did, the old thoughts and emotions came flooding back – the same guilt, anxiety and frustration as when I wrote it. I find the contents embarrassing, but they proved to be an invaluable resource to capture and trace the change in my mindset over that period. Reading them again, I am amazed at the capacity of our mind and body to evolve and recover.

The period of suspension and transition into a new role was a confusing and tumultuous time. I felt like an outside observer, watching the physical version of me attempting to come to terms with the confusing internal world I operated in. I recall some parts of this period perfectly, but other times are just blank. To return to the cocoon analogy, the grub was learning to be a butterfly.

The process of writing allowed me to express some of those emotions that I was too proud or embarrassed to share with others. Slowly, I was able to build some structure to my thinking, and the physical act of writing or typing made my thoughts visible. Revisiting the journal, I was struck by how changeable my mood was – the constant shifting from hope to anger to helplessness, from motivated to unmotivated, from free-flowing thought to practical, considered decision making. There were many days when my mind was like a runaway train, thoughts, feelings and emotions all rushing towards an unknown and undefined destination.

Of course what I have shared here only captures a small portion of my experience during this period. I selected passages that reflected my mindset at the various points along the journey and removed any content that was deeply personal or disclosed private aspects of my family life.

I underestimated the influence and impact my family had in sustaining me. The support, understanding and empathy shown by my wife, kids and extended family through this period was amazing. Sometimes I was impossible to be around, awkward in social situations, irrational and pig-headed. Our time together was punctuated with long periods of silence. I often felt like an outside observer of a world in which I was an active participant. While I was silent in a verbal sense, the internal noise was constant – a difficult concept to explain to loved ones. Remarkably, they maintained faith in me and this was to be the single most influential factor on my path to recovery.

The level of vitriol I directed at the police discipline hearing officer in my journal was intense. I have not shared some of the more colourful sections. The outcome was inevitable and while the process was frustrating, I had not thought I would be so affected by the comments he made. Almost on the first day of the journal, I conceded my career was over, so it is amazing to me that fifteen months later I was still fighting to remain a part of policing. Even though I knew that the conflict in my mind would not be resolved while I was a police officer, I still held out hope.

It also surprised me how long the suicidal ideation lingered. My memory was that I moved on relatively quickly from the Warrnambool incident, but the journal entries highlight my reliance on the 'escape clause'. I can clearly recall the original decision to complete suicide, but now it feels like looking back at a different life. I struggle to comprehend how I reached that decision with such clarity of thought and purpose.

Many journal reflections included the lyrics of songs I listened to while lost in my internal world. Music has always been important to me, mostly acoustic ballads – Paul Kelly, Colin Hay, Jimmy Barnes. Not long after the incident in 2014, I became obsessed with Paul Kelly and listened to his extensive back catalogue ad nauseam. There was one song in particular, 'If I Could Start Today Again', that struck a chord with me. It is a song about regret: if I could only go back in time, I would not make the same mistakes. This summed up my thinking – it was just a mistake, and if I could go back to before the car accident things would be different. But realistically, I would still have been an alcoholic, suicidal and deeply dissatisfied with my life, causing pain to the ones I loved. Going back would not resolve that. I needed to become visible, accept my shortcomings and move forward. This connection with music allowed me to explore the more creative aspects of my thinking, a much-needed reprieve from the analytical and critical thought patterns that dominated my psyche.

In this chapter, I reflect on how I attempted to make sense of transitioning from my role in policing to the next phase of my development. I describe the thought processes and internal language I developed to explain my experience. Having shared many conversations with others who have experienced a similar journey, I hope this will resonate with anyone who is going through a crisis and recovery process – whether they work in emergency services or any other industry.

Murdoch and the Blue Blanket

Following my spectacular fall from grace as a police officer, I spent many hours trapped inside my mind, trying to make sense of the circumstances I found myself in. As I reflected on my time with Victoria Police, I was searching for a way to explain my experience.

I had always considered myself to be well intentioned, to be someone who had strong values and morals and who did the right thing when it mattered. Serving the community through my role in policing for over twenty years, I had a significant impact on the lives of victims, witnesses and the underprivileged. But despite my commitment to the role, I never felt I was good enough; despite my achievements, nothing satisfied the negative voice within.

How did it come to this? How did I reach a point where my only goal in life was to serve that annoying voice who was with me all the time, chipping away, needling me and taking me to a place where there was no escape from expectation? There were so many positive aspects to my life that I ignored – my wife, children, extended family, my relative fortune in having secure employment and being physically fit.

In October 2014, I believed I was the only person who felt this way. The voice inside me, whom I have since named 'Murdoch', was a constant. 'Murdoch' is an imaginary orange horse from my childhood. I tied him to the rainwater tank stand in the backyard of our property in rural Victoria and spent many hours conversing with him, much to the amusement of my siblings. Fortunately, they could only hear one side of the conversation: Murdoch was always a voice only I could hear.

The second coming of Murdoch was far more sinister. It felt like this voice in my head controlled every aspect of my life and no matter what I did to make him go away, it was unsuccessful. He did not have a name back then; he was just part of who I was. It was as if there were two aspects of me. The person I wanted to be, aligned with my values and my desire to experience love, affection and friendship, and who allowed me to enjoy a mind that was not racing like an out-of-control projector in a cinema. And a second part of me that was the beast: Murdoch.

Murdoch was selfish, self-centred, egotistical, reactive to every thought that came my way. I tried to rid myself of him many times. He must be part amphibious, as my attempts to drown him with alcohol were unsuccessful. I tried to ignore him. I tried to reason with him. I even had many arguments with him out loud. I cannot tell you how many times I was asked, 'What did you say?' or 'Who are you talking to?' It was Murdoch every time. For periods of time, I could force him out, but he would always find a way back in. He is deceptive, cunning and determined; in my mind I was weak, subservient and scared. When I looked in the mirror, it was Murdoch who looked back at me. It was so much easier to buy into his rhetoric than to challenge my insecurities and fears.

This phenomenon is still with me, but in a different form. Murdoch and I live in relative harmony now, although he still has his moments. The key to this peaceful cohabitation is understanding that I do not have to act on the thoughts he conjures up. I have the power to choose what I buy into and what I let go. I have tried many strategies over the years; managing Murdoch is an ongoing process.

The second concept that I identified and named to explain my experience was the notion of the 'Blue Blanket'.

Most of us try to convince ourselves that we should be able to control what we feel. This is an absurdity. Policing has an emphasis on control. It needs to, for safety reasons. As police officers, we need to control many aspects of any situation to minimise the risk of injury and harm. But the one aspect we cannot control is our personal reactions and emotions. Our planned response to any incident does not include instructions on how to experience and accept the range of physical and emotional reactions you may encounter when involved in a traumatic incident.

The strategy I employed was to ignore those emotions or find another way to make them bearable. For me, anxiety – that horrible uncomfortable feeling of suspecting other people have noticed you are racked with fear or having an emotional reaction to a particular event – was never far away. I would get anxious about being anxious. My stomach would tighten. I would feel the adrenaline dump, the nausea, the shakes and dry mouth and then become more anxious about others noticing my reactions. Uncontrollable waves of anxiety would sweep over me. Why didn't anyone else feel like this? I just wanted to make it disappear.

Alcohol took my anxiety away for short periods. The hazier my mind became, the greater my reliance on alcohol. Escaping that confronting world, even if only for a short period, gave me hope. Of course this was not a healthy cycle. I am certain others could see the path of self-destruction I was on, but I had no capacity to self-reflect.

There was one place I could go to ease my pain, to lose myself in a world where I was accepted. I could immerse myself in a culture that treasured loyalty, a place where other like-minded people sought solace in achieving results 'for the greater good' to avoid having to face thoughts and emotions we could not control. This place was the 'Blue Blanket'. It was the comfort of the company of others who had experienced the challenges of policing and, rather than address those challenges, ignored the personal costs. In this world, reputation was everything: how many briefs have I completed, how many court cases have I won, how long since my last sick day, how many days off am I owed, how many times did I make myself available at short notice to be part of an early morning search warrant or arrest? These were the things that mattered inside the

Blue Blanket. It did not matter what was going on with the rest of your life; your reputation would be intact, and you would reap the rewards if you stuck it out for long enough.

You will not read about the Blue Blanket in a procedure or policy document, and it is never explicitly discussed in policing circles. Instead, we talk about 'the police family', as if this is a substitute for the actual families we belong to. The culture, rituals and symbols of policing reinforce the connection between all who have been part of the thin blue line. These are never more prominent than when we lose one of our own. If the death happened on duty, we speak about courage and sacrifice in an almost gladiatorial way. I have been to more police funerals than I care to remember, and each one has left me with a different reflection about that member and their particular policing experience. The importance of family and the ripple impacts such deaths have across the broader community is never lost on me.

The comfort of the Blue Blanket is difficult to describe. Why would you choose to hold on to your deepest fears and anxieties rather than express them to those closest to you? Sometimes we think that those outside the policing bubble will not understand or appreciate the experiences we have endured. We might want to protect our nearest and dearest from the graphic detail of what we confront in the course of our duties. Either way, we are anticipating and predicting how others will react. Who are we to decide what others can process, especially those who have committed to close relationships or friendships with us?

I could count on one hand the number of meaningful conversations I had with colleagues about mental health during my twenty years of operational policing. The most damning part of that is that I was a manager within the organisation and did not know how to discuss such issues with my staff. If anyone did inquire about my welfare, my answer was always the same – 'No, I am fine' – as I hurried onto the next operation. And I am pretty sure that those who enquired, while well intentioned, would have had little idea how to respond had I told them my true thoughts.

Whenever there was a choice between addressing my alcoholism or heading for the comfort of the Blue Blanket, I chose the security and comfort of what I knew every time. I had convinced myself I could manage both worlds, and that there would always be time for me – family, relationships, health, community – when I had finished my next investigation. I would tell myself this would be the last, that after that I would step back and it would be someone else's turn to step up. The reality was I would never allow this to happen. What if I let someone else in and they did a better job than me? Where would that leave me? Selfish and irrational, my thought was, 'If I don't do this one, it will not get solved!' Who was I kidding? I left my wife and children with a raft of hollow promises and feeble excuses instead of addressing my insecurities and fears.

There were many others like me. Perhaps we gravitated to each other, feeding off our insecurities and convincing ourselves that as long as we kept working and getting results our personal issues would resolve themselves.

The unwritten contract that if I worked hard, achieved results and committed to the cause then the Blue Blanket would save me from any predicament – personal or professional. The Blue Blanket served me well – until it didn't.

Murdoch and the Blue Blanket were strategies I developed to help maintain my cloak of invisibility.

I had accepted that my life would change because of the occupation I had chosen. Unfortunately, I also accepted I had little or no control over this change.

The Quadrant Theory

In trying to understand how I had reached a position where I considered suicide, I found it easier to think about how other people managed in similar situations than to turn the lens on myself. With Alex, I discussed many theories about why people did what they did. I spoke in the third person, discussing why people I dealt with through my work acted and behaved in certain ways. Having completed the highest-level human source management course available and combined with my experience of dealing with many witnesses, suspects, offenders and victims in my investigative roles, I had a strong understanding of human behaviour and motivations.

The first theory I proposed was simple: there was a scale from mindfulness to narcissism and we all move along the scale to some extent. In this model there were four quadrants, with quadrant one the mindfulness end of the continuum and quadrant four the narcissistic end. The pendulum represented the shifting nature of my experience. In recent years, I realised I had spent extended periods of time in quadrants three and four with little time at the mindfulness end of the model.

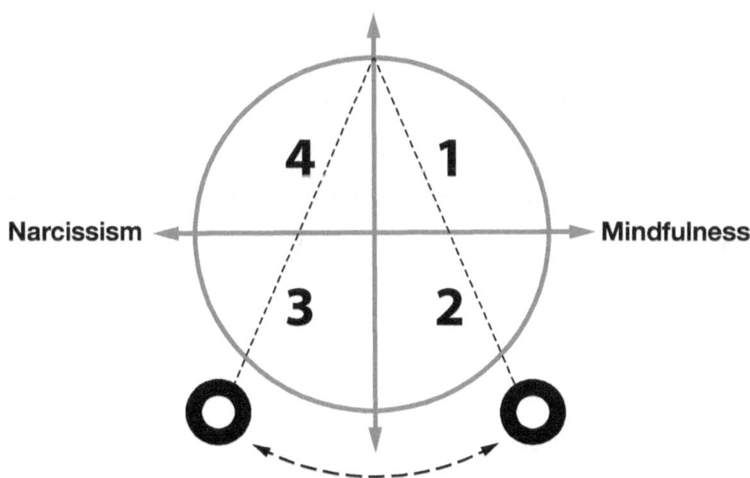

Quadrant 1. In this quadrant I was functioning at my best: sleeping well, looking after my diet, alcohol-free and engaged in relationships that matter to me. Work was not consuming me and I could manage my thoughts, living with Murdoch and the Blue Blanket in relative harmony. This is how I thought others lived their lives. I spent very little time in this quadrant personally.

Quadrant 2. The second quadrant was a danger zone for me. From here my decisions would either send me further along the narcissism scale or pull me back to becoming more mindful. In this quadrant I was just getting by, managing my alcohol to some extent and maintaining some semblance of a work–life balance. My conscience knew the right path to take, but I might decide to make work the priority and drift off to the third quadrant. It is difficult to be mindful when guilt, regret and frustration are the primary emotions.

Quadrant 3. When I was in the third quadrant, alcohol was prominent. I was obsessed with work and my unrelenting standards could tolerate nothing less than total commitment. My ego was at the forefront and Murdoch was in control. I was not living to my values. Avoidance, shame and escapism were prominent as I strived to present a competent persona in the workplace. I felt like a fraud. I could not be trusted, breaking promises and disrespecting the commitment I had made to my family and myself.

Quadrant 4. The fourth quadrant was a place I feared. Here I was manic. In this quadrant there was little sleep, paranoia, alcohol misuse and risk-taking, both personally and professionally. I was not a very pleasant person to be near and had no regard for my personal safety. When I was in quadrant four the silhouette was prominent, and my hypervigilance was extreme. Everyone and everything were against me.

When I first developed this model, I attempted to identify the triggers that caused the pendulum to move, at times violently, from calm, pleasant and engaging to angry, withdrawn and agitated. A simple incident could initiate a reaction that was often not obvious to anyone but me. For example, I could drive past an address that reminded me of a particular crime or investigation, lose myself in the thoughts associated with that investigation and find myself feeling as if I had returned to that traumatic time. In this way I could transfer from the first to the third quadrant with no discernible outside influence. Little wonder I was almost impossible to live with. There was no explanation or warning for the changes in behaviour, no consistency in who you may be engaging with from day to day or even hour to hour.

In the model, I saw mindfulness as when I was fully present and aware of myself and my surroundings. My thoughts were just that – thoughts – and they did not have to be acted on. I could step back and observe myself and not be overwhelmed by what was happening in my world. Mindfulness made practical sense, but I thought it would never work for me. I was certain no one else felt the way I did, and I had no explanation to account for my behaviours. This resistance to help-seeking was at the core of my discontent. Murdoch had convinced me I was special, that treatment may work for others but could never work for me.

At first I was unsure what to label the opposite end of the model. WebMD defines narcissism as 'extreme self-involvement to the degree that it makes a person ignore the needs of those around them'. Other definitions included 'self-centred', 'arrogant', 'lack of empathy' and 'in love with the image of themselves'. That was me when I was in the third and fourth quadrants. I am ashamed to admit that is where I was spending most of my time during the period leading up to 2014. The conflict with my values was key to where I sat in my model. But if I was being the person I wanted to be – a good husband, father and friend – looking after my physical and mental health and contributing to the relationships that were most important to me, I could shift this.

The challenge was that in my mind, to be effective at work, to be the best detective I could be, I needed to fully commit. That meant working against my values to achieve the outcomes I was longing for. I worked long hours, experienced stress, allowed my mental and physical health to decline and misused alcohol to project the image of an indestructible detective. There was nothing I couldn't do and if I did not take it on, who else would have the skills or dedication to successfully complete the task? I could always go back to my 'real' values after completing the next investigation or project I was working on. There was no balance. It was all-in or not at all, and I could not have my reputation tarnished by not succeeding. So my family and health suffered – you can always make it up later. But can you?

On reflection, this has been one of the most difficult concepts to reconcile. While it was apparent that I was deteriorating and taking greater risks to maintain my secret, I could not bring myself to challenge the position I was in. It was as if I had no capacity for reflection or review. Part of my defence mechanism was to shun any thought that I could not find a way through. At first the Quadrant Theory was my secret, a way for me to explore my inner world without exposing my mental health condition. Keep it invisible, at all costs.

* * *

My work with Alex had helped me consider that I moved through different stages of functioning. My thinking was not mature enough to engage with the model completely, but I was creating a framework that I could apply. The Quadrant Theory did not always make sense to me: when it felt too confusing and difficult I would return to my dysfunctional ways. At these times I returned to applying the model to those I dealt with in the work environment, rather than reflecting on my experience.

When my dysfunction and frustration were at their greatest, thoughts of suicide slowly infiltrated my thinking. This included planning the actual event. In this state, I was cold and detached, but strangely it gave me a sense of warmth and security. This was another contradiction I battled with as I sought to find a sense of my 'self'.

The pressure on my time was relentless. My role was inherently very reactive and required critical decisions to be made at short notice. These decisions impacted on the safety of my team members and the people we were dealing with. It was difficult to plan any given day as there would inevitably be a crisis that required attention. For many years I had made a list in my mind of what needed to be done that day, and if I did not complete the list in work hours I would catch up in my own time. I would either stay back late at work or work at home on the laptop. Every other manager at my level, like all the others before us, faced the same predicament. I was exhausted all the time and relying on alcohol to maintain some level of functioning – a release from the difficult emotions. Inevitably, someone would discover I was not the person I portrayed, that I was a fraud and not up to the role I had taken on.

As the pendulum swung to the third quadrant, my decision making would become impaired. I could no longer make concise, effective, ethical decisions. It severely hampered my capacity for intelligent thought and reflection. This was another anxiety to add to my list. What if my condition caused harm to someone else because I could not perform operationally to the standard required? Balance this against the option of disclosing that I was thinking of suicide, was a functioning alcoholic and had an orange horse named Murdoch running the show.

Alex had explained the notion of neural pathways: the more we use a particular pathway, the more engrained it becomes. I did some reading around this, although I was initially sceptical. I needed evidence – irrefutable, clear and concise evidence – before I could buy into any theory or treatment model. Comprehending the key concepts of neuroplasticity was beyond my capacity at that time, but the image of the brain having pathways made a connection, and I came up with another model – smoke and pendulums.

The sensation of heat in my brain was always strong. It often felt as if my brain was stuck in overdrive, processing images, thoughts, theories and strategies at a rapid rate, causing a fire within my brain. It was a unique sensation. If I attempted mindfulness or to connect physically through a body scan, there was this sense of heat coming from the physical place inside my head. I tried to see if I could feel my brain. If I lay on my back, still and motionless, scanning my body for sensations and reactions, could I feel it? I could feel my pelvis, my spine, my shoulders and other areas involved with movement, but could I conjure a sense of where my brain sat in my body? Where was it inside my skull? What shape, size and colour was it?

Through repeating this exercise, I created an image of my brain as a tangle of neural pathways with random junctions and connections leading in all directions. When I was functioning well, I was 'clear headed' and the pathways were obvious, with the junctions and connections easy to identify and navigate. When I had moved to the third quadrant, the heat in my brain caused smoke and the way through the maze was confusing, treacherous and nonsensical. Ironically, alcohol acted as a retardant rather than an accelerant. The more I drank, the more I was able to put the fire out, to find some clarity, to slow the burn from within. But while alcohol would suppress the smoke and fire for a short period, the back burn was intense: I craved more and more alcohol to control the smoke and fire.

Ironically, thinking of suicide was another technique to quell the smoke. It gave me space to plan a solution, ease the flow of thoughts, images and memories and move to a resolution phase. In this space I applied the basic principles of planning an operation – understand the aim and purpose, deploy resources and techniques to gather and strengthen the evidence, and then move to a resolution phase. But in this case resolution would not be an arrest: it would be a final, irreversible conclusion.

The idea of smoke and fire in my brain became an extension of the quadrant theory. All of this was going on while I continued to live a 'normal' life outside of my head. Escaping to this other world was a way to fill my mind with thoughts that did not take me back to those matters I did not want to deal with. My fixation on the silhouette reduced when I thought about suicide. I could feel the black blob, it was always there, but it would shrink back to a manageable size and influence when I distracted myself with thoughts of ending it all.

I considered my working life normal: everyone was busy and had responsibilities and difficult decisions to make. All police have seen shitty crime scenes and dealt with confronting situations; this was just part of the gig. Everyone else seemed to cope. But I was pretty sure most others did not have the background noise that I had. This was a significant flaw in my thinking process. I was forever comparing myself to others and assuming that my circumstances and reactions were far worse than any other individual could be experiencing.

The Alex impact

Alex was a constant throughout my recovery and he is still a part of my mental health plan.

Initially we focused on my alcoholism in our sessions. He had a very safe way of 'holding' me, accepting that I may relapse but making sure I was accountable and giving me the confidence to try again.

One of the many important concepts he taught me was that sitting with him for an hour a fortnight would not change much. There was much out of session work to do, and it would require a significant contribution from me. He accepted that my commitment would waver from time to time, and I am certain he had to delve deep into his kit of resources to maintain my interest. But he remained there as a constant, never judgemental, but with the skill and courage to call out my poor behaviours. There was a tightrope to walk – if he pushed too hard, I was likely to walk away; if he became an advocate for me, he would become another voice supporting my distorted feelings of being 'special'. Instead, he had an amazing capacity to provide an insight at just the right time to regain my focus and attention.

It was Alex who suggested I return to study, inspired me to apply for the position at Beyond Blue, assisted me in preparing for my interview, encouraged me in my transition to The Police Association and helped me develop my thinking and strategies around the BlueHub project. He gave me the confidence to believe that I could contribute productively despite my mental health condition.

When Alex first suggested I return to study, I thought he had lost his mind. I was a broken-down copper without a driver's licence who had failed his Higher School Certificate the first time around. Given my uncertain financial future and reluctance to let go of the Blue Blanket, committing to a course of study was the furthest thing from my mind.

We were discussing what my future might hold, Alex putting up well-thought-out, plausible solutions, me smothering them with the Blue Blanket. He then asked me: what would you do if there were no barriers to what you could achieve? No financial barriers. You could have any job you wanted, be accepted into any course you chose – what would you do?

He removed everything from the table we were sitting at to mimic a clean sheet and asked me to consider my options. This technique had a twofold impact. First, he had skilfully removed the notion of me returning to policing – he knew that the financial security was the biggest lure there. Second, he was asking me to return to my values and determine who I wanted to be in the world. By moving into the hypothetical realm and putting me in the driver's seat to choose, I sought solutions rather than focussing on barriers.

This discussion went on for many weeks. There was no lightbulb moment where I suddenly left policing behind, but seeking solutions created hope. Of course I still fell back into the negative and destructive thinking patterns, but step by step we were removing Murdoch's oxygen. Murdoch's chatter was still never far away, but it was now more of an uneasy coexistence than a domination.

The question most often asked of a new recruit is, 'Why do you want to join the police?' The standard response is, 'to help people'. When Alex asked me what I wanted to do in 2014, some twenty years after joining Victoria Police, my response was the same. But he gradually showed me over time that you do not have to wear a uniform to help people.

We decided I had strong communications skills, intellect for further study, and that developing greater understanding of mental health was a primary goal. As an investigator, I wanted to know what had happened – how did I transform from an intelligent, articulate and high-achieving member of Victoria Police into an anxious, suicidal alcoholic?

From the outset, I was not studying specifically to become a counsellor or psychotherapist. It was about allowing me to develop, to test myself in a safe environment and to explore options rather than shun them. To gain a better understanding of myself and how I may help others.

Alex expanded my thinking and would often recommend a book or a research article to read that we would then dissect in the following months. He had enormous humility, empathy, humanity and courage. He had an abundance of experience to share, and he took me on that journey with him.

I was fortunate to have found a clinician I related to. I tried others with varying degrees of success, but none seemed to grasp and understand my perspective as deeply and intuitively as Alex. He continues to be a significant influence on my thinking and evolution.

Family matters

I am fortunate to have a friend and mentor who is a leading expert in the treatment of post-traumatic stress disorder. He has treated many hundreds of emergency service workers and other clients impacted by trauma throughout his career. He has an outstanding ability to connect with his clients and is skilled in the use of evidence-based treatments. Although I have never been his client, we have shared many theories on the challenges faced by police and emergency service workers, from the systems issues that disrupt the treatment process through to the most effective treatment modalities. When I asked him what the most important factors in the treatment process were, he nominated a supportive and secure home environment as the most influential aspect. The use of evidence-based treatments, an accurate assessment of the presenting condition, the therapeutic alliance and the willingness of the client to be an active participant are all important, but this needed to be underpinned by support from family, friends and loved ones.

This was certainly my experience. Without the love and support of my wife and family, I am not certain I would have made it through the crisis I faced. The question I am asked most after delivering presentations on my experience is 'Are you still married?' Or, 'How did the family cope?' Obviously I have insights into how my actions impacted the family unit. One of Alex's techniques was to have me consider my experience from the perspective of my wife and children. And we have personally discussed these matters. But I will never fully appreciate what it was like to live with a person experiencing such an acute mental health crisis over such an extended period.

I did not have to live through the stress, hurt and helplessness that my wife and children were exposed to. I have not attempted to describe their personal experiences, as that is a story for them to share if they ever feel the need. They have been supportive of me throughout the writing process, acknowledging that it has been an important part of my recovery, but I respect their choice to maintain their privacy. Our collective experience continues to evolve. There are times when we reflect and wonder how we made it through, but mostly we appreciate our good fortune and focus on what we can influence. A little like the mental health continuum, there is an acceptance that not every day will be perfect, that as a family unit we will face challenges individually and collectively, but if we are open to sharing our love and experiences we can support each other through the inevitable challenges that will arise.

Families I have engaged with who have experienced a similar journey have observed that those closest to the person experiencing a mental health condition identify the changes in behaviour long before the impacted person is willing to accept that they were unwell. While my mental health concerns may have remained invisible in the workplace, my wife and children were well aware of them. They knew about my lack of sleep, angry outbursts, reliance on alcohol, exhaustion and tendency to remain mute and isolated. While I convinced myself my efforts to conceal my condition were effective, this was far from reality. There were many attempts to help me, but I was a reluctant participant in any strategy to improve my condition. I would sometimes agree to a quick holiday or weekend away, periods of abstinence from alcohol, various fitness regimes or a reduced focus on my commitment to work. While these strategies provided some short-term relief, they were not sustainable or effective. Meaningful change could only come from within, from accepting my condition and being willing to be a visible, open and active participant in the recovery process.

I cannot imagine what it must have been like when I first disclosed my suicidal intentions to my wife on that August morning in 2014, or how she was able to navigate her way through the broken promises, disappointments and frustration as my condition deteriorated over a period of years. Receiving the text message after the accident in October 2014, engaging with my managers when they attended her workplace on the morning of my accident, and enduring the uncertainty when I fled to Warrnambool. The emotional commitment to the treatment process, financial insecurity, exposure to dysfunctional systems issues, uncertain employment prospects – the impacts on the family unit were overwhelming.

Yet through all of this, there was an unshakeable confidence in our ability to endure. Some might consider it blind faith. When does such commitment reach the tipping point where the level of damage outweighs the possibility of a return to good health? I am certain that we were on the precipice of this tipping point on many occasions, yet through her calm, confident and loving nature, my wife was able to help my family navigate this tumultuous period. She often reminds me that, however difficult this experience was, I now have the opportunity to contribute to the family in different ways. Now we move forward with me as an active participant rather than as a disconnected observer. The way my wife and children supported me unconditionally has set the blueprint for us to meet life's challenges, whatever they may be.

PART IV

THE ROAD BACK

12.

Starting the Renovation

The transition to the next phase of my working life was a time of exploration and curiosity, as I attempted to navigate the thinking traps that had been such a burden in the past. I still did not have a full plan on how to manage my mental health going forward, but I had developed several strategies that I knew were beneficial. It felt like a renovation, adding some new features to the old structure to better serve my needs.

I had not made a conscious decision to be completely open about my mental health condition and history, but it was not something I would hide. I considered my mental health condition to be 'non-visible'. It was there, but unless you were aware of it there were very few outward signs.

It occurred to me that despite my ongoing studies and education around mental health, I needed to develop my own language to describe my condition. The clinical language did not really suit. It seemed to belong to another culture, a bit like how policing language is unique to that environment. 'Murdoch' and the 'Blue Blanket' are examples of the language I developed to allow me to better understand and explain my experience.

My quadrant theory provided a way for me to 'check in', to consider where I was within my model and observe the triggers that caused me to move between the quadrants. Of all the mental health theories I studied, this personal model had the most relevance for me. I drew on what I studied to complement my internal model, but I realised the more I thought about and considered my mental health the better chance I had of developing an effective method to manage it. This was far from a comprehensive plan, but internally, at least, I had made my mental health an important part of my everyday life, to make it visible in my internal world.

As I transitioned from a life of uncertainty back into full-time employment, two things shifted: my primary motivations and my understanding of the resources available to me.

Prior to the accident, my main motivation was simply to survive each day. There was no space to realise the extent of my condition or make any real effort to find a solution. That was why suicide was such an attractive option: it required little thought or self-reflection, just a clean, simple way to end the cycle of pain. Keeping my dirty secret and maintaining the web of lies and deceit was my primary motivation.

Other motivations included the material aspects of my life; I needed a good wage to provide for my family, the most effective way to increase my income was to pursue promotion, and promotion was achieved through hard work and sacrifice. There was a part of me that was motivated by the notoriety I enjoyed in my role as a detective. My world was not like that of others. I had the thrill of the chase, the satisfaction of solving difficult crimes and bringing some comfort to victims and families impacted by life-changing events. In my mind, to have the privilege of being involved in such investigations I needed to be fully committed to the cause, and I demanded this of those around me as well.

In short, my motivations had been based on the egotistical and materialistic facets of my life. My spectacular fall from grace forced me to find new motivations, to re-evaluate what was important to me when the fantasy world I had been living in was stripped away. Concepts such as love, emotions, personal reflections, learning and curiosity had been reawakened, and the challenge was to tolerate and manage my mental health condition while attempting to make sense of the changes that were going on around me.

During the final months of my policing career, Murdoch was in complete control. I can still hear him: 'You are super intelligent, no case can remain unsolved. If you persist for long enough, you will succeed. Look back on your results, swallow down the anxiety, make the sacrifice now and the rewards will come.' Alcohol was an insidious supporter of this narrative, and suicide was the dark angel that would be the only acceptable final chapter.

The narrative of my policing experience was both protective and destructive. To find the courage to confront violent and dangerous circumstances I needed to believe that I would be safe. I was well trained, had operational safety equipment and colleagues that would back me up no matter how challenging the circumstances. Physical confrontation was not my strong suit – it scared the shit out of me. I would much prefer to plan and ensure that I had all the contingencies covered than be at physical risk. Others thrived on the notion of resolving physical conflict quickly and efficiently through the use of force. The one unmistakable thread through these narratives was that you don't lose a fight as a copper.

I still vividly recall my first pub fight in a dingy inner-suburban establishment. It was in the first six months of my career – with a large, alcohol-affected male who had been refused service and was refusing to leave the premises. I was working with a senior member who was much smaller in stature than me but far more experienced. The male was verbally aggressive and had plenty of mates around him. We had called for back-up, and it was clear that this was going to resolve one way or another before they arrived. I had no clue what to do. The male looked terrifying, and the bar suddenly seemed very small. It was clear he was not going to leave on his own steam and he ripped his shirt off. I have never understood why men do that, but it did cross my mind to do the same. I am pretty sure my albino, skinny, tattoo-free torso would not have caused too many fears for our adversary!

Without warning, my colleague launched onto the male, like a leaping bear hug. My instant reaction was to do the same, and the combined weight of us brought him to the ground. We could control him to a point and fortunately his mates did not intervene. After what seemed like an eternity, we secured him with handcuffs and waited for back-up. I remained on top of him, attempting to keep him on the ground, while my colleague kept the crowd at bay. The adrenalin dump was massive. I was shaking, and my senses seemed to be alive to every stimulus that was around me. When we had secured the male into the van, the relief was palpable. My colleague congratulated me, telling me I was a team player, someone he would happily work with as I 'had a go'.

In hindsight, this was just another arrest. I would be involved in many more violent and challenging situations than this, but it stayed with me. My narrative changed that day. I walked a little taller and felt like part of the team. I could trust that those I worked with knew what to do and we could win every fight. My colleague most likely has no memory of this incident, but I etched it into my narrative. Under-resourced, undermanned and shit-scared, I had found a way through. I am pretty certain the offender we arrested woke four hours later in the cells and wondered why that tall, skinny, uncoordinated copper had kept holding onto him like a drowning man clinging to a life jacket. It was nothing to him, but important to me. I had survived.

The story I told myself about myself shifted, and as I moved into the world of investigations this narrative intensified. The more challenging the circumstances, the more effort I put in – the mantra was 'you never lose a court case'. If this meant time away from family, that was acceptable, as the narrative was to win at all costs. If sleep and diet became secondary, alcohol was used to manage my anxiety and checking in on my values was optional, I could make this narrative work. I did not label it then, but this was Murdoch's narrative, the dark silhouette that could push himself to extraordinary lengths to be 'successful'. What was missing was the 'real' me, the part of me that wanted to be loved and accepted for who I was.

My motivation was constantly changing, I relied on the policing narrative in challenging times, but there were times when I just wanted to be with my family. When Murdoch whispered, 'you are not good enough, you are a fraud, they will work you out', my narrative strengthened and I pushed those thoughts aside. I did not have the capacity to regulate myself to find a middle ground. The stronger my self-doubt and anxiety grew, the more tightly I had to hold onto my policing narrative. My story became that of a high-functioning alcoholic who had a special gift for crime investigation, someone to whom the normal rules did not apply. In my mind there was a tacit agreement between me and my supervisors: you keep getting results, we will support your 'specialness'. In reality no such agreement had been reached, but I was able to convince myself that this was my true narrative.

It was not surprising that when it came to seeking treatment for the symptoms I was experiencing, I had little or no motivation to comprehend or understand the reasons for my reactions. I was so focused on surviving that I ignored or avoided the intrusive thoughts, flashbacks and dreams. I could make them disappear with alcohol, and short-term relief was better than no relief at all. In hindsight, my response to the traumatic events I had witnessed was at the core of the symptoms I was experiencing. I had no will or desire to revisit the root cause of the nightmares and thoughts that were so real it was like I was reliving those horrible situations in high definition. The thought of being honest and disclosing my experiences to my employer, my friends, my family or even my clinician made me feel physically ill.

I was the antithesis of psychological flexibility. My thinking was rigid and determined – if you stick to the story, you will survive. Murdoch was able to reinforce this at every juncture to ensure that I continued to make decisions that on reflection seem illogical, immoral and nonsensical. Avoidance and escapism can shield you from the blinding light of an uncomfortable reality.

In the months following the accident, I had a desire to make someone pay for what I was experiencing. On reflection, I think this is why the suicidal ideation lingered for so long: it was less an escape clause at this stage, and more a way of seeking retribution or revenge: everybody would see what 'they' had done to me. I could channel my anger and allow all the horrific events I had witnessed to be destroyed with one simple action. My guilt, embarrassment and shame would be removed from my story; in a way suicide was about creating a false narrative that would be acceptable to others – the gun detective pushed too far by an uncaring and intolerable system.

During the period of suspension, I was able to re-evaluate many of the traumatic events that I had been involved in. In my discussions with Alex and through my studies, I developed a much greater appreciation of the impact that trauma can have on our functioning. For the first time I understood that exposure to repeated traumatic events can leave you depleted and can have a cumulative negative effect on your mental health and wellbeing. The memories and intrusive thoughts I had endured for so long could not be washed away with alcohol, avoided through isolation or removed through wishing them away.

As I reconnected with my body and my mind, my thinking became more flexible, Murdoch became less influential; the Blue Blanket was more of a throw rug than a weighted blanket. Alcohol use ceased, and while I was not able to identify this with clarity at the time, my motivation for change was shifting. There was no single 'line in the sand', no 'change now or else' moment. There was just a recognition that something had to change, that the inflexible thinking that had led to the all-or-nothing suicide scenario was not as attractive when I was able to view my world from a different perspective. Time and space had allowed me the room to shift; there was now choice where previously there had been none.

The irony is that all the ingredients I needed to better manage myself and my mental health were right in front of me. It was my attitude and willingness to avoid the obvious that was the greatest weakness. In my time with Victoria Police, I did not complete any meaningful mental health training – it was offered, but I was always too busy, too important to take the training seriously. Operational members saw it as another 'tick the box' activity to complete, forced on us by an unknowing and uncaring command structure. I would dismiss it immediately and race off to solve the next major investigation. Content and delivery are important, but it is difficult to engage an audience when they have no curiosity or interest in the topic.

Managing my mental health is up to me. I would challenge anyone to nominate a topic that has more freely available resources and information than mental health. And mental health is not confined to the workplace, yet many of us wait passively for an employer to deliver a generic program on mental health before we develop an effective strategy for managing it.

Like many of my colleagues, I held the view that if 'they', that is VicPol, broke me, 'they' should fix me. The concept of a shared responsibility between the individual and the workplace was foreign to me. Policing is one of the highest-risk occupations for mental health injuries – and each member can choose to take responsibility for their mental health, or they can choose not to. Unfortunately I took the latter option. It was not a deliberate, conscious decision, but I neglected my mental health.

This is not to minimise the important role of the employer. They have an obligation to provide a safe workplace and effective systems of work. Too often, in my experience in policing, mental health is secondary to the operational needs of the organisation. But there were many resources available to address and manage my mental health condition; it was my decision to ignore them. Colleagues, psychologists, managers, peer support, mental health training and welfare support were all readily available, but I didn't think they were relevant. Much of my time was spent proving myself, in an insatiable need to feel wanted and valued. Our culture did not engender trust in the system. In my world it was always up to me to do what I needed to survive. By the end of my policing career, I had managed to alienate myself from both the blue family and my own family.

When I began my role at Beyond Blue, I was determined to ensure that I had a plan to maintain my mental health.

13.

Beyond Blue and the Mental Health Continuum

On 15 February 2016, I started my first job outside Victoria Police in over twenty years. I had not worked for sixteen months, and although my mental health had improved considerably, I was apprehensive about my ability to work full-time at an acceptable level.

The strategies I used to manage my anxiety would be different in this new environment. There was no Blue Blanket with me this time, and I had not used alcohol since the incident in 2014. Murdoch was still with me, but I was able to observe him clearly; I could hear his chatter, notice it, accept it and move on – I, rather than Murdoch, chose which thoughts to act on. He was a part of me, but not *me*. I no longer had the burning desire to remove all feelings of anxiety or fear. I could sit with them even though they were uncomfortable. What was the worst that could happen? I knew how to monitor my reactions, accepting that everyone experiences anxiety and that I did not need to compare myself to others.

Landing a role at Beyond Blue was a miracle. I had initially contacted them to enquire about a placement for the Master of Counselling and Psychotherapy I was undertaking. A friend suggested Beyond Blue as a potential placement site. I soon discovered they did not offer placements, but I had a long conversation with the staff member who took my call. I told her about what had led to me leaving Victoria Police and that I was undertaking study in mental health.

The area in which the staff member worked had recently established a Police and Emergency Services program and had advertised for a National Engagement Manager. They were seeking someone with a background in emergency services, lived experience of mental health issues and some formal training in a mental health discipline. I was a bit shallow on the third aspect but had the other two covered. We continued the discussion and I discovered that a driver's licence was not a prerequisite, there would be some interstate travel and I might be required to share my story. I honestly thought someone was taking the piss. How could such a role exist? I had spent so many hours worrying that I was unemployable.

I prepared for the interview the best way I knew – by immersing myself in all I could learn about Beyond Blue. I tried to come up with examples I could use to highlight my strengths and capabilities and had decided that I was going to be absolutely upfront about the circumstances that led me to this position. I committed to sharing my experience, regardless of how uncomfortable it might be.

This was a very different experience to my interviews within the police force. Each position I had applied for during that period of rapid promotion followed an approach by a manager who was keen to recruit me. There was a process, but nepotism was alive and well. Police interviews had involved three people sitting opposite me, each with a notepad and a series of predetermined questions that would be asked in turn. It was not difficult to predict the topics that would be discussed. Often it was difficult to make any eye contact or read the reactions of panel members as they were usually head down and writing furiously, as if they had to transcribe every word uttered. Mind you, I ran several selection processes myself and did exactly the same thing. This interview was different.

The three of us sat in an office, each an equal, sitting around a table. We had a discussion, not an interrogation. This was not a memory test of what I knew about Beyond Blue; it seemed like they wanted to know about me. I shared my story. I was honest and direct and had no fear of being open and transparent. If my history was the reason I was unsuccessful, so be it. I would rather they know than carry another dirty little secret.

I was successful in my application and it transformed my outlook. I had hope again. Hope, Recovery, Resilience – three words I had read on a poster on the way into the interview. This was a workplace that lived up to the values it espoused. The interview was also the start of a wonderful friendship. My new manager, the interviewer, provided such a supportive and collaborative approach, my sense of worth returned. I could see how I could benefit their program and we discussed ways to manage my mental health as I transitioned back into full-time work. There was an acceptance that I had experienced a significant mental health condition, but so had many others and they were back in the workplace as productive and valued staff members.

My first genuine attempt to shift from the invisible to the visible had been rewarded in a way I could never have imagined. I couldn't believe the management at Beyond Blue would take the risk of employing me. I had disclosed a significant recent mental health injury, resigned from Victoria Police before they sacked me and did not have a driver's licence. This was not a great backstory, but despite considerable reputational risk they took the chance and gave me an opportunity. I felt indebted to the leaders who did so. I wanted to show that through openness, honesty and transparency their decision would be justified.

I established my routine: I would ride to work, shower, go for a walk and have a coffee. I started when the weather was fine and had the chance to watch the sunrise and appreciate each day as it began. There was no need to work on the computer once I had left the workplace for the day. Instead, I would ride home listening to music and prepare to share my day with my family over dinner. It was important for me to be connected with them as they had given me so much; this was their journey as much as it was mine. I planned meals, exercised daily, and went to bed and got up at the same time each day to establish a routine and to give myself the best chance of sleep. My weekends were spent with my family, actually present, not allowing thoughts of work to dominate. I kept up my sessions with Alex and continued my awareness through movement classes to stay connected to my body. I had peripheral vision; I accepted that I may have days when I experienced some of those old anxieties and stressors, but I knew if I stayed strong with my routine I could handle them without relapsing.

I undertook regular interstate trips as part of my role, and my manager and I discussed strategies for managing my mental health while travelling. I would use the flights as time to reflect and monitor how I was managing. Plane flights became one of the most enjoyable aspects of my role. In solitude, disconnected without guilt, I could use the time to plan for how I could be the best version of myself.

I am certain I was far more productive than at any stage in my last five years with VicPol. In the past, interstate trips had always meant a bender. Interstate detectives were only too keen to stitch up their compatriots with alcohol. Now I was travelling to every state, alone, with just my thoughts and a desire to be the best I could be. Thoughts of drinking came to mind ('Who would know? You could have a couple with dinner, it will help you sleep.') but I would answer them ('Thanks, but no thanks, Murdoch. I hear you, but I am not acting on your advice. My life, my choice.').

My new work environment was so different to what I had known. There was no threat to my safety, no chance I was going to be called out to some gruesome crime scene or have to manage a family who had just lost a loved one. I was not orchestrating an operation that involved hundreds of members and thousands of dollars of investment, where success or failure depended on my decision making. If I failed, it wouldn't potentially lead to the death of a witness or human source. The contrast reinforced the challenges of policing and how difficult that life had been. Shift work, deadlines, pressure from management, lack of resources, the list goes on. In terms of high-pressure environments, I could not think of a more dynamic, confronting and challenging role. My new role was structured, less reactive and did not involve trauma. Ironically, I spent more time planning to manage my mental health in a much less demanding role than I did in one of the most complex and challenging roles in policing. I was much more likely to be dragged into the 'three' on my quadrant theory in a policing environment than I was in my current role. Previously, I had the comfort of the Blue Blanket and the support of Murdoch. That was my mental health strategy. Policing does not stop; you work hard and wait for the rewards. How about working hard and being in the moment so you can experience the rewards, not escape them?

An example of experiencing a reward and not escaping: I recall a murder trial when we obtained a conviction without locating the body. It was a difficult time for the victim's family, as they were always hopeful their son would return. I spent many hours with the family through the investigation and a lengthy and complex Supreme Court trial that culminated in a conviction. I cannot describe the emotion of a courtroom when a verdict is returned. It is a unique experience and I was only a bit player. I cannot comprehend what it must be like for the family or the accused. In the moments immediately after the verdict, when you are with a grieving family, the emotions are priceless. Someone cared enough to fight for their boy, to hold the offender to account so that justice could be served.

I wish I had taken the time to sit in that experience, to notice my physical reactions. Where did my thoughts go? How did I process my response? How do you experience such an intimate interaction with another human and not have the capacity to reflect and consider your reactions?

My memory is that I just wanted to get out of there, get to the pub and celebrate, receive the accolades, satisfy Murdoch and that massive ego within. I relegated my family to second again; I would make it up to them when this was over.

I was determined this would not be my experience in my new role. I understood that by giving something of myself, I could form relationships and live in line with the values that were important to me. A structured and supportive work environment allows you to perform the role at a high standard and still achieve a balanced and rewarding life away from work. As I found out earlier, you cannot put a mask on in the workplace and return home and expect to return to the person you want to be. I needed to live to my values across all aspects of my life; the previous compartmentalised approach was intrinsically flawed.

I was required to give presentations to emergency service agencies and unions in each state across Australia. The presentations were on a framework for developing mentally healthy environments in the workplace and how to best manage the mental health needs of emergency service workers. My previous role gave me some currency and buy-in, and I could build relationships based on my experience in the sector. The communication skills I had developed as a detective and a source handler had prepared me well for interactions with the variety of personalities I was to engage with. But would that be enough to translate the message into action?

Early on, I was presenting to a combined group of emergency service workers interstate. It included representatives from each of the major agencies, from various departments, and a range of ranks. As I moved through the PowerPoint presentation, I could tell I had lost them. I didn't need to be a detective to appreciate that if napkins were being used to wipe sleep drool from mouths, rather than clean up after eating muffins, I was not really cutting it. The sun was beaming into the room; it was mid-afternoon and there was much nodding from the audience, not in appreciation of my words of wisdom but the reflex action when your sleepy head moves forward, blocks your airway and causes your head to snap back.

My manager had encouraged me to be innovative, to think laterally, to bring new perspectives to what could be a difficult topic to engage with. So, I abandoned the script mid-presentation and instead spoke candidly about my experience and what had led me to taking the role. I interlaced the key points from the presentation into my personal narrative using examples that resonated with the target audience. The shift in the audience was palpable. They were engaged; they could relate to the experience I was describing. I think most would have experienced similar feelings during their working life. This really brought home to me the power of sharing lived experience. When an audience can relate to a story, when they can empathise and reflect on their own experiences, the message becomes far more powerful. The cloak of invisibility was being lifted.

This was not a new concept. Beyond Blue has a speakers program that had been operating successfully for many years, one I am proud to say I remain a part of in a voluntary capacity. Many people have bravely shared their personal stories to change people's thinking about the true impacts of mental health issues across society. By speaking openly about my values and the strategies I employed to maintain my mental health, it tied me to this approach of openness. Practise what you preach. I can learn from experience, I can achieve change, I can be loved and valued despite my history. Without realising it, I was embedding the new neural pathways that Alex had been banging on about for years.

One of my first tasks at Beyond Blue was to bring together a senior representative from each emergency service agency and respective union body in Australia to a forum in Sydney. It was March 2016, and Beyond Blue were launching 'The Good Practice Framework for mental health and wellbeing in emergency service agencies', a project I had been heavily involved in. Fortuitously, this type of task suited my skill set in planning. It was like developing an operation order for one of the major police investigations I had managed. There was a clear aim and an end date to work towards. And as with police operations, sometimes you needed to think a bit from left field to achieve a result.

I attribute much of the success of the forum to the team's outstanding work in preparing for the event. For the first time in a long time, I felt like part of a team again, this time with no secrets. I attended many conferences in my role with Beyond Blue, but it was at this forum that I had a striking revelation. There were many excellent presentations across two days, but one in particular stood out for me. Mike Pietrus from the Canadian Mental Health Commission delivered a presentation on a program called 'Road to Mental Readiness'. In it, he shared his conception of the mental health continuum.

The version of the mental health continuum he outlined began with the notion that we often look at our mental health from a very fixed way of thinking – you are either well or you are unwell. Instead, he encouraged us to think about moving across a colour continuum, from green to yellow to orange and then to red. He described each section of the model and some strategies for managing being in each colour.

As I sat in the auditorium, my thoughts raced: had they stolen my idea? This was the quadrant theory flattened out! The green was my 1, yellow 2, orange 3 and red 4. We all move along the continuum just as the pendulum swings in an arc at the bottom of my model. The orange and red sections are closer to narcissistic behaviours and yellow and green is when we are more connected to our true selves – more mindful. Even the colours suited. Flames and heat at the red end of the continuum represented my brain when the smoke and fire were clouding all my thoughts. It is very difficult to see out or self-reflect when in the orange or red; that is survival mode.

The parallels to my model stunned me. Described in a clear and concise fashion, it was far easier to explain than my Quadrant Theory.

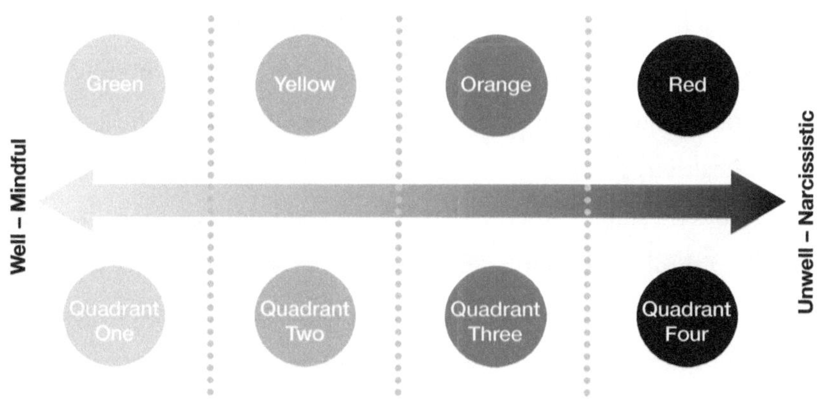

And it clearly resonated. In the lunch break, people were discussing the model and making jokes – 'You are always in the orange', 'You were in the red at that meeting yesterday'. It gave people a common language to discuss mental health.

For so long, people had been encouraged to have conversations about mental health, but it wasn't always clear how to have these 'difficult' conversations. The simplicity of the language of the mental health continuum was the key. Everyone could grasp it easily.

There were two big takeaways from this presentation for me. First, we all move along a continuum of mental health, and it is not possible to avoid stages where we experience anxiety. And second, the more time we spend in the green, the better our chances of living by our values and making good decisions – personally and operationally.

I returned to my hotel room and researched the mental health continuum. There had been many iterations, it seemed. But as I reviewed them, it struck me that there needed to be a greater emphasis on what keeps you in the green and how we identify that. Individuals have different backgrounds, unique experiences and a wide range in terms of exposure to trauma and emotionally challenging events. This was not just about emergency service workers. There is no argument they are in a high-risk industry, but everyone could benefit from thinking about mental health in this way.

There is no single 'thing' that will keep you in the green, or quadrant one. Despite all the resources available to take away your 'anxiety', there is one underlying truth – we will all feel shit sometimes. How I get there will be unique to me and my circumstances, how I manage it is my choice. Navigating the options available to manage my mental health and identify what works best is a matter for me. What I have learnt is that you need to be reflective and flexible, it is not set and forget. I have graduated through a series of theories and models; each was the panacea at the time but slowly faded in effectiveness. Mindfulness, meditation, exercise, diet, sleep strategies, narrative therapy, acceptance and commitment therapy, cognitive behavioural therapy, psychodynamic theory, schema therapy, motivational interviewing, self-help books. I have dabbled in each of these at different stages. There has been no one model or theory that has been sustainable for me; they all contribute to a library of resources that I draw on.

The concept of the mental health continuum has provided me with a simple framework to manage my mental health. Logic dictates that the longer we stay at the mindful end of the continuum, the closer we will be to the best version of ourselves. Accepting that we will move along the continuum, sometimes for no clear reason, is part of the journey. Like any skill, this takes practice and repeated effort to build confidence and competence. It requires reflection, self-evaluation, humility and empathy. It works best when you have like-minded people around you who can coach, advise and guide you when you may not be recognising the shift along the continuum.

* * *

I reflected on the mental health continuum in my hotel room after the conference. For the first time I could acknowledge that despite my condition I could still be a valuable contributor to a worthwhile cause. The Blue Blanket had been lifted somewhat: I'd started to outgrow it, the way a child outgrows a toy they had relied on previously. Murdoch was still in the background, though. I distinctly remember his voice that night: 'If there is ever a time to celebrate, it's now. Have a beer, who would know? You're back, you've made it!' Fortunately, I filed this phishing attempt by the master manipulator in the junk email folder of my brain.

Much like the rest of my experience, it was not a smooth ride to positivity and good health from this point on. I experienced times when I would revert to my old insecurities. Sleep was always an issue to be managed, and dreams and intrusive memories were never far away. When travelling interstate, I was still hypervigilant. I would go to great lengths to ensure that my movements were as confidential as possible. I never booked the same hotel more than once in the same city, used public transport where possible to avoid surveillance teams and paid cash rather than leave an electronic footprint. I subconsciously scanned the environment, looking for opportunities to deploy a surveillance team, for a safe route to 'clean' a human source before a meeting, or assessing people that seemed out of place. Old habits die hard. Much of this thinking was a result of my training and experience. The neural pathways gradually weakened, and over time I found I could have those thoughts and discard them without fear or insecurity.

My new workplace led to a change in my outlook. It was not as if I needed to make a conscious effort to discuss my mental health with my managers or work colleagues; it seemed almost like a natural extension of the work I was doing. I was immersed in an environment where discussing mental health was the norm. This was so different to the policing environment; it reinforced for me how difficult it is for those who have never experienced such a dynamic, confronting and challenging environment to comprehend the unique working conditions. I often used my experience in the investigative setting to make a point or strengthen my argument. My time at Beyond Blue was similar, except it was my lived experience of mental health in the emergency services that provided the basis for my contributions.

I was fortunate to be involved in establishing the largest ever survey of emergency service workers conducted in Australia, 'Answering the call'. Engaging with academics, agency leaders, clinicians and emergency service workers expanded my understanding and knowledge of the broader emergency services sector. I knew while my experience was unique, there were many aspects of that experience that were shared by others. This realisation gave me the confidence to weave my personal story into my engagement activities with the various stakeholders. There were many times when I was unsure and nervous, but when I took the opportunity to be open, to share my experience, to apply those lessons to the context we were discussing, the conversation was far more engaging and effective.

I was only with Beyond Blue for a short period – less than twelve months – but it restored my confidence and sense of worth. The staff I worked directly with were engaging, humorous, dedicated and smart. Despite my feelings of inadequacy, they took the time to integrate me into the workplace. Inevitably, I did experience fluctuations in my mental health during this period. But the strategies I had in place allowed me to build confidence in my capacity to manage my condition and still contribute to the team. They will have little understanding of the profound impact they had on my reintegration into working life: I will always be indebted to them.

While I cherished my time with Beyond Blue, the desire to return and improve outcomes for my former colleagues was burning brightly.

14.

The Police Association and Phoenix Australia

The Police Association Victoria (TPAV) was the next step in my journey. I had a deep desire to give back to those I had worked with, to ensure that my experience was not wasted and that others could learn from what I had endured. My work at Beyond Blue had eased me back into the emergency services sector and given me a greater appreciation of the magnitude of the issues across each jurisdiction and the unique challenges each agency faced. I was now comfortable sharing my lived experience as a tool to engage members in the discussion around mental health. It had also highlighted that the sometimes-adversarial relationship between unions and agencies was a barrier to presenting a consistent and meaningful message around mental health. One of the first challenges in my new role was to bring the collective resources of TPAV and Victoria Police together to improve the mental health outcomes of the membership. The union has an important role representing and advocating on behalf of members in industrial relations and discipline matters, to agitate for better working conditions and pay outcomes, and to ensure a safe workplace. But to achieve the best outcomes for the mental health of members, a combined, unified approach between unions and agencies was required.

Returning to the policing environment was bittersweet. While I was excited about the opportunity to help many people at different stages of their policing career, the shift also brought many reminders of the struggle I had endured.

The union environment in policing in Victoria is unique, with a membership density of 98 per cent, approximately 17,000 members and recognised political strength. The members look to their union for support and influence in times of need. Invariably, when members contact the wellbeing area of the union, it is a last resort. By this stage they have lost confidence in their employer and have a powerful grip on the Blue Blanket, confused about why the master they have dedicated their working career to is no longer meeting their needs. Stigma around mental health is still entrenched, and high achieving, committed, well-intentioned members find themselves in similar predicaments to the crisis I experienced. Fortunately, they don't all reach crisis point, but there are many who have and others who are well on the way.

I had little interest in the 'union' side of the membership when I was a serving member. If I never needed them, I was happy to have paid membership fees as insurance to have them available just in case I was ever in the shit.

From the journal entries I wrote after my incident in 2014, I was clearly frustrated, disappointed and disillusioned with the support offered. What did I expect? I had written off a company vehicle while pissed and been charged with a criminal offence. I had not reached out for support or assistance in the period leading up to the incident. When I had allowed my position to become so dire that it was irrecoverable, I expected the union to resolve my problems.

I recall my frustration at being suspended, and my vow that if I ever had the chance I would rectify the glaring gaps in welfare support, address the inadequacies of the disciplinary system and create a model that would support members through a case management approach. It was as if I thought no one had ever been through this experience before and that I was special and could identify gaps that no one else could see. Of course, this was nonsense. There was no mythical group of people dreaming up systems to harm the members, faceless people deliberately ignoring their needs to cause them hurt and pain. Managers were not taking deliberate steps to inflict as much suffering as possible. But at the time I had no capacity to step back and honestly reflect on my experience. It was simply too confronting and painful. In a bizarre way, it was easier to remain dysfunctional in the orange than endure the pain of experiencing reality in the green. Invisibility, avoidance, escapism and blame were all easier to tolerate than accepting that my circumstances were largely of my construction.

Response to critical incidents, workers' compensation, transition, education, superannuation pension – it was a steep learning curve to understand why these systems were so challenging for the end user. I was fortunate in that I had experienced most of these systems from the user's perspective and could now consider them from a different view point. My operational experience quickly became irrelevant; it was my lived experience of mental health and the systems issues that allowed me to agitate forcefully for change. The members I came into contact with validated and reinforced my experience and highlighted the need for improvement. There were many examples where the systems were failing and change was needed.

The mental health continuum had proven an invaluable tool: I regularly reflected on where I was on the continuum and what actions or events led me to that position. I concluded that beginning each day in the green required flexibility, attention and honesty. I needed to keep a check on Murdoch and his influence, discard the 'junk emails' he sent me, and accept that anxiety is a condition we all experience.

In March 2017, not long after commencing at the Association, I had my driver's licence returned after the two-year suspension period had expired. This, combined with the change of work circumstances, prompted me to review my mental health plan. This meant committing to taking the time to adapt and adjust my model of 'growing' the green. I required a vehicle for work and would need to drive into the office. I adjusted my daily routine to include a session at a local gym with an early opening time, and then a coffee at a regular haunt. This morning routine helped immensely. I also checked in with myself daily: would the decisions I took today be in line with my values? Did I live by my values yesterday? Growing the green also meant remaining in regular contact with Alex. I was continuing to study, and I ensured I was home for dinner each night with my family, making a conscious effort to engage, listen and be present. I remained alcohol-free and monitored my sleep. Importantly, I ensured that those close to me – my wife and children – knew my strategy and were comfortable in calling out lapses in my behaviour, and I listened to them.

My role at TPAV was intense – I had constant contact with members, management team responsibilities, projects and key stakeholders to manage and a team to lead. Sometimes I spent most of the day in the yellow or the orange: anxiety and stress were present but they did not need to dominate. In the past, the Blue Blanket was my security when I felt uncomfortable or challenged. I now had the 'green'; this was my safe place. If I maintained my strategy, I could tolerate the discomfort and return to start each day from a solid foundation. It is a strange experience knowing that you are preparing to feel a range of challenging emotions in a day but anticipating this from the relative calm and clarity of the 'green'. Monitoring reactions, thoughts and responses; instead of avoiding or merely tolerating these emotions, taking the time to experience them, to see them as part of the experience of living.

It was a privilege to share and connect with so many members experiencing the confusing and confronting world of a mental health injury. Many of the thoughts and emotions I described when I shared my experience resonated with them. The connection established simply through the sharing of a lived experience was remarkable. It was like it gave permission to those at their most vulnerable to find safety in sharing with another in an environment that was independent, confidential and empathetic – these were the key factors that enabled such intimate shared experiences. Having a sound knowledge of the systems such as workers' compensation, leave entitlements, superannuation, industrial relations and the discipline process provided an almost immediate relief to the member in crisis. They were clinging tightly to the Blue Blanket, but just releasing their grip to explore other viable options created the two most important components one needs in those circumstances – time and space. Time away to consider options, to check in with one's values and to reconnect with family and loved ones, and space to make important decisions in a safe and secure environment.

In 2017, Dr Peter Cotton conducted a review into the mental health of Victoria Police. I was interviewed as part of the review and I remained in contact with him as I moved through my roles at Beyond Blue and The Police Association. He would often describe post-traumatic stress disorder (PTSD) as being the most overdiagnosed and underdiagnosed condition in policing. Underdiagnosed because many members remain at work when they are unwell, fearful of the stigma of disclosing their condition and of the risk to their career and livelihood. Overdiagnosed, as many members believe they have PTSD without properly understanding the assessment criteria. This is compounded by the culture of policing: talk of 'breaking' people and the notion that the only acceptable mental health injury is PTSD.

This accords with my experience. Many members I interacted with clearly had significant symptoms of PTSD yet continued to push through and remain at work. There were also those who would seek a diagnosis of PTSD as if to prove the seriousness of their condition. Major depressive disorder, an anxiety disorder or alcohol dependency simply would not do – it had to be PTSD. Most times, the need for a diagnosis was driven by the workers' compensation system, a model in which PTSD is recognised as the pinnacle of mental health injuries. There are states and countries that have enacted presumptive legislation to support those diagnosed with PTSD, to ensure they don't endure the adversarial nature of the workers' compensation scheme. This only reinforces a diagnosis of PTSD as being seen as a catch-all for those who experience a trauma-related injury.

What was the purpose of the diagnosis? Other than for workers' compensation, what use is a diagnosis of PTSD? It certainly assists with research and allows the type and severity of injury to be recorded, but for the patient, what does it do?

I was not that concerned about what they wanted to call my condition. I knew I felt like shit and I wanted to feel better. A focus on the seriousness of the diagnosis provides further fuel for the flames, gives strength to Murdoch and pushes me to quadrant three or orange, whichever model you choose. A fixation on the diagnosis was detrimental to my condition. There is a perception that once you have a diagnosis of PTSD, it is a lifelong condition; it will always be lurking, waiting to pounce the minute you sense a trigger or stimulus.

There were the usual pressures of a hectic work schedule, on-call requirements, demands for my time, and limited resources. I certainly received my share of well-justified criticism for not getting back to people or not maintaining contact, but my mindset had shifted somewhat. In my previous working life, I would have viewed this as a failure, as a personal attack on my dedication to the role or as an inability to manage competing interests. But my focus had shifted. To provide the best level of service, I needed to be well, mindful of my condition and concentrating on matters I could control, not becoming fixated on matters out of my control. I increased our resourcing significantly, became better at prioritising risk and improved systems to enable better referral processes for those requiring clinical assistance. There were obviously some instances where I failed to meet the external expectations. Internally, I could accept that I am not perfect, that I may make mistakes, but ultimately I could manage my mental health in a demanding and confronting role.

The mental health continuum provided some fascinating insights. After a period, it became apparent that most meetings I had were with members in the 'orange' or 'red'. This was not their fault – it was merely a product of the condition they were experiencing. But interestingly, where I was on the mental health continuum had a significant bearing on the outcome of the conversation. If I was also in the orange, the standard of the conversation would deteriorate. I would buy into the narrative that it was the system's fault, that if we could take 'them' on, we could win. 'They broke you – stick with me, we can fix you.' This invariably ended in a poor outcome. The short-term comfort from aligning forces to take on an enemy, taking sides and directing the member into an adversarial response was far easier than a conversation that challenged some of those long-held, dysfunctional beliefs. Inadvertently this guided the member into a solution that might provide short-term relief but would not address all the underlying issues that led to the presentation.

When I was in the green, I could provide a more calm and nuanced perspective. What is most important to that person? There is a process, but they have choices; how they navigate the process is up to them. I can provide the information and some broad advice around options, but it is not my role to manipulate and direct a preconceived outcome, simply because it is less confrontational or challenging. It was during these discussions that the benefit of lived experience and the very basic understanding of the clinical process I had obtained through my study was most beneficial. The irony is that the member involved invariably made a decision that was best for them and their family. During these discussions, it was apparent that the notion of the Blue Blanket resonated. It was not another splintering of my mind that I had cast on others; it was a way of placing words around an experience that is inherently difficult to describe.

During my time at The Police Association I finally developed some leadership skills. I am still far from the most effective or dynamic leader, but I shifted considerably from my previous leadership style. It was no longer keep up or move on, taking sides, trying to be the most popular, chasing accolades and recognition at every turn. I learnt that as a leader you need to give something of yourself if you want others to come with you. To accept that individuals have different needs and expectations, to be flexible, and to challenge the norms of the working environment.

During my time with Victoria Police, I thought being a good manager meant being able to teach the technical skills of the role to junior members. To mould them to be just like me, to have the same work ethic, to be dogged and determined and to rely on the strength and comfort of the Blue Blanket. Perversely, this method worked, and was convincing when I used this philosophy as the core of my presentations to selection panels. I failed to consider how junior members would interpret my actions. It was my choice to work ridiculous hours, stay back to finish a brief or get in early to get ahead on an investigation. It was my choice how I spent my private life – if that was with Murdoch in a haze of alcohol and escapism, that was up to me. I didn't stop to reflect on how this might influence others. The example you set is the example they follow.

Early in my time at Homicide I recall my manager saying – 'family first, go home and spend time with your family, there is always tomorrow'. We may have finished at 3 am and decided to regroup at 11 am. On returning to work, you would discover that the manager had been there since 7 am, doing the menial tasks, attempting to make our lives easier so we could concentrate on the investigation. This was a well-intentioned and noble position to take, but it had an undesired outcome. The hidden message was that to be the best you needed to get back in early and get ahead; family can wait, the investigation would not. I wanted to be as respected and as successful as my manager, and to do this I had to mirror his work ethic. It created an unsustainable and competitive environment where no sacrifice was too great – after all, the Blue Blanket would reward me in the long run.

We can successfully manage mental health conditions within a workplace. I was the living example, giving confidence to others to be open with their experiences, using the shared experience of the work context to build confidence and tolerance. Spending time with staff individually and collectively led to greater understanding of the role and discussions about how we could not only improve service delivery but also improve as people. The staff knew of my mental health history, and that sleep was often an issue, and I encouraged each member to develop their own individual strategy to manage their mental health. My role was to bring those parts together in a workplace environment. It was a tremendously rewarding and gratifying experience to develop a cohesive and high achieving team, each contributing equally to the end goal.

I was fortunate during my time at The Police Association to be given scope to develop the BlueHub Project. We obtained federal government funding for a three-year period to pilot a model of care that would provide evidence-based treatment to Victoria Police members through a single point of contact. An intake and assessment model was established to link members to a specialist clinician who was familiar with the policing culture and able to practise evidence-based modalities. A key component of the model was providing independent and confidential access to treatment options that operated under a best practice model. It also included a quality assurance overlay and the capacity to capture data for research.

We selected Phoenix Australia as the partner for the BlueHub project to provide the clinical and research expertise to bring the model to life. I am uncertain if such a model would have appealed to me when I was struggling to come to terms with my experience. But I do know that it being independent and confidential would have removed many of the barriers. In my role at The Police Association, it was apparent that access to appropriate care was the single most pressing issue for members in crisis. Having confidence that the clinician you engage with understands the environment in which you operate and has the skills and experience to manage a trauma-related injury is an important incentive to engage.

I spent four and a half years at The Police Association, managing the delicate balance between my personal mental health needs and the needs of the members I was assisting. Despite the traumatic and challenging periods, the plan I developed to monitor and manage my mental health proved to be effective. There were periods when I was overwhelmed, but I maintained a sense of safety, knowing that if I followed my plan, I could tolerate the difficult periods. There were also many rewarding experiences, assisting members through their most desperate times, challenging their thinking and witnessing recovery and resilience.

The role was all-encompassing. As well as directly assisting those members I came into contact with, the BlueHub project highlighted that there were many pathways to improve outcomes in the sector.

As with Beyond Blue, I appreciated the opportunity that was offered to me by The Police Association. There were many reasons not to take on a person with my history. It takes courage to take a risk and make that decision. It was the insight, support and trust that accompanied that decision that made my time with The Police Association a time to cherish.

* * *

In mid-2020, I began working with an executive coach. A close friend connected us, and we agreed to meet to see if a professional relationship could be beneficial. Before long, I realised I had added another resource to my mental health strategy. In one of our first sessions, we developed a clear aim for my professional future. My goal was to be 'the driver of sustainable change in mental health outcomes for emergency service workers, achieved while maintaining personal values, standards and growth'.

We discussed my role at The Police Association and the potential for that role to achieve my goal. We explored other options and organisations that would help me achieve my aim. This was a new way of working for me. My coach provided insights, challenged my thoughts and encouraged me to explore the curious and creative aspects of my thinking. My traditional way of approaching a career change would have been to wait for a position to be advertised and then apply. With encouragement from my coach, I developed a strategy in line with a role that I could see would be most beneficial to me and my potential employer.

I first came into contact with Phoenix Australia during my time with Beyond Blue. Phoenix Australia is recognised as the National Centre of Excellence in post-traumatic mental health and has a strong history of involvement in the emergency services sector. In developing the BlueHub project, I worked closely with the Phoenix Australia project team to establish the operational component of the model. I had identified that developing models of care had a greater capacity to influence a broader section of the emergency services community. My work at The Police Association, while rewarding, was also demanding and reactive. There was little scope to explore the more creative aspects of my thinking. It was very much concentrated on service delivery. While the role was rewarding, I realised that there were other opportunities that would allow me to live more in line with my stated aim.

Phoenix Australia had won the tender to develop the Victorian Centre of Excellence for Emergency Worker Mental Health. This was the ideal opportunity for me to explore and expand my thinking into a broader market, to have influence and input into service delivery, clinical education, training and research. With encouragement from my coach, I developed a plan to approach senior management at Phoenix Australia and ultimately was successful in obtaining a position.

I began with Phoenix Australia in August 2021 and continue today in the role of Deputy Director, Responder Assist, the marketing name developed for the Centre of Excellence for Emergency Worker Mental Health. I also lead and assist with projects that involve emergency service agencies nationally. This has expanded my horizons, generated new ideas and opportunities and enabled me to promote the use of lived experience in developing and designing training, policy and models of care.

I have continued to develop my theories around mental health and how we can best support emergency service workers, their families and the clinicians who treat them.

Many of the staff at Phoenix Australia are aware of my back story. The work environment is supportive, with a focus on maintaining the wellbeing of staff. My personal model for managing my mental health, based on everyday attention, sleep, diet, exercise and reflection, has served me well. And I now have a whole team of mental health specialists in the workplace that I can reach out to if I need to discuss a particular issue. I remain focused on my personal relationships and outside interests, my coach and other mentors are sounding boards for my thinking, and my family remain as my constant support.

Certain events can take me back to my previous life. I still have contact with friends and colleagues from Victoria Police, many of whom I have supported through their own experiences of managing a mental health condition. Every day I make the conscious choice to look in the mirror, to remain visible, and to navigate and accept the changes in my emotional state. If I continue to practise my model, I am confident this will bring the best version of myself.

PART V

DISCOVERING THE INVISIBLE OBVIOUS

15.

Everyday Attention

At first after my accident, I felt like everything I had achieved in my career had been a waste of time. Over time my thinking has shifted on this. No one can take away the results I achieved, the friendships I made, the wonderful people I met both within and outside Victoria Police through my role as a serving member. Nothing can change the impact I had on the families of victims, and on witnesses and loved ones I supported through the most catastrophic periods of their lives. I am indebted to them for sharing their experiences with me.

I worked with many great people. They tolerated my inadequacies and supported my left-field thinking. And the support I experienced on returning to The Police Association in 2017 was amazing. I feared I would be labelled a 'nuffy', but in countless interactions since that time I have felt nothing but love and support from police members I met throughout my career. They rarely bring up my sudden departure from their lives without notice early on an October morning in 2014. They respect that I needed to find my own way through.

I have delivered many presentations to different workgroups, sharing my experience and casting some light on what not to do. By far my favourite presentation to deliver is to the graduating members at Detective

Training School at the Academy. I can still recall myself sitting in that position all those years ago, telling myself that mental health problems did not apply to me. *Don't they know how special I am? Mental health is an excuse for those who can't keep up. Push it down, find a way – push on.* I hope that by sharing my story I can shed light on the importance of managing your mental health, particularly in a role in which trauma, stress and confrontation cannot be avoided.

Many officers have managed the inevitable fluctuations in their mental health during long and successful careers in policing. They are human, like the rest of us. From my observations, it is those who can leave their egos at the door and maintain an effective work–life balance who manage most effectively. These people are often the foot soldiers I used to denigrate, the members who did the same work without seeking glory and self-promotion, who took a long-term and balanced view of their career and recognised the importance of their life away from work. The work was no less important to this group. In fact, they were often more effective, in a quiet, considered and compassionate manner. They did not need to strut, big-note or seek adulation. They led a meaningful and connected life in line with their values.

One of my squad mates from the academy in 1994 started his life as a detective the same day as me at the same office in 2002. Quiet, considerate, intelligent and humble, he was one of the most esteemed and skilful investigators I ever worked with. He remained a divisional detective, shunning the career opportunities I craved and walked over people to reach. He maintained an excellent work ethic, achieved outstanding results, and is the equal of any detective I worked with in the crime department. He remains at that same divisional location to this day – confident, content and satisfied in having contributed enormously to the community. He has a lovely family and a simple plan for transition out of policing. I am not suggesting that it was all smooth sailing for him. He has had his challenges too, but he had a simple goal and developed a plan to achieve it – in line with his values and with the support of those he loves.

That career path would never have suited me, but I could have taken a step back and learnt a little from him. We each have different pathways, but the ability to plan, to be clear on your goals and priorities, to live according to your values and to be flexible with your approach to managing your mental health is paramount in managing a career – in policing or any other high-pressure environment.

An experienced colleague who is recognised as one of the most highly skilled investigators to have worked with Victoria Police has an adage: 'The answer is always in the file.' This meant that if you reviewed a file long enough from different perspectives, eventually an answer or hypothesis would come to light.

I had been over my personal experience so many times, I was blind to the obvious. If you ignore your mental health in a high-risk industry, you increase the risk of mental health injury. And if you actively take steps to hide your condition and deceive others, the risk increases exponentially. It seems so perfectly obvious in hindsight. But it was invisible to me.

There is no doubt that the greatest risk to my overall health in the policing environment was a mental health injury. Yet I didn't complete a risk assessment or apply any preventative strategies: I just had a bloody-mindedness to push on regardless of the cost.

As I gained clarity in my thinking, I developed a personal model of care and I hoped that some of the lessons I learnt could be adapted for a wider audience – a blueprint for others to consider.

In many high-pressure environments, such as the emergency services, there will never be a model that completely removes risk. Exposure to traumatic events, critical incidents, violence, fear and hard conversations is a given in policing. But steps can be taken to reduce the risk. By implementing a model that encourages individuals to be more accountable and alive to the risks presented, we may reduce the severity and frequency of those injuries.

This model represents the synthesis of my thinking since that cold October morning in 2014. Had I followed these four steps during my career in policing, I may have avoided some of the heartache and distress I caused my employer, colleagues, wife, children, family and friends.

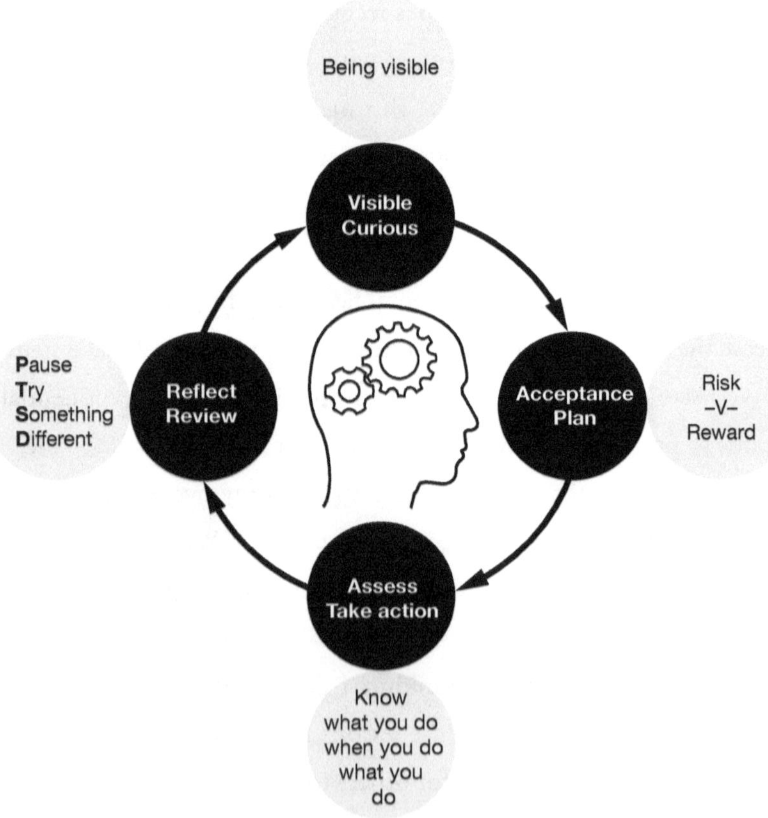

With everyday attention as the core of the model, the four key pillars are:

Being visible

Risk versus reward

Know what you do when you do what you do

Pause. Try Something Different

These form a checklist that we can run through every day in our heads, and in the chapters that follow I explain how to use them effectively.

* * *

Commitment involves the acknowledgement that change starts here or not at all. That concrete, humble steps are best. Small is good. Over and over is good. Being responsible for building larger patterns is good. It will lead to remarkable progress. You can indeed pursue your dreams.

—Steven Hayes, *A Liberated Mind*

This quote sums up the essence of 'everyday attention'. It is so easy to be caught up in our hectic daily lives. How often do you ask someone how they are and they reply by mentioning how busy they are? This was me, forever seeking out the next challenge or problem to solve. Mind you, on most occasions I had not finished the last project or investigation I had started ... Awareness of my actions and the impact on others was non-existent. Invisible. I might have wanted to be the best and to serve the community, but what the outcome looked like and how it was to be achieved were far from clear. My 'plan' was a series of individual, ad-hoc, short-term goals based on reducing the pain and anxiety that consumed me.

The crisis in 2014 forced me to spend time with myself. I could no longer run from the consequences of my actions. The stark reality was that there was an arduous road ahead with no conceivable solution. Reconciling my appalling behaviour in a cloud of anxiety, grief, anger and frustration would require a new approach. With seemingly endless reminders of the traumatic events I had endured around me, my first aim was to survive rather than flourish.

'Everyday attention' was almost forced upon me. At the time I had no appreciation that this concept would become the building block for my return to an improved level of functioning. In the days and weeks immediately after the accident, I was in daily contact with Alex. He supported me to build on the foundations we had discussed: making choices that were in line with my values. He gently reminded me to understand my options, select a pathway and have a clear goal. Most of the time I was lost in my confusing and confronting internal world, but there were periods of clarity. Not every minute had to be a crisis, and in those small moments I could make a choice.

Learning to trust myself and build self-confidence was an arduous task. At first sitting quietly and experiencing the thoughts, emotions and reactions that overwhelmed me was a considerable achievement. Over time I learnt that it wasn't the opinions and beliefs of others that were important; I had the skills and capacity to make choices about how I lived my life. Abstaining from alcohol was one achievement that allowed me to build self-confidence. I made a choice, took action and followed through with it, despite the constant temptation to revert to my old ways. As the length of my abstinence grew, it became a measure of my capacity for change, a constant I could refer to when I had doubts in other areas of my life.

Reconnecting with my body was another important step in my restoration. This went deeper than just the physical act of returning to regular exercise. Becoming more aware of my posture and movement was what provided the greatest benefit. Over the years I had been fortunate to have been introduced to and educated on the Feldenkrais model of awareness through movement. My sister had proven to be an excellent teacher in this respect. I checked in with my head position, orientating it in relation to my shoulders and spine, noticing the depth and pace of my breathing, expanding my peripheral vision, feeling where my pelvis sits in relation to my spine. These simple observations developed into a library of signals that I could interpret to better understand how my physical being was interacting with my anxiety-based responses.

Both abstaining from alcohol and becoming more aware of my physical being could only be achieved through focusing on small actions each day. If I could catch thoughts about drinking, I could redirect them. If I sensed a tightening in my chest, I could remind myself that this was a normal physical reaction for someone with my condition, not a heart attack.

Step by step I built a platform of stability, with exercise, diet and sleep the key focus points. With repetition, I was creating small footholds, periods when I could tolerate the dissonance I was experiencing. There were many setbacks. Sleep was the most difficult challenge, and there were times when I did not feel like exercising, when I had to drag myself out for a walk or to the pool for a swim.

Alex's words resonated: 'What you do is your choice. What you put in your mouth, how you decide to spend your time, how much you exercise is up to you.'

As I focused on the small things each day, the foothold became stronger. Everyday attention allowed me to build a platform of safety. I previously described this as my cocoon. In it I could tolerate the troubling thoughts and have a sense of safety when I became overwhelmed.

It was isolating, demeaning and frustrating, but it was tolerable. It was also a choice: the alternative was a return to the destructive, avoidant behaviours that had dominated my life previously.

I knew I needed to change, but there was no quick fix. Entrenched thoughts and patterns developed over many years of dysfunction needed to be 'rewired'. Through small, deliberate steps I was able to make a tiny shift every day. Maintaining this awareness or visibility of my mental health enabled me to take further small steps and the new thoughts and habits to grow and flourish. I do not view myself as a survivor. I have endured a life experience and been able to adapt, learn and grow.

Everyday attention is at the centre of my model, the building block on which each of the other components is founded. The model works as a whole, with each part interacting with the next. Having a capacity to focus on the small decisions I make every day and to analyse and reflect on the fluctuations in my mood, reactions and emotions has been central to my development.

16.

Being Visible

If the meaning of visibility is to be seen or to be obvious, in a policing sense I did everything I could to be visible. My reputation and achievements were there for all to see, and I ensured I maximised any recognition that came my way. But ironically in my internal world I was completely invisible: I was lost in my personal battle with Murdoch, with no capacity to confide in anyone, even those closest to me, about the extent of my distress. Alcoholism was just one driver of my deceit. My absolute fear of confronting or at least trying to understand my symptoms was so deep-seated that I thought a single ultimate solution that enshrined my hard-earned reputation was the only palatable outcome.

Taking ownership of my mental health condition was a challenging and confronting experience. Having the courage to accept and address my inadequacies and share my world with those who love and support me was a giant step. I first needed to learn to be visible to myself, visible in my internal world. Defining concepts such as Murdoch and the Blue Blanket allowed me to make some sense of how my mind operates. It gave me a language for describing my inner experience.

When I started sharing my story, I discovered that I was not alone, that many others had walked my road: not the exact route, but a similar one. I discovered how much empathy, love and support is available when we have the courage to share our experiences.

Being visible is now a key part of my mental health plan. I continue to deliver presentations on mental health to various audiences, and my role at Phoenix Australia ensures that my mental health remains a priority. This doesn't mean that I relay my story to everyone I come across or mention my lived experience in every work setting. But by being open and visible about my mental health, I have a quiet confidence that I can bring something of value to both work and personal circumstances. While I may not be an experienced clinician or academic, I bring another important variable to the discussion through the lens of lived experience.

The conversation

We don't want our first conversation about mental health to
be when we are in crisis.

I have used this quote in almost every presentation I have delivered since my time at Beyond Blue. Following the presentation, the question I am asked most is why I did not seek help earlier, or why my managers or colleagues didn't intervene. Why was I so determined to remain invisible?

I explain that I had engaged with a clinician, Alex, before my crisis, but that I was there for the wrong reasons. For therapy to be beneficial, the individual must commit to the therapeutic process, give something of themselves, challenge the inflexible story they have created. They need to be open to new ways of considering the world and where they fit within it. To be visible. Therapy can be challenging and confrontational. It will test the narrative you have created. It will ask the simple question:

is what you are doing now working? (If it was, you probably wouldn't be seeking help through therapy.)

Answering the second part of the question – why no one else intervened – is harder. How could I be so dysfunctional in almost every aspect of my life yet still present a confident and capable persona in the workplace? Was I really able to hide my struggles? Did people notice? And if they did, why did they keep my secret? Why did the system work against me?

Truthfully, if anyone had approached me I would have blown them off, as I had no interest in confronting my challenges. I barely shared it with my wife and did everything I could to avoid sharing it with my clinician. Why would I share with a manager or colleague?

But when I reflected on the many colleagues I had seen endure a struggle similar to mine, it came to me: 'We don't want our first conversation about mental health to be when we are in crisis.'

During my time as a serving member, I saw many fellow members struggling and did nothing about it, primarily because I did not know what to do – I had no plan and didn't know what resources were available.

Over the years, I had created intricate plans for interviews and human source meetings I was involved in. I had run through the conversations in my mind before they happened, attuned to the language someone used and identifying how I could use their words to make a point at strategic times. There were contingencies and behavioural observation questions to test if they were being deceptive. All of this for conversations that involved aspects of my work life, yet I never considered a plan for a conversation about mental health. I had no plan for what to do if someone found the courage to open up to me and disclose that they were struggling, no idea what resources were available or how to keep them safe. I simply avoided the conversation and remained invisible.

Clearly I was not alone. We did not talk about mental health at work. I am not suggesting this is the case in every working environment, but I have heard similar accounts from people in many different disciplines and cultures.

If someone has reached a crisis point, it is challenging to start a conversation about mental health. The damage has been done and the dysfunctional thinking patterns are well entrenched. Prior to my time at TPAV, I did not know what to say or do to support someone in that predicament, and they did not want to hear it anyway. When each party is in the orange or red, attempting to find a solution, this is hardly the optimal starting point. When we are in crisis, we want to isolate and we tend to see others (such as the organisation we work for) as the enemy. In my case, I had black and white thinking: either the Blue Blanket kept you safe or 'you are only a number'. This common phrase in policing refers to the registered number each member has, a unique identifier that is only ever allocated once. From a member's perspective, it conveys pride and importance, but to an employer you are just one of many, disposable, replaceable, transferable. These two competing narratives – that I was either part of a 'family' or a disposable asset – kept me stuck in a negative spiral.

So why is it so uncommon to have discussions in the workplace – particularly in the emergency services – prior to a team member reaching a crisis point? There are many issues at play. Many people fear that if they disclose a mental health condition it could be a 'career killer'. In my case, disclosing my thoughts or feelings would definitely have affected my career. Police members are required to carry firearms and there is significant accountability to ensure a member is in a suitable condition to make effective operational decisions while armed. If you cannot carry a firearm, it becomes common knowledge that you 'are not right'. There are very few meaningful roles for those who cannot perform operational duties.

I also had to overcome the strong notion of being the helper, not the helped. Police see themselves as problem solvers, people who can make the best out of shit situations. They have experienced many challenging situations and been a guiding light in difficult times. I knew firsthand how sharing your expertise and experience built confidence and trust with victims and their families: it provided reassurance that there were skilled, experienced, determined investigators on their side. To place myself in a position where I was reliant on others for support was foreign to me. It did not fit my narrative of the indestructible, independent, self-reliant persona.

Much of the focus at present is on training colleagues and managers to have conversations about mental health. I am often asked what would have changed things for me. How could they have created an environment where I was comfortable to disclose the extent of my condition prior to reaching crisis point? Given my background and my single-minded determination to be self-sufficient and to put my trust in the Blue Blanket, I am uncertain that any environment would have been 'safe' for me to disclose. I loved what I did, I was good at it, and it gave me financial security. Why would I give it up without fighting as hard as possible to maintain it? From a personal perspective, it made strategic sense to remain invisible.

A framework for conversations can be provided, but it still requires two people to be willing to engage, to take a risk, to forget embarrassment and ego and to connect with one another. This is challenging in any environment. I struggled to be vulnerable with those I loved. Why would you take a risk in exposing that vulnerability to a colleague or, even more confronting, a manager?

The easiest way to justify your shit behaviour and hide the symptoms of a mental health injury from those closest to you is to lay the blame elsewhere. For me, that was the workplace. I could easily create an enemy that was the cause for my ills, despite the major determining factor being my behaviour and unwillingness to confront the issues facing me. By creating this enemy, it further solidified the chasm with the workplace. It was an easy pivot to create an enemy, and why would I approach the enemy for assistance?

While it is imperative that colleagues and managers have the skills to invest in a conversation about mental health, it is ultimately the attitude and capacity to engage of the person experiencing the condition that will determine the outcome. You may have the most skilled, empathetic and compassionate intent, but if the other party has no willingness to engage, then the chances of the conversation being beneficial are minimal.

Logically, if the conversations can take place prior to the person reaching crisis, then there is a greater chance of a positive outcome. It is best to create an environment where discussing mental health is considered as normal as discussing your physical health, where shared knowledge of the subject and the mental health continuum permits the participants to use a common language.

This is the notion of visibility coming to life. We need to have the capacity to look internally as well as externally, to engage with our mental health, to be open to the shared experiences that will allow for meaningful conversations to take place. The external world includes our family, friends and loved ones. Being visible in one of these domains naturally extends into the other aspects of our lives. In my case, visibility with my family allowed me to mend fractured relationships, visibility with friends and loved ones opened a world of support that was previously inaccessible, and visibility in my workplace has enabled me to become a productive, valued member of my team.

'My bucket is full'

I have heard this phrase used frequently to describe how repeated traumatic events pile up until the person reaches the tipping point. Often they will mention that there was one critical incident that was just too much to bear and that this led to a crisis. The person might have experienced a career of challenging traumatic experiences, which they coped with – until the one that tipped them over the edge.

This was not the case for me, but everyone is different: we all react differently and process our experiences in unique and individual ways. Personal experience is always valid.

This phrase started me thinking. How can we determine how many critical incidents one can tolerate before reaching a crisis? Why can some people seem to tolerate a lifetime of exposure to trauma and others appear to have little tolerance? Is it just the individual or does the number of incidents attended matter too? The problem is there are too many variables, not least of which is the reaction of the individual involved.

Here's an example from my time at Homicide. Our team used to be on call for a week at a time, starting on a Sunday night. I would start the week well rested, looking forward to work with excitement and anticipation. Attending a crime scene was educational and fascinating: an opportunity to learn new skills and strategies from more experienced members. I looked at the crime scene from an investigative perspective and we attempted to elicit as much information as possible from witnesses. No task was too menial. I just wanted to be involved, to be part of the team. My interpersonal relationships were strong.

But by the time I reached the third or fourth job for the week, towards the end of the seven-day period, my attitude towards the crime scenes and investigations would have shifted. I was exhausted from the hours worked on the previous investigations and disconnected from my family, as I had hardly been home. I no longer looked at a traumatic crime scene as an opportunity to solve a crime; instead, I was questioning why people did this to each other. Why did this shitty job have to happen when I was on call? Conversations with victims' families became a chore rather than an opportunity to connect with humans experiencing grief.

So, what had shifted? Was the job at the end of the week really that challenging, or was I impacted by what I had experienced earlier in the week? Why did some scenes stay with me like a set from a movie scene that I could step back into at any time and others simply vanished from my mind? I am using Homicide as an example because that was my experience. I know when I was tired or frustrated, Murdoch came to the fore. I enlisted those avoidant behaviours to survive another day.

As I pondered this, I returned to thinking about the mental health continuum. Could it be that where we are on the continuum at the time a critical incident or trauma occurs influences our response? This would suggest it is not the number of critical incidents that is important so much as how we are managing our mental health at the time of any given incident.

Could it be that where we are on the mental health continuum dictates our response to trauma? When I was in the 'green' at the start of the week, I could effectively manage a tragic event that had significant consequences and a ripple effect through an entire community. My role was as a leader, as someone who could be relied upon under adversity to provide an example of how difficult feelings and emotions can be managed in an operational environment. I could access my plan to remain flexible and visible around his mental health.

By the time I attended the incident at the end of the week, my outlook had transformed. I was in the 'orange'. Without a clear plan to reflect on the impact of the trauma earlier in the week, I simply continued on, ignoring the shift in mood and the drift along the continuum. This was reflected in the way I engaged with others and the manner in which I went about my tasks. I was only concerned about the investigation outcome, with no ability to engage or show empathy with those impacted by the event. This version of me did not accord with the one seen at the start of the week. I wanted to be the shining example of how to manage a traumatic scene, yet inexplicably I acted in a way that was not in line with my values.

Acknowledging my response to the initial trauma and taking steps to share this response may have allowed me to identify that I was in the 'orange', that my role was in a high-risk environment, and that it was likely I would have a response to such a traumatic event. Having an awareness of this may have allowed me to present differently, acknowledging that it was going to be a difficult day, a day when he needed to be more in tune with my reactions to the incident. Perhaps I may have had enough insight to consider stepping back from the next investigation or taking a lesser role, or discussing my reaction with my manager. My grip on the Blue Blanket ensured this would never happen.

Whether it is the number of incidents you attend (the bucket scenario) or where you are on the continuum when you attend an incident that dictates your response, what is important is that it generates a conversation about mental health. At the core of this is the question: which version will you choose to present when you are next involved in a critical incident or traumatic event? By continually reviewing where we are on the continuum, we have a greater chance of remaining in the green for longer periods and recognising when we are not in the green and how we need to modify our behaviours. To be seen as a leader and exemplar of how to manage your mental health in times of crisis requires practice, patience and reflection.

I hope this example can help shift our thinking from mindlessly filling a bucket and waiting to see what happens to taking stock each day to ensure that the level of the bucket is managed.

17.

Risk Versus Reward

Whatever your choice of career, the reward for the work you do is an important consideration. This is often more than financial return; personal development, your interest in the role, job satisfaction and working conditions all contribute to the reward matrix. But as with any reward, there is always risk attached.

The idea of the three Rs – reward, risk, resources – is used in many disciplines to guide people in decision making.

Simply put, the three Rs are a framework for considering a particular challenge.

1. Understand the goal, or **reward**, you are attempting to reach.
2. Identify the **risks** that may impede you reaching your goal/reward
3. Assess the **resources** that can mitigate the risks.

These three components sum up the thought processes that accompany everyday operational decision-making for police officers. And they can be applied in many other fields as well.

Like many officers, I considered policing a job for life and thought rewards would come if I worked hard and stayed the course. I didn't take the time to reflect and consider whether the benefits I had identified at the start of my career were still as important to me as I moved through my career. My risk profile increased as I moved into the world of high-level investigations, but so did the rewards. These were primarily selfish – prestige, reputation, financial, buying into the narrative driven by Murdoch. I did not consider the risk to my mental health and personal relationships in such a confronting, high-pressure role. My issue was that I never undertook a realistic assessment: were the rewards still outweighing the risks?

A common example of the three Rs process in the policing context is the use of firearms. Every operational member is required to carry a firearm, a high-risk undertaking. The many rewards that come with a career as an operational police member are accompanied by risk: you will carry a firearm and you may be expected to use it. Significant resources are enlisted to ensure members remain competent and capable in the handling and use of firearms. Regular training increases the likelihood that if an officer is required to discharge their firearm in an operational setting it will be done in accordance with the law and internal policies and be used as effectively as possible to minimise overall harm to all concerned.

Personally, I loathed the biannual training sessions we undertook to practise our firearm skills and operational safety tactics, but I knew they were necessary to reduce risk. The chance of me ever having to discharge my firearm was minuscule. However, it was appropriate and necessary to ensure that I was trained and prepared for such an incident if it occurred. Fortunately, I was never required to use my firearm. This was not through any brilliant planning or foresight; in my experience it's just luck – who is working a given shift on a given day – rather than any particular skill that prevents such an occurrence.

When comparing the training and preparation that was undertaken to mitigate the identified risk of carrying a firearm to the risk of a mental health injury, the contrast is palpable. The research is clear: a police offi-cer is far more likely to sustain a mental health injury than to be involved in a firearm incident. Each of these events can be career-ending and may cause a serious injury, whether physical or psychological. This does not diminish the risk that either of these components represents; it simply highlights the lack of attention, or visibility, that we apply to our mental health, despite it being an identifiable risk.

So how do we develop a plan to mitigate the risk of mental health injury? There is a general acceptance that a career in policing will involve exposure to events that have the potential to cause a mental health injury. Organisational factors such as shift work, lack of resources, unsupportive leadership and challenging work environments can add to the level of risk. Developing skills to manage our mental health is far more complex than taking aim at a target every six months to improve our muscle mem-ory. Do we invest as heavily in managing our mental health as we do in training in a specific skill to improve our operational safety? It is not as simple as mandating mental health training. There is a view that training is something that is 'done' to you, rather than an exercise in which you are an active participant. The development of mental health training would benefit from a greater emphasis on co-design, of establishing what is important to the end user, rather than feeling that an indiscriminate expert has advised what is best for you.

Emergency service agencies spend significant time and resources developing programs and initiatives to assist emergency service workers in preventing, managing and recovering from mental health injury. My experience was that these resources did not suit my particular needs, and for myriad reasons I refused to engage. This attitude was common among other members I encountered in my various roles after leaving the force.

We each have to decide what value we place on our mental health and how much time, energy and effort we are willing to invest in preventing or managing a mental health injury. I dismissed the offerings from my employer and hid my condition. I had developed no other plan to manage the symptoms I experienced other than to employ the dysfunctional and destructive strategies of avoidance, escapism and numbing my senses through alcohol. Resources *were* available, but I chose not to use them. When forced to engage, I acted in a way that was detrimental to any positive outcome; deceit, disrespect and dishonesty are of no value in a therapeutic setting.

It took some time for me to appreciate what an effective plan for managing my mental health might look like. In the early stages, prior to the accident, when I had periods of clarity and sought to find ways to manage my condition, I relied on strategies I had attempted previously without success. I would aim to arrive home from work on time, try to manage my workload, strive to be more involved with my wife and children, increase my exercise and decrease my alcohol intake. I would plan to take a brief break with my family when I had leave and remind myself to engage with my extended family. But I'd tried all these things many times during my years of dysfunction. Murdoch and I knew that these strategies would never last in the long term, that I would eventually fail and return to the lies, fantasy and ego-driven methods that drove much of my behaviour.

'Everyone has a plan until they get punched in the face.' This quote from Mike Tyson summed up my attempts to develop a plan for my mental health in the policing environment. The limited awareness I had of my condition was not a match for the rude awakening that comes with experiencing a debilitating mental health condition. Avoiding any support from my employer or colleagues and relying on my limited knowledge of mental health left me susceptible in every way. Avoiding and ignoring my condition only amplified the intensity of the symptoms I experienced. When I reached crisis point, my plan was inadequate and ineffectual.

There are many resources available to those who choose a career in the emergency services. Whether an individual elects to access the resources available within the agency or prefers to pursue options outside the agency is a matter for them. But either way it is imperative that they have a plan to manage the risk of a mental health injury in a high-risk environment.

Attempting to develop a plan when you are in crisis is a confusing and confronting prospect. When every part of your being is focused on simply surviving, it is difficult to make informed and considered decisions about which resources will best suit your needs. In my time of crisis, I had all the components of a mental health plan at my fingertips, but I ignored them. I had unconditional love and support from my family, but I shunned it. I had colleagues, managers and friends who would have dropped everything to assist me, if only I had the courage to be visible. I had a trusted and experienced GP and a skilled therapist but refused to let them into my world. The aspects of my life that I had control over – such as sleep, diet, exercise and alcohol consumption – were sacrificed in my insane pursuit of excellence and egotism. I had not developed a plan to share with trusted supporters who were aware of the risks I faced and of the need to monitor and manage my condition. How could I expect anyone to intervene when I had been so determined to mask my symptoms from everyone?

If I had applied the three Rs strategy before reaching crisis point, there might have been a very different outcome. By taking the time to consider what I was trying to achieve and what level of risk I was willing to accept, I might have been able to develop a plan that prevented the extent and duration of my symptoms. I chose not to engage with the resources made available by my employer; my biggest regret is that when I sought an alternative, I did so in a secretive and underhanded way. I was determined to resolve my own issues, but it was not until I let others into my private world after the accident that I could make progress.

The plan I have now evolves and matures and is very different from the plan I had at earlier life stages. I am certain it will be different again in three, five or ten years' time. One strength of my current plan is that it includes a diverse range of resources I can rely on: my wife, children, extended family, friends, former and current work colleagues, mentors, clinicians, GP, an executive coach – the list goes on. I have developed this network over an extended period and these relationships are strengthened through the shared knowledge and acceptance that mental health is a key priority in my life. I do not write my plan on an A4 sheet of paper that is reviewed annually. It is a fluid and organic daily evaluation of where I am at and which of the available resources will be most beneficial at that point in time. The diversity of the resources is crucial to the success of the plan. I rely on different resources in different settings: for example, if a particular work-related incident is impacting me, an ethical dilemma perhaps, then the people I reach out to will be different to who I reach out to if there was serious illness in my family.

I have become a resource to others who embrace the concept of visibility around their mental health and who seek guidance and support. I have a clear pathway to clinical care should that be required, and those closest to me are aware and capable of initiating this aspect of the plan.

The most important resource in my plan is *me*. I make the choices each day about how I want to live my life, from simple reflections on my values to what I eat and whether I exercise. If I isolate myself and refuse to engage, that is a choice. If I do not practise 'everyday attention' and drift back to a world of ego and narcissism, that is also a choice. If I refuse to listen to the advice and guidance provided by trusted family and friends, that is a choice. Being open and honest with myself and others about my plan and how I engage with the resources available to me is the single most important thing I have learnt to do. That is a choice. And we all have the power to make it.

18

Know What You Do When You Do What You Do

*Our best chance for positive outcomes is to be aware of what
we do, how we do it, and our clear intentions.*

—Lesley McLennan and Julie Peck, *Moving from the Inside Out*

It is 1 am and I have just returned home after a sixteen-hour shift, having begun at 7 am the previous morning. The house is quiet. My wife and children have been asleep for many hours. The crime scene I spent twelve hours at is now embedded in my brain, along with the graphic images of an assault victim from a domestic violence incident. I've spent the past hours providing support to family members and witnesses. The event was challenging, but I also saw it as an excellent opportunity to showcase my skills.

Scenarios such as this played out many times in my career. The circumstances changed, but exposure to traumatic events and the emotional aftermath that those affected experienced repeated many times.

The way I managed my mental health following such events varied through the different phases of my career. In short, I didn't have a plan. Other matters that were influencing me at the time generally dictated my response.

For example, early in my career, I would have seen such an event as a fantastic opportunity to follow the lead of the more experienced members and develop my skills at managing such an event. I would likely have discussed the matter with my wife on waking the next morning and shared my enthusiasm and learnings with others when I returned to the workplace. In my early career, I didn't yet have children, my physical exercise routine was well established, I maintained a network of friends and family outside the job, and lack of sleep from a 'quick changeover' had minimal impact on me. At this time, the responsibility for the investigation and court processes lay with the senior member or a specialist squad; as a junior member my responsibilities were more limited, and I had support from senior members and managers to assist with the investigation.

I had no formal plan for managing my mental health in mind. I did not reflect on how I reacted or what worked well for me. If the effects of experiencing a traumatic event lingered, I had no explanation for this, just an understanding that it was 'part of the job'. There was no noticeable difference in the demeanour of those I worked with, which sent the message that this was just another investigation to be undertaken and completed.

As my career developed, along with my focus on crime investigation, I became front and centre at the crime scene and I would have been keen to show off my ability to manage a complex investigation. As the informant, I was responsible for the court process, and I probably would have been required to attend a hearing the following morning. Instead of arriving home at 1 am, I would have ensured that all the paperwork was completed for the court appearance and might have arrived home at 3 am. I would be up again at 7 am, gone before the family was awake. My focus was on preparing for court and ensuring the investigation was completed to the absolute highest standard.

By this stage, my personal circumstances had changed. We had children and my narrative had changed; I thought the sacrifices I was making were required to achieve the best outcome for victims and their families. By observing senior members in the past, I knew that this was required to achieve the optimal outcome. My workload outside of this investigation would also have been bringing additional pressure. The first protective components to fall away were exercise and sleep. I felt invigorated and excited during these phases, determined to grow my reputation and standing. I had no plan around my mental health, and the gradual shift into relying on the policing family was well underway.

The specifics of the cases may have changed, but on attaining my goal to become a detective the frequency and intensity of such incidents increased. One investigation would morph into the next and the initial excitement and enthusiasm waned as these types of investigations became the norm rather than learning experiences. I was far more capable, confident and efficient now and could manage such events effectively, as the senior investigator that junior members looked up to. The abnormal had become normal. I was not shocked by much and no longer felt a need to share these experiences with others. It was just another investigation: follow the process and achieve a positive result. Being more competent and familiar with the processes, it no longer took me additional time to complete the paperwork. These hours were now spent using alcohol to ward off the exhaustion and to maintain the narrative that dreams, flashbacks and intrusive thoughts were my new normal. Sacrificing time at home, avoiding sleep and exercise and using alcohol were my go-to strategies. I didn't choose this consciously – but because I had not learnt to reflect on my reactions, it had become the norm.

As I moved into a manager's role, my responsibilities shifted again. I was now teaching others, introducing them to the chaotic world of crime investigation. My inability to share responsibility was my greatest weakness. I thought I needed to be present for all the important aspects of the investigation to ensure we completed them to the right standard. At home I now had three young children at school and my wife was working. The investigations I was involved in on any given day dictated how involved I was in the day-to-day functions of the house. It was investigations and policing first and family second. Every time. Finishing work late, alcohol to numb the pain, poor sleep and an early rise to return to work became the standard. I was desensitised to the graphic nature of the work I was involved in and I felt no need to share any aspect of my professional life with my family, other than to reinforce that it was my employer who dictated the long hours and time away from home. I didn't mention that much of the fault lay in my inability to say 'no' to any request, in order to maintain my precious reputation.

The examples above did not occur in a neat sequence: there were fluctuations along the way and periods when I experimented with different resources to help manage the symptoms I experienced (although I never considered what I was experiencing as 'symptoms'). I presumed that everyone else coped with the same issues in their own way. I never stepped back and took stock of how I was feeling or whether the job was providing the level of reward required to justify the sacrifices and risks. My two lives were stark; family and work were separate and distinct, with family life coming a distant second. I regularly finished work at 1 am and returned to it by 7; anything less than that would have been a failure in my mind.

Knowing when to take action, to enact a plan, is the most difficult aspect of my model. We often want to avoid involving others in our personal lives and our internal worlds. I told myself that if I could push through to the next block of leave or to my next days off, I would enact my plan then. Invariably, this never occurred. Such maladaptive coping strategies bring temporary relief, and the urgency to act is diminished. It's a bit like planning to paint a house. It can always wait, but when I finish, it will look brand new. On the other hand, the longer I leave it, the more difficult the task becomes. As I mentioned in the previous chapter, I had most of the components of a plan to manage my mental health available to me. But the more I shifted into the unplanned responses of avoidance, escapism and alcohol, the less visible those resources became. I always had the idea that at some stage, I would need to address the issues I was facing and change the way I lived. I thought promotion and changing work locations would be a catalyst for this, but repeated failures showed that this was a flawed strategy. Genuine change could only come from a deeper examination of why I felt the way I did.

Of all the interesting and challenging investigations I had the opportunity to be involved in, I never chose to investigate how I was in the world – even though it would have been the most rewarding investigation of all.

George Bonanno introduces the concept of 'coping ugly' in his excellent book *The End of Trauma: How the New Science of Resilience Is Changing How We Think about PTSD*. The premise is that the way we cope will differ from situation to situation. A strategy that has worked previously may be ineffectual at a different career or life stage. At times, we need to do whatever we can to get through; it may not be part of our predetermined plan or may even seem counterproductive. But if it works in that moment, for that circumstance, it may be the best outcome we can hope for.

We all will have had experiences of 'coping ugly'. The question is: have we been able to identify this and know what we are doing? For example, in the scenario I discussed earlier, if I arrive home at 1 am and my family is asleep and access to the other resources I have identified is limited, I may need to adopt a short-term course of action to alleviate some of the anxiety and stress being experienced. If I choose to sit on the couch and have a couple of beers to 'wind down', that is a choice I make. In and of itself, this is not what would be seen as a conventional response, but if it assists in providing some relief to reduce the symptoms being experienced, it may be the best we can do at that time. The skill is in identifying that this is not a response that can become our norm. I tried 'coping ugly' for many years, and the repeated use of unconventional responses led to harm.

An alternative response may involve acknowledging and accepting that there will be times when 'coping ugly' is all we can manage. We need to know and understand the course of action we are taking, identifying that the actions we take are part of our overall plan. The steps that follow are aimed at addressing the core issues of why and how you came to be feeling so helpless and overwhelmed. It may be that on identifying a circumstance of 'coping ugly', the next step is to talk with one of the trusted resources that forms part of your plan. As we have been visible and open about our mental health and the risks we face, those around us will understand the meaning of 'coping ugly' and what are required as follow-up activities. It may be as simple as returning to an exercise regime or creating time for an activity with loved ones. It may involve enacting the process for accessing clinical support, an agreed pathway that has previously been discussed and identified. Knowing what you are doing and why is crucial in this process.

The model I have developed relies on all the aspects blending together. 'Know what you do when you do what you do' cannot work in isolation from the other components of the model. The benefits of understanding what you are experiencing and how you are managing your response are amplified if we share that knowledge with others. To go back to my example, imagine I arrive home at 1 am and sit on the couch and destroy six beers before going to bed. I say nothing to my wife the next day and when questioned about why I was drinking by myself in the early hours of the morning, I respond, 'What does it matter? I'd just worked sixteen hours, surely I deserve some time to myself.' This response is received as well as you might expect, and before long there is a conflict about my drinking and long working hours. This conflict then becomes the catalyst for further maladaptive responses, as I feel more isolated and unsupported than before.

But if there was a clear plan in place and both I and my wife were aware of the model and familiar with phrases such as 'coping ugly' and 'know what you do when you do what you do', the conversation the following day would play out differently. There would be acceptance that my role places me at high risk of my mental health being impacted. The drinking the previous night was clearly my way of coping with the distressing events of the incident I attended, rather than a reward for working long hours. We could then discuss the reasons behind why I felt the way I did and what steps I could take to prevent this from becoming my standard response when feeling stressed and anxious. If I needed to enact my plan to engage with clinical support, this would be done in a considered and supportive manner. It does not mean that I would have to go into great detail about the particular incident I attended if I was not comfortable with that, but there is a shared understanding that my work exposes me to troubling events. This is the three Rs in action. Understand the rewards of the work that I do, identify the risks, and access the resources required to mitigate them.

The diversity of the resources available and ability to access a resource you are comfortable with are key to the success of this model. In the above example, I might see my clinician and discuss in detail some of the specific aspects of the incident that caused me to react the way I did. The fact that I want to protect my wife from the graphic detail of my work does not diminish our trust or the strength in our relationship. There are matters that I discuss with my wife that I would never discuss with anyone else. Equally, there are matters that I discuss with others that are unique to that particular relationship. For example, my discussions with Alex are very different to conversations I have with my closest friends, but they each serve important purposes.

Having a diverse group of resources available to meet your needs increases the probability that regardless of the challenging circumstances you face, there is someone who is willing and capable of sharing your experience.

'Know what you do when you do what you do' is a quote that has stuck with me since I completed the highest-level human source management training while I was with Victoria Police. Dr Mike Webster, a psychologist from Canada, used the quote to reinforce the importance of being mindful of what technique you are applying in any situation. 'Know what you do when you do what you do.' If you intend on applying a strategy, be aware of the potential outcomes that flow from the use of that strategy.

Not only did I not have a plan, I had no concept of reflecting on what it was that I was actually doing to cope in the policing environment. I was 'doing' plenty, most of it destructive and dysfunctional. I did not consider what worked well for me to manage the stress and anxiety I was exposed to; even if there were periods of clarity, I was unable to identify what it was that I was doing to achieve that outcome. On face value, the strategies I employed were nonsensical – alcohol misuse, poor sleep, no exercise, avoidance, isolation, fantasy. I clearly had no concept of what I was doing, as on any measure this response was always going to lead to the same devastating outcome.

Avoidance and escapism were my key strategies to avoid the pain, frustration and fear that consumed me. There was no structure to this response, merely a strategy to do whatever I could do to survive and then worry about the consequences of my actions later. My solutions were short-term and ill-conceived, with no real conscious choice. The quick fix was the overriding factor for every decision.

With a plan in place, one of the greatest challenges is understanding when to activate the plan and act. My desire to push through challenging periods to achieve results needs to be tempered with an ability to acknowledge and identify when my symptoms are impacting the quality of my emotional and physical experiences and the experiences of those around me. Identifying and understanding the resources available is critical when planning a response to fluctuations in your mental health. This includes taking the time to notice what works well and adding these strategies to your toolkit of resources.

19.

PTSD: Pause.
Try Something Different.

The last component of the model is perhaps the most important. As well as being visible, having a plan and knowing when to use it, we also need to have capacity to reflect on and review the outcome. Are we living a life in line with our values? Can we step back and consider the worldview of others? Are we being the best version of ourselves?

'Pause. Try Something Different' is my wordplay on PTSD. It represents the capacity to reflect on and review what actions we are taking to manage our mental health. This is crucial in developing a model that is flexible and adaptable enough to mean you can thrive in challenging environments. We need to regularly stop and ask, 'Is what I am doing working?'

If I had had the courage during my career to step back and evaluate some of my actions, the answer would have clearly been that they were self-destructive and irrational.

Did I really expect that I could choose to take on one of the most challenging roles in policing and not experience any discomfort or dissonance? The level of pain and anguish I felt was also being exacerbated by the choices I made. But at no point did I properly take the time to assess whether there was another course I could take; in fact I had a fierce desire to avoid self-reflection at all costs. The idea of taking time away from the workplace to create the space needed to process my reactions, to share my concerns with my family and loved ones and to consider that my role may well be having a detrimental impact on my functioning was frightening. As brave as we were in an operational sense, having the courage to take the time to reflect on our personal lives was not something I had witnessed in the policing environment.

I repeated the same mistakes and accepted that this was how it had to be. As my condition had an increasing negative impact across all aspects of my life, the idea of stopping to reassess became even more unlikely. This led to me seeking a solution that would end the problem completely, rather than manage it.

It is so obvious in hindsight that reflection and review are crucial to any plan to manage my mental health. This is now part of my 'everyday attention'.

Each day I take the time to assess my day, to acknowledge and understand my fluctuations in mood and temperament. I explore new tools that I may add to my list of resources to help manage my condition, and I discard activities that perhaps were beneficial in the past but are no longer of value.

We can only assess the effectiveness of our plan and the resources available through reflection and review. As with a post-operational assessment after a major investigation, we need to monitor our progress. The major difference is that with a mental health plan the assessment is ongoing. The cycle of the model continues; there is no endpoint where we reach a perfect world. This process requires courage, honesty, persistence and patience.

My perspective on post-traumatic stress disorder changed as I developed my thinking in relation to mental health. At first the diagnosis was something I feared; now it is a condition I know how to navigate and manage. Everyone's experience of PTSD is unique. I was fortunate not to have been as severely impacted as others whom I assisted on their journey. I would not attempt to compare my experience with that of those who have suffered to a far greater extent. But I do have a deep understanding of how severe PTSD can be and how hard it is to quantify. There is such a variety of symptoms, occurring over extended periods of time with different levels of intensity. Individual experiences vary enormously, with distinct features of the condition being prominent in some cases and not others.

Many people are living a life dominated by trauma-induced injury and have not experienced relief from the solutions presented. Almost without exception, those who present with a trauma-related injury experience other conditions too. Alcohol misuse, sleep disorders, anxiety and depression are common. Some people require in-patient admission, while others do not. Each experience is individual. PTSD is real. It is debilitating, frustrating, scary, challenging and confronting. But one thing I have learnt is that it is rarely ever constant. Like the mental health continuum, it moves back and forth along a scale of intensity. Can we identify what leads us to the more acute end of the scale and what we do to move to the more manageable end of the scale?

Time and space are critical. Creating space and allowing time to take stock, to reflect and examine your responses, to take a breath and absorb an experience. Is your plan working? Is there another strategy you can apply?

Pause. Try Something Different.

My play on PTSD is based on the same principle as the quote attributed to Albert Einstein: 'Insanity is doing the same thing over and over and expecting different results.'

The message is simple, but enacting it is far more challenging. The first component, 'Pause', means taking a step back, marking a point in time. This is very difficult when your mind is racing, when you are doing what you can to get through a day.

It's common to set a fictional marker sometime in the future. Perhaps you say to yourself, 'I will get through to the weekend and deal with it then' or 'I have to finish this investigation, then I will take a breather'. Pausing in real time takes skill and courage, and like any skill it needs to be practised.

This is why connecting with our body is so important. I was introduced to the concept of awareness through movement developed by Moshé Feldenkrais, but there are many alternatives – yoga, breathing exercises, Pilates. If we can take a moment to check in with ourselves physically, we have a chance of creating that space.

Consider the mental health continuum: it is very difficult to pause and make effective decisions when we are in the orange. It is far more achievable in the green. We can be aware of the continuum and accept that a difficult period will test our courage to make the decision to pause. But we can remind ourselves that if we keep pushing through, we will only get the same result as last time. Pause. Breathe. Try Something Different. Again, easy to say, hard to do. Much depends on where you are on the continuum.

Consider the experience of reading a magazine from the Sunday paper. You are sitting in your favourite chair in the sun, comfortable and relaxed, taking the opportunity to reflect, relax and read. You come across a self-help article about a new exercise regime or diet, or the latest in yoga or Pilates, and you think, 'I could do that.' You are in the green, open to new ideas and willing to consider new strategies and techniques to improve yourself.

Now consider you come across the same article the next day. In a policing context, Sunday's paper is still on the messroom table at the station, and you have just come in after the first shitty job on the divisional van. The sergeant is all over you for outstanding correspondence and you have a court case this week you have not prepared for. You can feel the anxiety welling up. You are gulping it down to stay afloat, your mind is foggy, and you are just waiting for the next shit job to come in. You dismiss the article as new-age crap: 'How could that work for me? I'm a copper; they have no clue what I go through!'

Are you able to pause in this moment? Can you try something different, check in with your body, collect your thoughts, reflect on what your inner Murdoch is up to? Manage the junk emails? Remind yourself: guilty about the past, anxious about the future, I can only control today. Are you able to identify that you have drifted into the orange and need to try something different to return to the green?

This simple example – of the same article experienced differently depending on the circumstances – illustrates how where we are on the mental health continuum dictates our responses. If we are in the green, we have a greater capacity to pause and consciously apply a different strategy. If we are in the orange, it is harder. Before we know it, the feared outcome has arrived, and we are pushed further into the mire.

Like exercising a particular muscle regularly, it gets easier with practice and as part of an overall health plan. It is amazing how much time there is to think, to observe, to experience the world when we are not so caught up with our internal conflicts. The number of thoughts that run through my head is the same as it has always been. But I have become far more adept at 'filing' them – junk emails are dispatched, important information is kept, and some thoughts are held in abeyance for me to return to when appropriate. There is no need to dwell on the negative, matters that are out of my control or catastrophes that will never happen. I can also share my inner world with others now, externalising my internal thoughts without fear of judgement or embarrassment. I acknowledge and cherish times of clarity and endure and persist through the times of confusion.

Epilogue

Metaphors have long been a part of my internal world. Storytelling is a great way to share a thought or message, to emphasise an important point in a presentation. Of the millions of thoughts that pass through my head, very few materialise into anything of substance, but I am always searching for ways to better explain my internal experience to an external audience.

In 2021, during the Covid-19 epidemic, our family moved from suburban Melbourne to the Macedon Ranges, undertaking a 'tree change' like many other Melbournians who wanted to escape lockdowns. This had been a long time coming for my wife and me, both raised in country Victoria. We had spent most of our adult years in the same suburb of Melbourne, but we had contemplated the shift to the country for several years. For me, the lure of space and some separation from the constant reminders of my previous life in policing was an underlying contributor. And now we were in a new life stage; our children were no longer as dependent, and they were moving into the next chapters of their respective life journeys. It was important for us to maintain a stable home base for them, from which we could access work. We selected the Macedon Ranges due to their proximity to Melbourne and our love of the area.

As I travel to and from my new property and when I walk to the rear of the property to feed the horses each day, there is one constant – Mount Macedon. The beauty of the mountain had always struck me, but I have developed a deeper appreciation of it through going about my daily tasks. No matter the season, the mountain stands staid and solid, absorbing and enduring all that goes on around it. Destructive windstorms, occasional snow, searing summer heat waves, potential bushfires and human intervention all impact on the immediate environment, but the mountain is a constant.

When the weather is fine and the sky is a deep blue, its majesty in the flat landscape is something to behold. The mountain will always be impacted by external forces, primarily the weather. Some days it is just a light fog or cloud that hovers around the apex; other days the cloud is so thick, you cannot even make out the shape of the mountain. As I consider the constant change in the external forces that impact on Mount Macedon, it reminds me of my experience of mental health.

There are days when the sun is shining, and the sky is a brilliant blue – in my world I am in the green and all is good. I take the time to enjoy this period for what it is, understanding that it is a moment in time and as much as I would love my experience to be like this all day, every day, this is life, things will change. On other days there are light clouds that float around the top of the mountain, obscuring the view. I equate this phase to when I have moved into the yellow: I have my plan, but I also acknowledge that I will experience shifts in my mood and outlook.

On the cold, dreary, cloud-laden days when the peak of the mountain appears and disappears amongst the never-ending cycle of clouds pushed along by the prevailing wind, I am taken to my time in the orange, where it is uncomfortable and unpleasant, but if I stick to my plan, the blue-sky days will return. When there is a serious weather event and it seems like the mountain almost becomes angry, I am in the red. The noise of the wind is dramatic and creates a theatre of impending catastrophe. It is easy to be caught up in the drama and to be dragged along. But as I take notice of my physical and mental self and enact my plan, it becomes another life experience that can be tolerated, particularly if I have a visible, well-practised plan in place.

I now appreciate the clear blue days so much more. There is a beauty and calmness about Mount Macedon that reminds me that if I persist for long enough, then these times are there to be enjoyed. The weather will change, much like our mental health. Then I ponder – are those special clear days so special without the contrast and acceptance that they are but a point in time? A point in time to be embraced and acknowledged, but a point in time nonetheless. No matter how much time, energy and effort I dedicate to managing my mental health, I cannot avoid the periods when the weather becomes more threatening and confrontational. What I know is that my method of having a plan and paying attention every day to my mental health allows me to both enjoy and endure all the stages along the continuum of mental health.

I am certain there will be another metaphor that materialises in the coming months, and that too will provide me with the opportunity to continue to explore my internal world and develop strategies to bring that world to my external experience. I will continue to evolve and develop; some metaphors will be worth sharing, others will just be a series of thoughts to be discarded. The benefit is that my experience is something I can embrace, to share and make visible to others, pausing, taking the time to consider new options and alternatives.

* * *

For a long time, I never thought I would make it here. I have been so for-tunate to develop and grow as I have moved through the various stages of my life. It has not been a steady, incremental path to a place where every day is bliss. There have been many experiences I wish I did not have to endure, and many regrets, but accepting that there will be challenging periods that will test every fibre of your being is part of living.

When I say I have made it here, I want to be clear that I have not 'made it' – whatever 'it' is, I still have much to achieve. I have always dreamed big and I have now changed my goals to be aligned with my val-ues, but I am still determined to pursue important work goals. My role with Phoenix Australia, a leader in post-traumatic health, allows me to help develop models of care that will better accommodate the mental health needs of emergency service workers. A key aim is to bring the experience of the affected members to the centre of any model we create, to keep sight of who we are designing these programs for.

There have been other changes. Our family has completed a move to the country, and our children are now adults. I can only hope that having watched my challenges with mental health they have a much greater understanding and appreciation of the need to develop a plan to manage their own. Me chirping away about my latest theory is only white noise to them now, but I am certain my relationship with them would not be as strong had I continued the path of destruction I was on – if I were here at all. My wife accepts my left-field thinking, bizarre dreams, strange sleeping habits and occasional lapse to the orange and red end of the con-tinuum as part of my life experience. As always, she is there to guide, advise and support me. I would like to think that in return I can now offer her some much-needed support.

Not every day will be perfect. Life is complex and challenging, and by taking time to reflect and review, we can always find ways to improve.

Ignorance and avoidance will lead to the same path I have travelled previously. Having the courage to look internally and see what is important to me is crucial to my ongoing development.

I use the mental health continuum as a way of gauging my mental health status. I can accept a period in the orange or red, knowing that if I stick to my plan I will return to the green. Everyday attention gives me the best chance of starting the day in the green.

I am now part custodian of two horses, thanks to my daughter, and along with my wife share the responsibilities of maintaining them. The likelihood of this occurring in 2014, when I was stuck in my own self-importance, was negligible, but Orbit and Maisie are now part of my mental health routine. It is ironic that Murdoch was an orange horse. There are many lessons to be learnt from Orbit and Maisie that are metaphors for my mental health. If I take the time each morning to spend time with them while feeding, to build a connection, to be in their presence, this effort is reciprocated. They are engaged, listen, follow commands and are easily managed. If I ignore them, rush to feed them and leave again, they are more unpredictable and difficult to handle. Like Murdoch, if I take the time to be with him, accept he is part of me and listen to but not act on his suggestions, we have a great relationship. If I ignore him, treat him as if he has no influence and is unimportant, he will strike out. Perhaps there are actually three horses in the paddock on our property: Murdoch is tucked away in the background, rugged in his blue blanket, still to be cared for and acknowledged but no longer at the forefront of all I do. It is time spent considering my mental health from different perspectives that allows me to continue to evolve. It is difficult for this type of thinking to occur when I am invisible.

Remaining visible is an ongoing process, and maintaining honest and open communication is central. The story I tell myself about myself has transformed; my outlook has changed from 'me against the world' to me as part of a team, working to maintain the best version of myself. Indirectly, this helps others to be the best versions of themselves. I have morphed into a positive influence on others, where in the past I was holding people back and creating a dysfunctional culture that could not be sustained. The more I give of myself, the more open and honest I am about my experience and the learning from it, the greater influence I can have on others to create change. The years of avoidance and fear of others finding out my dirty secret have been inverted and those same feelings now inspire me to continue a path of assisting others and developing accessible systems of care. As Alex said, 'You don't need to wear a uniform to help people.'

Internally, thoughts, images and memories used to reverberate with intensity, and the harder I tried to force them out, the more congested the space in my mind became. Space is so important to me: now my thoughts can come and go with freedom. When people observe me now, they see a difference. People tell me I seem taller, lighter, relaxed and content.

For now, my model is effective, although I still experience challenging times. Relationships take time, effort and patience, and I am not easy to live with. Sleep is still a problem I continue to work on, but I start every day with a keen anticipation of living through the experiences that day will bring. I recently came across a song by Jimmy Barnes, 'Til the Next Time', in which he describes his experience of waking during the night with his wife beside him. He alludes to his past trauma and says he spends many hours in bed looking at the backlit digital clock, watching time pass by, enduring a racing mind. He accepts that this is his lot on many nights. But his wife will wake, and they will move forward together through the day until the next sleepless night – 'til the next time'.

There will always be a next time, but if we manage our mental health such experiences can be tolerated. And that is okay.

I now have balance in striving to be the best I can be in both my personal life and my working life. I no longer feel a rush to reach the next step in my career: there is time to experience this stage for what it is, and it is amazing what opportunities present themselves. Where once I would remain at work, attempting to catch up or get ahead, I now look at those hours differently. What did I achieve in those two extra hours at work? What if I had spent them exercising, sleeping or connecting with my loved ones? Which would be most beneficial to me? When I reflect on those additional hours going over and above, I did not really achieve much. By that stage of the day, I was exhausted, unproductive, frustrated and overwhelmed. When I returned the next day, those problems would have seemed much more resolvable with the benefit of sleep and a rational mind. Improving the visibility of my mental health, both internally and externally, has increased my creativity and productivity. Adapting my working habits to suit my personal needs has improved outcomes across all aspects of my life.

To summarise what works for me, the foundation is my close relationships with my wife and my family. They are what is most important to me, and I can create a model that works to this strength. I consider myself as being part of a team, a team to help myself learn and grow and hopefully a small part of many teams that assist other individuals in their mental health journeys. There is one inescapable truth: the time I spend with my own thoughts will always be mine. Having a team around me allows me to make better decisions to manage these thoughts, but they will always be there. How I choose to react to them is up to me and me alone.

Policing will always be important to me. It is part of my identity. But at last I recognise it is just a part, not all of me. Other people have taken my place and there will be others who take theirs. I have been fortunate that my experiences have allowed me to be part of the process to improve outcomes for those in policing, in emergency services and more broadly in the community.

When I stand in front of the mirror in the morning, there are still different versions of me reflected. If I take the time to look a little deeper, the person I aim to be is in there. By engaging with those who are important to me, working on a flexible plan of managing my mental health and having the courage to accept that I do not have to like every part of me, I increase the chance of being the best I can be. Sometimes my imaginary friend Murdoch is there in the background, but only when I choose to see him. Part of me; not me.

The death hours are no longer as prominent. The silhouette has been reduced to a small space in the centre of my chest, deprived of influence and strength by me being visible about my mental health.

The best part of my day is early in the morning, having a coffee with my wife while looking out at the horses. Taking the time to listen to the sounds of the various animals and birds that are such a change from the hustle and bustle of a city coming to life. Mount Macedon sits in the background, a subtle reminder of the constant external changes we experience each day. This life is the polar opposite of where I was in October 2014.

It seems so obvious that this is the course of action I should have taken years ago. My model for managing mental health may not be for everyone, but I hope that there is some aspect of this story that resonates enough for you to become more visible in how you approach your own mental health in your everyday life.

Reflections from My Mentors

Ron Iddles OAM, former Victoria Police Homicide Detective

It was around 2005 that I first met Tim. He was seconded to the Homicide Squad, Missing Persons Unit, to investigate people who had gone missing under suspicious circumstances. It became evident once I got to know Tim that he was totally dedicated. It wasn't surprising that he rose from constable to eventually taking on the rank of Detective Senior Sergeant before his accident.

What stood out initially was his focus. He was analytical and a very good thinker. And he always wanted an outcome. In fact, Tim was often two or three steps ahead. He had the ability to sit down and not just read something but analyse it and pick up when something didn't sound right or add up. He was brilliant. Just brilliant.

He was highly respected by his peers, managers and senior executive. Anyone who worked with him would all say the same thing. He was somebody who strived for perfection. Strived for results. And in the end that took a toll on his life.

At Homicide he had an almighty sense of trying to give the victim's family an answer. He put pressure on himself to solve each case so that the loved ones could understand what happened to the person who passed away. He was always committed to families. And if the phone rang and it was a witness or a family member, he wouldn't think twice about getting in the car and driving out to see them. Unfortunately, Tim's own family took a backseat in his determination to give the victims' families some sense of peace. You have to give a lot of yourself to do this but as Tim found out, the more you give the greater the impact it can have on your own life.

I was the person who picked him up from Warrnambool when he tried to commit suicide. While we worked closely together, I hadn't seen it coming. And I look back and kick myself because if you're going to work closely with someone, they are things that I think you should see. But that's the point of his book, too. If you cover up your struggles (and remember, he was a great detective) and don't put your hand up when you need help, you're no help to yourself or anyone else important to you.

Tim was renowned for his ability to absorb knowledge and information and then pass it on. He was someone who probably could have gone on to the top; just his ability to think, strategise, understand the changing environment. He was always ahead of investigative processes and always wanted to try something new. He was one out of the box.

When I took over as Secretary of The Police Association of Victoria (TPAV) in February 2014, I started to realise that there were serious issues around members' mental health and emotional wellbeing. I wanted to change the way we engaged with members. The way in which we looked at mental health. So I thought of Tim.

Having been let go by Victoria Police, Tim had found his feet at Beyond Blue as the Police and Emergency Services Engagement Manager. We had kept in contact, and I knew he was doing great work there, so I approached him to take on the role of manager of the welfare section of TPAV. Here was someone who had been through policing, had fallen over, had rebuilt his life and now was well respected as a speaker and trainer in relation to mental health issues.

Tim was instrumental in setting up BlueHub – a central resource for members to access to support their wellbeing – as well as breaking down the stigma of mental health by presenting to police officers around the state and interstate. Rather than an academic, here was someone who could stand up and say, 'I know what the job did to me, here's what happened, and I've implemented all of these strategies and plans.' He was very well accepted.

Ron was my supervisor and mentor for much of my time as a detective with Victoria Police. He was a member of Victoria Police for thirty-seven years, twenty-five of them with the Homicide Squad. In 2014 he took on the role of secretary of The Police Association Victoria. We have maintained contact since he retired and, unfortunately for him, he is often the sounding board for my latest strategy or left-field idea.

Alex Zannoni, retired psychotherapist, trauma and grief specialist

My first impression of Tim was that he came across as being quite solid but also very fragile, brittle. And that got me intrigued. With that, I started to think that, yes, this is quite a damaged man. He was at a crossroads.

Initially he was trying to outsmart me, and I thought, well, let's cut the BS here. Because, you know, we've been around the block a few times, you and I: different blocks, but nonetheless, we've intersected on various areas such as trauma and depression, anxiety. And so once that little dance was over, I thought we could get down to business.

He had been to see other therapists of different persuasions. And I made it very clear at the beginning, as I did with a lot of people with serious and chronic addictions, whether it was alcohol or any other type of drug (legal or illegal), that if you're coming to see me, the aim was total abstinence. And Tim understood that. I would say to him that it's okay if you fall off the wagon as long as you don't fall under the wheels. You can get back on the wagon without any judgement.

So, a lot of the work we were doing at the beginning was to gradually pull back from the alcohol use. Really start looking at the basics, like diet, exercise, sleep; sleep is crucial. Get the foundation right. And once we've got that down, then we can start doing some necessary deep work to look at how and why this disease has evolved. What happened?

The word 'recovery' has always been a bee in my bonnet. If you hyphenate it to re-cover, what the hell are we covering? It's not a case of covering something. Sure, you can cover a wound initially for it to mend, but at some point you're going to need to rip the band-aid off. So, it's not about covering something. It's about having a good look at the wound. And I think that's a crucial thing that Tim was willing to do. His capacity to front up and converse about all this, when a lot of people won't; they'll disengage.

When he had that serious knockback and ended up at Warrnambool, and Ron was looking after him for that twenty-four-hour period, it really didn't disturb me. Because I thought, it's the path he's on. It's what I expected. The fact that he quickly re-engaged with me shows the strength of the man. Even at his darkest moments, he was still able not just to engage with me but to re-engage with himself and connect with that part of himself that was far healthier. I thought, well, you can handle this. You've got the architecture. Ultimately, it is the person who needs to take the responsibility once they have the knowledge to start moving. Tim understood this.

This is one of the reasons I suggested that Tim start a journal.

Memory is fallible, people naturally forget a lot of things – especially when faced with trauma. The purpose of a journal is to remember the nitty-gritty of life. That's why journals are so powerful. You can see through Tim's entries that they were incredibly powerful for him. He was brutally honest. But it was important for him to remember what he was going through and learn from it.

The more we talked together, the more it became apparent that his ideas and theories around having a plan for your mental health could help a lot of people. It's also why I suggested he write a book. There is a lot of rubbish out there; people are pandering to the quick-fix solutions. What Tim is putting forward is that if you want sustained solutions and a better life, the reality is we deal with challenges every day. But you can deal with it from a position of strength, and wisdom, and information.

Information is another word I like to hyphenate. In-formation. We are constantly in formation. We never reach the light on the hill. It's there to guide us and get us through the terrain. Tim would echo this. His journey is ongoing. What Tim realised is his journey was never about avoiding suffering. It was about not falling into the trap of unnecessary suffering, and developing the skills to deal with genuine suffering, which we all experience. It's the deal we make with life.

Alex has been a counsellor for over twenty-five years and for eighteen years operated a private practice. He specialised in the treatment of trauma and grief and treated many workers from the emergency services and health industries. He has a keen interest in the areas of neuroplasticity and brain-based psychotherapy and retired from private practice in 2019. I was a client of Alex's from 2009 on an ad hoc basis, but the treatment process flourished from 2014. I remain in contact with him in his retirement, and what was a clinical relationship has morphed into a friendship focused on new learnings and personal development.

Patrice O'Brien, former Chief Community Officer, Beyond Blue

Reading Tim's book was an incredibly powerful experience for me. Prior to reading it, I'd already known Tim's story pretty well. I first heard about it in 2016, when one of my staff members recounted it to me, having inadvertently come across Tim and realising he might be the perfect candidate for the seemingly impossible role we were recruiting for in Beyond Blue's Police and Emergency Services Program. When he interviewed for that role, I heard Tim's story firsthand for the first time – raw and honest, in a way I'd never really heard anyone communicate before. After appointing Tim, I heard him tell his story countless times to varied audiences, usually full of police and emergency services personnel – where the impact of his story was always profound. And I heard him tell it, maybe the most impactfully, as his parting 'gift' to Beyond Blue, when he shared his story in heartbreaking detail with Beyond Blue staff – his way of saying thank you and, more importantly, his way of using his story to influence all who worked at Beyond Blue, in how we undertook the important work we were doing.

But despite having heard Tim's story all these times, actually reading it in detail, especially the diary entries, was a different experience entirely.

Upon my first reading, I found myself getting so engrossed in the story that I almost lost track of the real life connection I had to it. This was never truer than in the section of the book where Tim was applying for the job at Beyond Blue. I found myself fervently hoping that he'd get the job, almost shouting at the book – *just give him the bloody job. Imagine the difference it will make to his life!* Only to remember that I was in fact 'in the story', and the decision about whether to give him the job – or not – was one that had rested squarely on my shoulders.

Reading Tim's book enabled me to truly appreciate the profound role that Tim's employment at Beyond Blue played in his recovery. It made me reflect on the role of leadership and the decisions we make as leaders that affect people's lives. It was powerful realising, in hindsight, how unwell Tim still was and what a precarious point in his recovery he was at, when he applied for the role at Beyond Blue. I wonder, had I realised the depth of Tim's ill health, whether I would have made the same decision. I like to think – and I certainly hope – that I would have.

But leadership is not easy. When we are making decisions about people, we have to make the best decision that we can for the human being sitting in front of us – and also for our employer, our teams, our customers and the community we are working to serve.

We did a lot of due diligence before employing Tim and fortunately it stacked up. We repeatedly heard that, despite the challenges he had faced, Tim's reputation was intact and he continued to be held in high regard; employing him would in no way detract from the important work we were doing. In fact, it would do the opposite!

Tim's book reminds me that it is much harder to practise the kind of leadership I aspire to if I am not at the 'mindful end' of the continuum. As a leader, if you are already feeling under strain, anxious or withdrawn, you are more likely to be focused on yourself (at the narcissistic end of the continuum, in Tim's words) than thinking about the people around you. It takes the everyday attention that Tim talks about to ensure that we can show up each day, ready to lead in a way that aligns with our values and able to have as much positive impact as we can, as we make the myriad of decisions that cross our paths.

Leadership reflection aside, I'm so pleased, in every way, that we decided to recruit Tim. Working at Beyond Blue for just shy of twelve months, the impact Tim had, particularly considering what he'd just been through, was mind-blowing! Less than three months into his Beyond Blue employment, Tim had already – almost single-handedly – ensured that every single police and emergency service agency in Australia was represented at a national industry conference focusing on mental health. This included an incredible five police commissioners! In the same period, Tim established mental health networks of police and emergency service agencies in almost every state and territory. These achievements were game-changing, flipping the script on how police and emergency service agencies engaged around mental health.

Tim brought incredible qualities to his work at Beyond Blue. The dogged persistence he'd applied to solving complex homicides remained, only now moderated so that he could look after himself as well. Tim had this incredible nous and intuition to understand what would work – and what wouldn't – in a way that I've seen very few people have. He had this way of knowing what to say, what angle to take, to get people to listen, even if it meant he had to adjust his messaging on the run.

What Tim achieved at Beyond Blue was truly inspiring. It progressed our work with police and emergency services beyond what anyone could have hoped for. For Tim and Beyond Blue it was a mutually beneficial experience. Tim took Beyond Blue leaps and bounds in terms of credibility in the police and emergency services sector and what we were able to achieve. And in turn, Beyond Blue was an important part of Tim's recovery. The work gave him access to every police and emergency service agency in Australia. It was the launching pad to enable him to make even bigger changes at The Police Association Victoria and then Phoenix.

Very few people in the mental health sector have had the individual impact that Tim has had on police and emergency service mental health. Tim has relentlessly driven sector-level change and he is just as passionate today as when he walked through the Beyond Blue doors all those years ago. As well as these big picture changes, Tim has also given so much of himself and his own time to help countless individuals who have found themselves in a similar position to the one he was in at the beginning of this story. Tim is a visionary change maker, who consistently pushes the boundaries and makes things better.

And all of this was only possible because of Tim's perseverance to get well. One of the most powerful parts of Tim's story is the responsibility that he has taken for his own wellbeing.

There is no doubt that Tim was luckier than many. His strong family bonds; the unconditional support of his loving parents and siblings, his wife and his kids; finding the right clinical support in Alex; his incredible intellect and his work ethic all played a role in helping Tim get well. However, even with all these protective factors, the fact remains that while these things could help Tim, only he could truly find a way through.

Once Tim decided that life, not death, was the option he wanted to pursue, he needed to find a way to painstakingly get through each day, picking his way forward until a future path was clear.

As outlined in this book, Tim realised that the only way forward was truly looking into himself and examining his own behaviour, his own shortcomings, his own maladaptive coping strategies. Tim's story is one of true courage – the tremendous bravery that it takes to stop and look our own challenges in the eye cannot be underestimated.

It's important to remember as well, that this is a real story, not a fairy tale. Tim didn't just one day magically get better and leave the bad days behind him. Keeping well is something that he works at every single day. That is, I believe, one of the key messages of Tim's story.

I saw an example of this in the very early days of Tim's time working at Beyond Blue. He'd recently returned from an interstate trip. The next day he came and sat in my office and shared with me some of the negative thoughts he experienced on his return flight. Tim was so open – there was no chance that he was going to make the mistake of hiding everything he was going through from his employer again. Tim says that Beyond Blue was a great environment to work in (and that is true!), but Tim also contributed to that. So determined was he to not make the same mistakes again, that he truly influenced the culture by his own openness. On this occasion, Tim and I talked candidly about what was on his mind and what strategies he was going to use to keep looking after himself. I was his manager, not his psychologist, but there were simple things that I could do – creating an environment to ensure that he felt safe to keep talking openly about his condition at work and providing practical support, so that he could effectively navigate any work challenges impacting his mental health.

Tim writes in this book about some of his strengths – about being analytical, about having a great understanding of people and their motivations – I too see these strengths in Tim. In Tim's greatest time of need, I see how he turned his own strengths in on himself. He used his deep analytical thinking and his ingrained and learned ability to understand people, to better understand himself; to better understand depression and anxiety and the hold they had on him. He used these resources to ultimately chart his way out of the darkness that had enveloped him.

We don't all have the same strengths as Tim, but we do all have our own unique attributes. Tim's story is a model for all of us, for how we can identify and harness our inner strengths to help ourselves through life's inevitable challenges.

Many people reading this may never get the pleasure of meeting Tim. These people will be missing out on meeting a true treasure. I only got to know Tim during his recovery, not at his most challenging times. When

I read his book, I cannot marry up the arrogant, difficult man he de-scribes, with the lovable larrikin I know today – full of funny stories, killer one-liners, constant wisdom and kindness and an enormous heart. What a loss it would have been to the world if we'd lost Tim on that ter-rible day in Warrnambool.

Through our friendship, I've not met Tim's wife and the kids, but I feel like I know them through how much he has told me about them. I'm so glad for them that they got their husband and dad back. They truly deserve it after the unconditional love they showed him.

When Tim and I catch up now, he's full of stories of sitting on his verandah, building a shed or feeding the horses. These simple pleasures have become part of the routine Tim practices to look after himself. The work that Tim puts into staying well is unrelenting and I continue to be in awe of how hard he works at it.

I wish Tim many more of these simple pleasures and moments of gentle joy – of seeing the light dappling on the deck, of feeling the breeze on his face. Tim is, quite simply, one of my heroes. I am beyond proud to have played a small role in his story, and prouder still to be his friend!

Patrice was responsible for my recruitment to my first role back into the work-force at Beyond Blue. She was a member of Beyond Blue's executive team during the time I worked there. We formed a strong relationship while at Beyond Blue, and once I left she remained a mentor and trusted friend.

Acknowledgements

It was always my intention to maintain the privacy of those that were involved in my experience, and this is particularly the case with my family. Any attempt to quantify the positive influence that my wife and children had and continue to have on my life experience would grossly understate the reality of the impact they have had. The love, care, empathy, forgiveness and inspiration they provide have taught me so many lessons. The enduring memory of my experience was of taking many small steps, individually and collectively, in a supportive and loving environment in which we accepted that we all have imperfections. Repeated actions to build trust; understanding that we all have days when we are not at our best; and accepting the hand life has dealt us and working together to find solutions that suited our needs.

The death of my beloved dad in August 2023 illuminated the good fortune I was blessed with to have the support of my immediate family in challenging times. Mum and my siblings provided unconditional support for each other in our own unique way as we experienced the personal grief of losing a loved one. Expressing our feelings verbally is not a great strength of our family, but the sense of love and connectedness that comes from simply being in company with each other is immense. In many ways the connection in our family remains invisible in the verbal sense, but throughout the experiences I have described, the unconditional love and connection was present through the unique bond that we share. My family never criticised or judged me for my actions; I only experienced unwavering support and encouragement that aided in building my self confidence to find a way through.

The trust and friendship that was afforded to me by the many staff I worked with in my roles at Beyond Blue, The Police Association Victoria and Phoenix Australia have been remarkable. The sense of safety and empathy in these workplaces allowed me to develop a strategy to manage my mental health that worked for me. I hope I was able to contribute in a meaningful way to their culture. The enduring friendships I have from these organisations is testament to the mutually beneficial nature of these relationships.

To all the members of Victoria Police, past and current, I can only admire the work you do. Remember the work you do is important; it does make a difference and I am not sure there is any other job which provides the level of satisfaction and reward that policing offers. To the many members who had the courage to share their mental health journeys with me, I will be forever indebted. My aim is to highlight the mental health risks faced in policing and, with a sound plan and a commitment to be visible with our mental health, it is a career to be embraced and enjoyed.

Lastly, I wish to acknowledge the many people who provide a listening ear, sound advice, empathy, inspiration and guidance. This includes work colleagues, mentors, life-long friends, executive coach, clinicians — the people who are part of my everyday plan. I would not have had the drive or motivation to finish this project without the input from each of them. Again, I will not name them individually, but their influence has been profound.